BMW M Series
PORTFOLIO
1979-2002

Published jointly by

BROOKLANDS BOOKS LTD.
P.O. BOX 146, COBHAM,
SURREY, KT11 1LG. UK
sales@brooklands-books.com

ROAD & TRACK
1499 MONROVIA AVENUE,
NEWPORT BEACH, CA 92663. US
www.roadandtrack.com

A-BMMRT   Printed in China   ISBN 185520 6277

The *Road & Track* Portfolio Series is an exciting new group of publications covering some of the most exciting automobiles for the enthusiast. In each Portfolio, you will find feature stories, road test narratives and complete specifications along with performance data. For the serious enthusiasts, the Portfolio series is an excellent reference for collecting, restoring or buying the car of your dreams. Happy reading!

Thos. L. Bryant
Editor-in-Chief
Road & Track

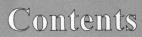

BMW M1

Racing defines the breed

BY PAUL FRÈRE

As PROUD AS BMW is of its sporting image, the M1 project would not exist if CSI rules did not specify that 400 examples of a production car must be built before it can be homologated for racing in Groups 4 or 5. Originally, the Bavarians had hoped that adding a turbocharger and stretching the rules to the limit would have made their 3.0CSi coupe at least a match for the Porsches. But the BMW's size and its front engine consistently defeated their efforts to supplant Zuffenhausen's supremacy and led to management's decision to produce a completely new car. The M1 was designed entirely in keeping with requirements of the racing version; that is, the Group 5 car was planned first and a production model derived from it to make a practical road car. The latter would be likely to attract wealthy customers without racing ambitions, yet would retain all those features that can't be changed when a production car is modified to Group 4 or 5 specifications. This is reflected, for example, in the suspension of the production car conforming to modern racing practice except for its rubber bushings, where the racing version uses spherical Unibal joints. Also, production bodywork is externally identical to the racing version, except for its lack of fender flares and smaller aerodynamic aids.

Principal differences between road and racing M1s are in the engine department, suspension and running gear. For example, in addition to its Unibal joints, the racer's suspension features special spring/damper units, adjustable anti-roll bars, wider wheels, brakes with adjustable pressure distribution and, of course, racing tires. Nevertheless, all pick-up points and alternatives remain in their original locations.

In its standard form, the 3.5-liter engine develops 277 bhp and has the same bottom end and bore and stroke dimensions (94.0 x

84.0 mm) as the latest production 6-cylinder used in the 635CSi. The M1 engine differs from the 635CSi's primarily in its 24-valve, twin-camshaft cylinder head, a production version of the twin-cam head developed for the coupes that ran the 1974 IMSA series, among others. Also unique are its Kugelfischer-Bosch injection system and its distributor-less, fully electronic, flywheel-triggered ignition system.

In Group 4 form, output is increased by nearly 200 bhp to 470 via the usual tweaks. This is the approximate output of cars running in the Procar series, all-BMW events in which Grand Prix stars race against experienced private owners. In Group 5 trim, the same engine is turbocharged to yield approximately 800 bhp and its piston displacement is reduced to 3.2 liters. Taking into account the CSI supercharger factor of 1.4, this reduction brings the engine into the 4.5-liter class, which allows a minimum weight, without fuel, of 1025 kg (2260 lb). Other racing modifications include revised gear ratios, a reinforced clutch and a differential with a higher locking factor than the street version's.

ends, for whatever the refinements incorporated in the latest Pantera (admittedly costing about half the price of the M1), the difference between the two cars is akin to a first development prototype versus a final product. The BMW is an unexpectedly refined car, especially bearing in mind that the street version is derived from what was conceived as a racing car, rather than vice versa.

The cockpit is devoid of unnecessary frills, but is quite well equipped, with a typical BMW instrument panel including a speedometer reading to 280 km/h and a 9000-rpm tachometer—this being the limit for both Group 4 and turbocharged Group 5 engines. The central console incorporates various switches, a rather vast cubbyhole and controls for the radio and air conditioner. There are four adjustable air outlet grilles. A loudspeaker is fitted in each door, and a locking glovebox is situated between the seats. However, as usual in mid-engine cars, barring some notable exceptions, there is no room in the cockpit for larger items: coat, briefcase, or the like. The Recaro bucket seats are

The M1 is not part of BMW's regular production program; the 635CSi continues as the top sporting model. Indeed, the M1's official manufacturer is not Bayerische Motoren Werke AG, but the company's racing organization, BMW Motorsport GmbH. All the street versions are built by BMW Motorsport though only some of the Group 4 cars are to be built there, others being assembled by recognized racing organizations in various countries from parts supplied by BMW Motorsport. This is mainly to save time, as BMW Motorsport does not yet have facilities to produce all the cars required for the Procar series—the only European races, except Le Mans, they can enter before production reaches 400 units. To achieve this figure, the premises of BMW Motorsport are being considerably expanded, but by early February of this year fewer than 180 M1s had been built.

In any case, interest created by the car and the number of orders for its street version (at 100,000 DM or approximately $60,000 apiece) are such that production will probably not be limited to the first batch of 400 cars. The intention is to continue production at the rate of two cars per day even after CSI homologation has been obtained. For cars of this type, price seems to be of minor importance and certainly the M1 is not a cheap car to manufacture: Virtually none of its components, except for the engine cylinder block and bottom end, come from the standard production program. And quite apart from this, the car incorporates many items that are over-engineered for the road version. This is evidenced by the fact that the Group 4 version, ready to race, is only 50 percent more expensive than its road-going counterpart. Nor is the manufacturing procedure particularly cost-effective: For example, the raw fiberglass body is fabricated in Turin by Ital Design, then sent to Baur in Stuttgart who fits the body on a tubular space frame supplied by BMW Motorsport, and then it goes to Munich for final assembly.

The result, however, is a striking 2-seater coupe with a marked resemblance to the De Tomaso Pantera. Indeed, performance is comparable to that of the Pantera GTS. But there the comparison

adjustable for reach and rake, and a telescoping steering column is fitted; thus most drivers should find a comfortable driving position. However, head room is limited and some drivers might find that with a helmet on they want a lower seat. The padded 3-spoke 14-in. diameter steering wheel is extremely pleasant.

Driving out of the center of Munich toward the *Autobahn* was no problem at all. The only embarrassment in city traffic comes from the attention you receive. First and 2nd gears of the ZF 5-speed gearbox are comparatively low, giving maximum speeds of 49 and 74 mph, respectively, at the 7000-rpm redline. Also, the 24-valve engine is almost as flexible as its 12-valve production counterpart. Thanks to the twin-disc clutch, pedal effort is not excessive. The brakes are not over assisted, the gear change is light and positive and the fairly high-geared steering is never heavy—not even when parking. It feels a little dead at town speeds, with little return action, but becomes just splendid when the M1 is used as it's meant to be. Typical of many mid-engine cars, rear quarter vision leaves something to be desired, so the electrically adjustable mirror on the passenger side is much more than a luxury.

Even less expected than the engine's remarkable tractability is the excellent road noise suppression. This is about the last thing one would expect on a car running 7-in. wide front and 8-in. wide rear wheels, shod with 55 and 50 series Pirelli P7 tires, respectively. On this score, the BMW is superior to a similarly shod Porsche Turbo, for instance. The ride is quite comfortable, even in the lower speed range where high performance sports cars usually don't excel—a luxury the BMW can probably afford thanks to its sophisticated suspension geometry. And at high speed, comfort can only be rated as exceptional.

Naturally it is only on the open road where the M1 really comes into its own—and there you soon find that traffic and visibility set limits far below the car's true potential. Therefore I arranged to round off the drive with a session at BMW's test track where the car could be fully extended, and where it was also possible to do some performance testing, far from police and other traffic. The handling course was closed, but for a car of this caliber, it is useless anyway, being much too slow. The speed track is really ideal with two parallel straights of approximately 2.2 miles linked by two loops incorporating a long 95-mph left bend and faster and shorter right-handers, each slightly different from the other. On these curves the M1 was undoubtedly better than any road car I have ever driven. It is capable of approaching race car cornering speeds, and even at the limit it is easily controllable. After a few practice laps, I was accelerating hard into the straight with the tail well out. Even when cornering at high speed, closing the throttle abruptly produces no drama, just a slight, easily checked tuck-in which experienced drivers welcome.

Track testing also gave the tiger in the engine a chance for an outing. Though the engine meets all European emission and noise requirements, it revs eagerly to its 7000-rpm redline where an electronic revolution limiter protects it against over-enthusiasm. And it delivers its power smoothly and progres-

sively—as do all BMW engines. It's not a "cammy" engine, coming on with a bang, with nothing in the lower ranges. It pulls smoothly from 1000 rpm in 5th gear (equivalent to 24 mph), and accelerates from 25 mph (or about 1050 rpm) in that gear, reaching the end of the kilometer in 33.5 seconds, only 0.6 sec slower than a Porsche Turbo 3.3 will do in top gear.

Neither is the engine excessively noisy. Sound damping is excellent and any mechanical, intake or exhaust noise reaching the occupants is neither obtrusive nor tiring, whatever the speed. Conversation remains possible up to the car's maximum, and the low wind noise helps to keep the general noise level acceptably low. Consequently, there is every reason to use the engine as it is meant to be used, and what happens then is best told by the following acceleration figures:

Time to speed, sec:

0–50 mph	4.5
0–60 mph	5.9
0–80 mph	9.6
0–100 mph	13.3
0–120 mph	19.7
0–130 mph	24.9

Time to distance, sec:

0–1320 ft (¼ mi)	13.8
0–1000 m (1 km)	24.9

Up to 130 mph, the M1 is fractionally slower than a Ferrari 365BB 4.4-liter (the current 5.0-liter does not seem to be any faster than its forerunner) and slower by a slightly larger margin than a Porsche Turbo 3.3 (though the Porsche I tested was not air conditioned). However, the M1 beats the Pantera GTS and the old lightweight Porsche Carrera 3.0. Over the standing kilometer, the BMW is one of few current road cars beating 25.0 sec, a

performance achieved, to the best of my knowledge, only by the Porsche Turbo 3.3 (24.0 sec), the Lamborghini Countach and the Ferrari BB, which equal the BMW at 24.9 sec.

Such performance makes first-class brakes really essential, and on this score too the M1 is outstanding. Not only is the boost just right, but pedal effort matches the grip of the wide Pirellis to produce very short stopping distances. Also, repeated hard use failed to produce any fade.

The only performance figure unobtainable on the test track was maximum speed; however good the exit from the loop at either end, the car was still accelerating at the end of the 2.2-mile straight. So off I went to the twin track, 3-lane *Autobahn* connecting the Nürnberg to the Salzburg *Autobahnen*. On a Saturday afternoon, conditions were hardly ideal to time a 160-mph-plus sports car, but in one direction a kilometer was covered at 163 mph with the car apparently striving for one or two more, while in the other direction I got a best timing of 162 mph with the car still accelerating. This certainly confirms BMW's figure of

162.8 mph because, given a completely clear run in either direction, my test car would probably have averaged slightly more. BMW's figure, by the way, is 3 mph faster than the maximum speed I timed for the Pantera GTS, 2 mph faster than the 3.3-liter Porsche Turbo and 10.5 mph slower than the Ferrari 365BB.

BMW's times for 0-60 and 0-120 mph are 5.3 and 19.0 sec, respectively, perhaps indicating that I was not quite brutal enough with the clutch when getting off the mark. On the other hand, though the drivetrain took many standing starts with utmost equanimity, I found myself suddenly without any drive when gently releasing the pedal at a traffic light, just a quarter mile from the factory. A clutch lining had collapsed because of excessively countersunk rivets and I was just able to crawl to the factory gates. "Well, we've learned something," was BMW's reaction. Once arrived, I had another surprise, but a pleasant one: Items I had deposited in the fair-sized trunk at the extreme rear of the car were not noticeably warm, despite their proximity to the engine compartment. Apparently the seal between the two does its job efficiently.

Summing up my impressions, I would say that, although the M1 was designed specifically for racing, in its street version it is no less practical than any of its direct rivals of similar configura-tion. And it outscores them in two important departments: ride and handling; in the latter it has no rival anywhere. In its home country the M1 will inevitably be compared to the Porsche Turbo. The Porsche, with its two occasional seats and good interior stowage space, is an altogether more practical car which also scores points for its remarkable detail finish and tremendous acceleration. However, compared to the M1, the Porsche is not quite as comfortably suspended. Neither are Ferraris immune from BMW competition, because among enthusiasts the M1 will benefit from being basically the same model as the racing version, a car likely to be highly successful in international competition.

PROCAR
BMW rolls its own race of champions
BY JOE RUSZ PHOTOS BY THE AUTHOR

IT'S BEEN CALLED the IROC of Europe because in some ways BMW's Procar Series does resemble our own International Race of Champions. Both series provide identically prepared cars to a select group of drivers who compete in a series of races winning prize money, a championship title (based on accrued points) and, in Procar, other prizes like BMW automobiles. But while IROC's Camaros are owned and maintained by the promoters (Roger Penske and friends), only five Procars belong to the BMW factory. The remaining 15 to 20 cars are owned by independent teams who buy the 150,000 Deutsche Mark ($80,000) M1 coupes from BMW Motorsport and groom them to series specs for the 9-race championship.

Then there are the drivers, true champions in IROC, the great, near great and those who wish they were either in Procar. In other words, IROC drivers are points leaders from the major forms of motor racing (USAC, NASCAR, Formula 1, IMSA) whereas Procar pilots include five F1 drivers (the fastest qualifiers from the Grand Prix accompanying each Procar race), plus other "highly qualified private drivers" and "young talents." That covers a lot of ground and the disparity between Procar chauffeurs is at times, mind boggling. But then, there may be the same diversity of skill in IROC, or so say some of its competitors.

Both series are designed to be supporting races, held in conjunction with a major motor race. For IROC, this may be a Champ car, stock car or road race; for Procar, only a GP. What is the *raison d'être* of each championship? In IROC the emphasis has always been on the drivers and in determining who is best. Some of that same thinking is evident in Procar where "talented drivers now have the possibility of competing with the world's best racing drivers under the same conditions." *C'est vrai,* but I'm sure that if pressed, even Jochen Neerpasch, BMW Motorsport's boss, will admit that the ultimate goals of Procar are to promote the new M1 coupe and to test its mettle in competition. Es-

pecially the latter, as promotion or no, Bee Em Vee should have little trouble selling the 400-or-so road-going M1s they'll produce each year. No, what Motorsport wants is a chance to wring out their future World Makes racers so that when they finally return in 1980 (what a spectacular Daytona 24 Hours that'll be), the Müncheners will be ready to take on the Stuttgarters with no holds barred. All right, but in the meantime, why has BMW chosen a showcase series instead of a genuine road racing championship as its arena? Because at this time only about 80 of the 400 production M1s needed for Group 4 homologation have been built. So there's no place for the cars to compete. Besides, what better way to get attention than to be the second ring in the Formula 1 circus?

This brings up the politics of Procar vis-à-vis FOCA and FISA. I doubt if even the CIA can discover the sort of deal BMW has struck with the Constructors, specifically Bernie Ecclestone. But Ecclestone's imprimatur is on the Procar brochure and Max Mosley, Bernie's right-hand man, is handling the series' organization and regulations. So one can assume that as goes F1 (or FOCA), so goes Procar. This was apparent at Zolder, Belgium where it was rumored the debut of the M1s would not take place because FISA regulations prohibit F1 drivers from competing in another race held within 24 hours of a GP. When confronted with this question, FISA's president, Jean-Marie Balestre, was nonplused and said the problem, if any, was between BMW and FOCA. Then he pointed out that the 24-hour rule was flexible by an hour or so in either direction. But the real strength of the FOCA/Procar alliance was tested in France where the race organizers told Ecclestone they wouldn't allow the Procar race to take place. Bernie's alleged reply: "Then don't expect a GP."

One hopes Procar will have smooth sailing from now on, because it is an exciting concept. There are the M1s, driven by Paul Frère and described in an accompanying article. All I'll say

Elio de Angelis (left) outdrove many more prominent competitors, including Clay Regazzoni (right), to win the Zolder opener.

Procar pas de deux by Clay Regazzoni (leading) and Toine Hezemans.

is that they are magnificent specimens of modified Group 4 machines, worth more than just a passing glance in the paddock. A few of the cars were built in the Motorsport shops, but most were constructed at March Cars in England because BMW couldn't handle the volume. There are about 20 racers at present (Procar rules allow for 24 entries at every race except Monaco) and 19 of them showed up to qualify at Zolder.

Because Procar rules ensure that the first five starting positions go to the fastest F1 competitors in the first F1 qualifying session, Jacques Laffite, Clay Regazzoni, Mario Andretti, Niki Lauda and Nelson Piquet sat at the front of the grid. Behind them was the 1978 Deutsche Rennsport Meistershaft runner-up Markus Höttinger, the quickest of the Procar qualifiers (as opposed to F1 qualifiers), who shared the third row with Piquet. Then came F1 drivers Hans Stuck and Bruno Giacomelli, then GT superstars

Toine Hezemans, Dieter Quester and other well-known European drivers who were joined by yet another GP pilot, Elio de Angelis. For the record, Gilles Villeneuve and Jean-Pierre Jabouille had been among the fastest qualifiers in that first F1 session, but their Michelin contracts kept them from taking part in the Goodyear-supported Procar series.

Although Laffite, Regazzoni, Andretti and Piquet were aboard works BMWs (painted white, red and blue), Lauda was in his own Marlboro-sponsored M1 prepped by Ron Dennis. One wonders what sort of deal the former World Champion has with the Procar folks, because Niki appears to be a staunch and vocal

Driving the Group 4 BMW M1

WHEN I DROVE BMW's road-going pride, glory (future) and headache (production delays) a few months ago (R&T, June 1979), Jochen Neerpasch, chief of BMW's sport involvement, promised he would let me drive the Group 4 version; the opportunity came sooner than expected. At the beginning of May, I ran into Dieter Stappert, the Bavarians' racing manager, in the lobby of one of the better Paris hotels. "When can I drive the Group 4?" I asked him. "Next Tuesday if you like," he replied. "We will be testing on the small pit course at the Nürburgring to get our cars right for the first of the Procar races which takes place in Zolder at the end of the week. The course will also be open to any of our customers who might want to come." As I had an appointment in Frankfurt the day before, this suited me magnificently.

Though the M1 was mainly designed as a basis for a turbocharged Group 5 car to challenge Porsche's supremacy in the World Championship of Makes, the Procar series is limited to the normally aspirated Group 4 version. But the cars present at the Ring differed from the prototype shown in the catalog and exhibited at various shows by a large rear airfoil. According to Group 4 regulations, a rear wing may not be added, so

before the model can be homologated by the CSI, every one of the 400 M1s produced will have to be delivered with that appendage, even if owners who run their cars on the road (and they will be the majority) don't have any use for it. It is a highly efficient, sharp edged spoiler, but neither the German government nor any other responsible authority will ever accept it on a road car; yet another loophole to be filled in the CSI regulations.

Having been designed primarily with racing in mind, the Group 4 version of the M1 is much closer to the basic model than is the case with most Group 2 and 4 cars. It has simpler, lighter interior trim, plastic side and rear windows, Heim joints in the suspension and different springs, dampers and anti-roll bars. In addition, the car dispenses with the brake booster but has adjustable front/rear distribution, wider wheels and tires, quicker steering, a deeper front spoiler and, of course, a specially tuned engine driving through a beefed-up clutch and a gearbox having a choice of ratios and its own oil cooler.

The increase in power, up from 277 bhp to 470 bhp at 9000 rpm, is obtained by straightforward means, but the basic car is heavier than hoped for, so it has not been possible to get the weight of the

Group 4 version down to the class minimum of 2215 lb; it is still 155 lb overweight.

The car I drove is one of those which would be entrusted to the Grand Prix drivers. It had just been tested, set up and finally passed by BMW's test driver and protege, Manfred Winkelhock, also an up-and-coming Formula 2 star. The short circuit around the start/finish line and pit area of the Nürburgring is nearly 2 miles in length and much more useful than one might think. It allows quite high speeds to be reached on the two straights, with sharp applications of the brakes at either end. The turns include two left-hand and three right-hand bends; one is very slow and the others are of the 3rd-gear variety, including one with a hump. The only feature missing is a very fast bend.

Because of the last-minute arrangements, I had no racing equipment with me, but the car looks so little different from the street version that my civilian clothes did not seem improper, even though they did not match the helmet I had to borrow from Winkelhock. With the luxury of a sliding seat, it was not too difficult adjusting it to suit my longer legs and arms but, for a car of this sort, I found the driving position surprisingly upright. I would have preferred it more reclining, but the luxury features stop short of providing rake adjustment. There is no redline on the tachometer, so an electronic limiter set at 8500 rpm is used in all cars running in the Procar series. Similar 24-valve engines have

Serious battle injuries failed to stop Wolfgang Schütz's M1.

because one display of exuberance eliminated Höttinger and Stuck as they fought for the lead. Another knocked out Markus Hötz and Walter Brun and ultimately Albrecht Krebs who, along with Sepp Manhalter and Wolfgang Schütz, was involved in a gigantic 1st-lap tangle. Manhalter soldiered on to finish in 7th place, 1 lap down, while Schütz struggled with a broken chassis and an evil handling car that finally crashed 2 laps from the end.

Regazzoni looked promising for much of the race or at least until De Angelis worked his way up from the back of the pack to take over the lead. From then on it was Elio, followed by Hezemans who relegated Rega to 3rd in the 49.3-mile event.

Only seven cars finished the half-hour contest, a fact that profoundly disturbed Neerpasch, Procar's proud papa. The number of crashed cars was upsetting, but especially unnerving were the mechanical breakdowns. Andretti's, Giacomelli's and Lauda's M1s suffered terminal ailments that may have been related to failure of the 6-cylinder engine's harmonic balancer. An acceptable woe, if it had been BMW's fault. But Neerpasch and his staff theorized that the breakage occurred when the engines were run up against their rev limiters (set at 8500 rpm), resulting in shock forces that caused undue vibrations (and hence damage) in the powerplants.

Things were not much better at Monaco where Lauda bounced his M1 off Regazzoni's racer to win the second round of the Procar series. Stuck, man in a hurry, was a bit more flamboyant and severely crunched his Procar after rolling it onto the Armco. Only the catch fence kept the car from careening into the crowd.

Look at the bright side, Jochen. The race-going public loves Procar even if a few drivers and the Motorsport mechanics do not. And if it's sympathy you need, call Jay Signore. He's Penske Racing's competitions manager who's responsible for straightening 15 bent Camaros five times a year. ◆

supporter of the series. Not so some of the other F1 drivers whose dispositions at Zolder were undoubtedly affected by the drizzle during the 45-minute practice and qualifying session held the day before the Procar race—and possibly pressure from FOCA. Mind you, of the GP lot, only Lauda had ever driven an M1 before, so most found this wet welcome to be a less than ideal accompaniment to a sorting-out session.

Fortunately, the weather sorted itself out by race day, although the 19-car field was diminished by two after Piquet's and Franz Konrad's cars suffered cooling problems during the pre-race warm-up session and were withdrawn. But no matter, because the 17 survivors provided enough excitement to keep the usually blasé F1 qualifying-day crowd on its feet. It was the stuff that makes closed-wheel racing so spectacular—plenty of drafting and, alas, body contact. Maybe a bit too much of the latter

been run up to 9200 rpm in BMW's racing coupes, but it was thought that with no competition from other makes to be faced, limiting the revs to 8500 would probably help conserve the engines and save us a lot of expense.

Though it's so different, the Group 4 M1 reminds me of the D-Type Jaguar. Its flexibility and refined ways are more expected in a touring car than in a racing machine. The clutch is not particularly heavy and is reasonably progressive: nothing of that "in-or-out" variety; the gear lever feels just the same as in the road version and as the engine is also surprisingly flexible, getting off the mark is almost as easy as with any road car. The M1 I drove was rather overgeared for the small circuit, 5th having to be used only for a short distance on either of the main straights before braking became imperative, but acceleration in the lower gears is what you'd expect from 380–390 bhp per ton, including me and some fuel on board. The factory claims that, with that sort of gearing, 100 km/h (62.5 mph) is reached from a standing start in 4.5 seconds. For the road version, their claim of 5.6 sec was better than the 6.3 sec I got, but even allowing for that, the push in the back is impressive.

After getting the feel of the car for 2 or 3 laps, I found myself braking later and later, getting nearer the limits and generally improving my lap times while analyzing the car's behavior. The more I did so, the more I was surprised by its civilized manners. The higher-than-stan-

dard geared steering is still quite light by racing car standards, beautifully smooth, but magnificently precise. Lacking a vacuum booster, the brakes naturally require a fairly strong push and they were probably what I liked least in the car. They are too spongy to inspire the confidence required to leave your braking to the last yard when coming up to a corner at 155 mph or so, which is probably what the M1 does at the end of those straights. But I really liked the pedal layout which allows extremely easy heel-and-toeing while the perfectly guided gear lever is just pushed or pulled from one notch to the next.

With 12.5-in. wide rims (the widest allowed by the regulations) at the rear and 11.0-in. rims at the front, the area of rubber in contact with the road is not all that extravagant for a comparatively heavy car, which makes it easier to find the limit and, of course, brings down the cornering speeds, compared to Formula 1 standards. So for someone familiar with well shod, high-powered road-going sports cars, it is easier to get the hang of things at the wheel of an M1 than in a single-seater. In the case of the BMW, things are made even easier by the complete absence of vices. Set up as it was, the M1 felt almost completely neutral and it was astonishingly insensitive if, for instance, the throttle was suddenly shut when cornering fast. Only if the car was turned into the bend with the brakes still applied quite heavily or if enough power was applied to break the rear-wheel grip,

did the tail tend to come out. But this certainly does not indicate excessive understeer, as the car did not show the slightest reluctance to go around the one hairpin corner of the course.

This corner also emphasized the astonishing flexibility of the engine. The first time I came to it, I selected 1st gear (dog-legged to the lower left) but soon found that I was wasting my time, as it was surely quicker to stay in 2nd and save a change. From 3500 rpm and even lower, the engine picks up cleanly and vigorously until it reaches 7000 rpm; by then the gates of the stables are wide open and the horses stampede out until the tach reads 8500 rpm and the rev limiter checks their rush. However, there is no suggestion that the fireworks are over, and setting the limit at 9200 as would be done for an "open" Group 4 race would surely further improve lap times, if only by saving the occasional extra gearchange or allowing the use of lower overall gearing. As it was, after only 7 or 8 laps (they stopped me after I completed only 9 or 10), I was within 3 sec of the times turned by Winkelhock who did all the development testing of the prototypes, and I was certainly not taking any risks, nor can I claim to be in daily practice—yearly would be more appropriate. So this *must* be a very easy car to drive. And it is well ventilated too, which makes so much difference not only to how much you enjoy such a drive, but also to the fighting spirit a driver can muster in a hard race.

—Paul Frère

Some driving machines are more ultimate than others PHOTOS BY JOE RUSZ

GIVE ITALIANS CREDIT for developing the exotic car concept, but leave it to the Germans—BMW, specifically—to bring it well nigh to perfection. The BMW M1 is the sort of car that enthusiasts dream about, and for good reason. It has all the elements of a proper exotic car: a powerful, high-technology engine located amidships, a suspension resplendent of racing practice, aggressive styling, the right combination of sounds piped into a well engineered cockpit. But what's so extraordinary about the M1 is the lack of compromise it requires of its driver and passenger. Unlike several other super exotics that come to mind, here's a car that's superbly finished, quite comfortable, tractable as you'd like, yet blindingly quick in a straight line or otherwise. It's an exotic you could live with. Alas, only if you're well heeled to an extreme, however, because the U.S.-legal BMW M1 we tested set a new record for these pages as to list price for production cars: $115,000. No matter, because for most of us, exotic cars are dream stuff anyway and what good is a dream if it's attainable?

Genesis of this particular dream came with BMW's deciding back in 1976 that its 3.5 CSL wasn't quite competitive enough in Group 4 racing. By October 1977, we saw fruition of this with R&T's cover subject that month, the BMW Lamborghini E-26. Why Lamborghini? Simple. Neither the BMW factory nor BMW Motorsport GmbH, its racing division, had capacity to produce the car in any quantity, and Group 4 and 5 requirements say 400 cars within 24 months or no homologation. Time passed, and our next feature on BMW's exotic was in June of last year, when Contributing Editor Paul Frère sampled an M1, and yes, by this time the code-name E-26 (and Lamborghini's production assistance) had gone by the boards. Paul spoke highly of the car, calling it "unexpectedly refined, especially bearing in mind that the street version is derived from what was conceived as a racing car, rather than vice versa." And although the M1 has been in competition, production numbers have limited it to the Procar Series, a European version of IROC in this country, and to an occasional IMSA effort.

But what of the "production" version (if this mundane term can apply to something as rare and exciting as the M1)? First, its lines haven't changed since Giugiaro set them down in 1977; in fact, it's his Ital Design firm in Turin that still fabricates the fiberglass bodies. The bodies travel to Stuttgart next where the frames are fitted, and BMW Motorsport in Munich completes the assembly of all street versions. In addition, the handful of cars entering the U.S. legally have yet one more step in their manufacturing process. Our test M1 came from ACI, Automobile Compliance Inc, a Harbor City, California firm whose specialty is importation and legalization of cars otherwise unavailable in the U.S. market.

BMW M1

We noted back in 1977 that the M1's bodywork wasn't all that breathtaking a design, but our bright red-orange test car has a purposeful look from the front three-quarters that says BMW unmistakably, and its side window treatment is nicely taut if not especially original. The rear looks a bit busy with its louvered glass, cooling vents and multi-surface development, but its soft, rounded contours carry a purposeful appearance as well. The overall design has a blend of tautness and Teutonic opulence that looks particularly striking in impeccably finished fiberglass.

All this fiberglass envelopes a steel space frame that incorporates fore and aft bulkheads, the floor panel of the passenger compartment and a roll-over structure. ACI adds the necessary fed-crash bumpers with so little change of appearance that our plan of showing before-and-after photos proved pointless: The original appearance is retained with a mere 3.0-in. increase in length, 2.0 in. at the front and 1.0 in. at the rear. The front bumper was split horizontally and sectioned a bit to narrow it for clearance. From it a pattern was pulled which was used to lay up a layer of Kevlar, five layers of fiberglass and a steel backup bar. The latter is attached to energy absorbers taken from the Fiat 131, and these hydraulic struts are mounted to longitudinal structures of the M1's frame which have been gusseted and reinforced to take the added load. A similar scheme prevails at the rear, only here the hydraulic struts are from a Chevrolet Caprice, chosen because of their shorter stroke than those of the Fiat 131 (and hence, less clearance constraints). Seems that load transfer at the rear goes directly into the main frame, and the shorter stroke is acceptable.

Other structural modifications include a pair of tubular steel bars welded in each door to its hinge plate at the forward end and latch plate at the rear. These together with a gusseting of the rear bulkhead behind the seats and added tubular cages around the two rear-flank-mounted fuel tanks take care of the side-intrusion regulations. Legalization adds a total of 175 lb to the M1's curb weight, bringing it to 3325 lb.

Suspension is typical racing practice, with unequal-length A-arms, coil-over shocks and a 23-mm diameter anti-roll bar at the front. The rear suspension is similar, but with additional upper and lower longitudinal radius rods and a 19-mm anti-roll bar. Tires are Pirelli P7s, 205/55VR-16s on 7-in. rims at the front and 225/50VR-16s on 8-in. rims at the rear; wheels are cast alloy with a distinctive ventilated disc look. Speaking of same, the brakes are ventilated discs of diameters (11.8-in. front, 11.7-in. rear) befitting a car of the M1's performance capability.

The M1's 6-cylinder 3453-cc engine uses the dohc, 24-valve crossflow head developed for the BMW coupes that campaigned the 1974 IMSA series. Other noteworthy features of this over-square engine (93.4-mm bore, 84.0-mm stroke) are its Kugelfischer/Bosch mechanical fuel injection, dry-sump lubrication and digital electronic ignition system with flywheel sensor. In Euro-

AT A GLANCE

	BMW M1	Ferrari 512BB	Lamborghini Countach S
List price	$115,000	$85,000	$85,000
Curb weight, lb	3325	3615	3250
Engine	inline 6	flat 12	V-12
Transmission	5-sp M	5-sp M	5-sp M
0–60 mph, sec	6.2	5.5	5.9
Standing ¼ mi, sec	14.5	14.2	14.6
Speed at end of ¼ mi, mph	97.0	103.5	100.5
Stopping distance from 60 mph, ft	156	140	131
Interior noise at 50 mph, dBA	79	72	85
Lateral acceleration, g	0.858	est 0.850	0.852
Slalom speed, mph	62.7	61.2	63.6
Fuel economy, mpg	13.0	est 10.0	11.0

pean trim, the production engine produces 277 bhp at 6500 rpm and 243 lb-ft of torque at 5000. ACI's Jas Rarewala estimates that desmogging cuts maximum horsepower by some 15 percent (which mainly affects top-end performance), but he's confident from mid-range flow measurements that peak torque is essentially unaffected. U.S. emission standards are met by fitting two Ford dual-brick catalytic converters in place of the single large muffler orginally filling the rear of the car's underside. The forward portion of each catalyst handles NO_x reduction; the rear, HC and CO oxidation. There's also selective air injection that injects air upstream during warmup to promote catalyst light-off, then switches downstream between the two converter types to give each HC/CO converter its necessary oxygen. The only other engine modification is a bit of enrichment to its fuel injection; this, to give the forward NO_x converters their necessary oxygen-starved environment once they're lit.

But don't be concerned that all this emission-control hardware bogs the M1 down, because the car is still a stormer. We had opportunity to test it before its desmogging as well as after, and it impressed us both times with the effortless way in which it posted really spectacular performance. Time from 0 to 60 mph after desmogging was a super quick 6.2 seconds, a scant 0.2 sec off its original figure. Even at the top end, the 0–120 mph time rose by only 1.2 sec (22.8 versus 21.6 sec); and note, there are only a handful of cars that will reach 120 mph within the confines of our test track. Indeed, the M1 is just a tad faster in the quarter mile than the Lamborghini Countach S tested in December 1978, but a bit off the mark from the Porsche 930 Turbo tested in June of that year. For instance, M1 quarter-mile figures were 14.5 sec and 97.0 mph; quick indeed, but not the 13.7 sec and 106.5 mph of that delightfully outrageous 930.

This is part of the appeal of the M1—somehow it doesn't feel outrageous. It's a low car, at 44.9 in. overall height, so getting in demands a certain agility. But in place, only those taller than 6 ft will encounter any head-room compromise. The leather-trimmed interior has that blend of luxury and starkness that's typical of BMWs, and the driver faces a full bank of instruments and a particularly handsome leather-wrapped steering wheel; the latter perfectly located. In typical mid-engine-car tradition, the pedals are offset to the right a bit, but only the narrow space between clutch and dead-pedal to its left presents an ergonomic challenge of any sort. Succinctly, it's a cockpit designed for the enthusiast driver, with every control and instrument in good proximity. Outward vision is what you'd expect for a mid-engine car: fine forward and to the forward flanks, but limited at the rear three-quarters and hampered at the rear somewhat by the louvered hatch. Heating, ventilation and air conditioning controls are built into the center console; in fact, 320i owners will feel right at home because ACI replaces the German-labeled panel with an English-labeled one from the 320i.

The shift feels right at home to BMW owners as well (the knob is standard BMW issue), and it's an excellent linkage with crisp, positive throws and excellent definition of the five forward speeds

and reverse. Befitting the car's racing pedigree, the shift patte has 1st to the left and back, out of the H, but somehow in a car this character it doesn't seem out of place. And compared several other exotic cars that come to mind is the superb over level of fit and finish of the M1's interior. No mouse fur in sig here, thank you.

However, he who travels in style such as this also travels lig because the only provision for luggage is a bin located behind engine bay, sealed from engine heat but measuring only 6.2 cu There's also a small lockable cubbyhole nestled in the re bulkhead between the seats.

A twist of the key, and the engine fires to life with a throa burble enhanced by the catalytic converters replacing the ori nal muffler. A proper sound, although members of your lo constabulary might feel otherwise if you abuse it at all. T engine is a perfect model of a smooth 6-cylinder around tov displaying tractability that would put several less powerful e gines to shame. It'll dawdle all day at 1500–2000 rpm witho protest, if for some strange reason you felt the need of this, ye push on the throttle and you're pinned back in the seat with characteristically BMW turbine sound behind your head. Ev during all-out acceleration testing, the car gives the impression being understressed. You ease into the clutch at 3500 rpm, ju enough to light the P7s off the line, then hold part-throttle ur 4500 when the car catches up, then nail it to 6700. Upsh through one of the best mid-engine linkages, and you're on yc way to an exciting ride.

Brakes and suspension are fully up to this level of perfc mance. Panic stop distances from 60 and 80 mph were 156 a 270 ft, respectively, with the tester's only negative comment bei a relative insensitivity to modulation of the quite light pedal. O 0.5g stops from 60 mph, for instance, required only 22-lb pec pressure, perhaps a bit low for a car of this character. On the otl hand, as expected, there was not the slightest trace of fade in : stops from 60 mph, and certainly the M1's brakes didn't g extensive time to cool in between.

Handling is everything one would expect of a race-br suspension: Our objective measurements on skidpad a. through slalom posted figures of 0.858g and 62.7 mph, respe tively. Around the skidpad, a gradual throttle would bring the c to an understeering stance just slightly that side of neutral, a lit punch would kick the tail out and a liftoff would tuck the front ever so gradually. Through the slalom, the suspension and ti reacted with only barely perceptible lean, and only a nibble at t steering wheel told how close the M1 was to the limit. A bit extra throttle caused a slight squat that translated into add grip. All as effortless as can be, yet at speeds that wou embarrass lesser suspensions (not to say our tester).

The ride is typical BMW, with considerable suspension tra (especially for what is essentially a race-car suspension) a excellent compliance over large irregularities. High-frequen compliance is hardly Cadillac Seville, but then this is a suspe sion—and, in general, a car—that telegraphs to its driver inform tion of the tire/road interface that matters.

But enough. We came away appreciating just how refined. exotic can be, how much pleasure it can provide. Whoever t lucky owner is, we hope attainment of a dream doesn't lessen sweetness.

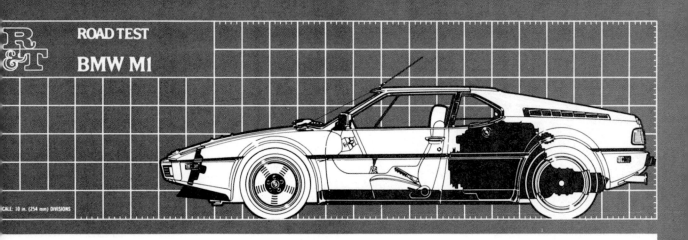

SCALE: 10 in. (254 mm) DIVISIONS

PRICE

List price $115,000
Price as tested $115,000
Price as tested includes importation and safety, emissions & damageability certification

IMPORTER

Automotive Compliance Inc, 25518 Frampton Ave, Harbor City, Calif. 90710

GENERAL

Curb weight, lb/kg ....3325.........1510
Test weight ....3405.........1546
Weight dist (with driver), f/r, % 45/55
Wheelbase, in./mm ....100.8.........2560
Track, front/rear ....61.0/62.0...1550/1576
Length ....174.7.........4437
Width ....71.8.........1824
Height ....44.9.........1140
Ground clearance ....4.9.........125
Overhang, f/r ....39.9/34.0...1013/864
Trunk space, cu ft/liters ....6.2.........176
Fuel capacity, U.S. gal./liters ....30.6.........116

INSTRUMENTATION

Instruments: 280-km/h speedo, 9000-rpm tach, 999, 999 odo, 999.9 trip odo, oil press., coolant temp, oil temp, fuel level, clock
Warning lights: oil press., coolant temp, alternator, brake sys, low fuel, rear-window heat, seatbelts, hazard, high beam, directionals

ENGINE

Type ....dohc inline 6
Bore x stroke, in./mm ......3.68 x 3.31 ...93.4 x 84.0
Displacement, cu in./cc ....210.........3453
Compression ratio 9.0:1
Bhp @ rpm, SAE net/kW ....est 235/175 @ 6500
Equivalent mph / km/h 152/245
Torque @ rpm, lb-ft/Nm........est 243/330 @ 5000
Equivalent mph / km/h 117/188
Fuel injection............Kugelfischer-Bosch mechanical
Fuel requirement ....unleaded, 91-oct
Exhaust-emission control equipment: 3-way catalyst with selective air injection

DRIVETRAIN

Transmission ....5-sp manual
Gear ratios: 5th (0.70) 2.95:1
4th (0.85) 3.59:1
3rd (1.14) 4.81:1
2nd (1.61) 6.79:1
1st (2.42) 10.21:1
Final drive ratio 4.22:1

ACCOMMODATION

Seating capacity, persons 2
Head room, in./mm ....34.5.........876
Seat width ....2 x 20.0.........2 x 508
Seat back adjustment, deg 30

CHASSIS & BODY

Layout ....mid engine/rear drive
Body/frame.........................fiberglass/tubular steel space frame
Brake system ..11.8-in. (300-mm) vented discs front, 11.7-in. (297-mm) vented discs rear; vacuum asst
Swept area, sq in./sq cm ....502.........3239
Wheels...............cast alloy, 16 x 7 front, 16 x 8 rear
Tires ....Pirelli P7; 205/55VR-16 front, 225/50VR-16 rear
Steering type.............................rack & pinion
Overall ratio ....na
Turns, lock-to-lock 3.1
Turning circle, ft/m.............42.7.........13.0
Front suspension: unequal-length A-arms, coil springs, tube shocks, anti-roll bar
Rear suspension: unequal-length A-arms, longitudinal radius rods, coil springs, tube shocks, anti-roll bar

MAINTENANCE

Service intervals, km:
Oil/filter change.....................7500/7500
Chassis lube ....none
Tuneup 15,000
Warranty, mo/mi..........................6/6000

CALCULATED DATA

Lb/bhp (test weight)..........................14.5
Mph/1000 rpm (5th gear).....................23.1
Engine revs/mi (60 mph).....................2600
Piston travel, ft/mi..........................1435
R&T steering index..........................1.32
Brake swept area, sq in./ton 295

ROAD TEST RESULTS

ACCELERATION

Time to distance, sec:
0-100 ft 3.2
0-500 ft 8.0
0-1320 ft (¼ mi) 14.5
Speed at end of ¼ mi, mph 97.0
Time to speed, sec:
0-30 mph 2.5
0-50 mph 4.9
0-60 mph 6.2
0-80 mph 9.8
0-100 mph 15.1
0-120 mph 22.8

SPEEDS IN GEARS

5th gear (6700 rpm) 156
4th (6700)...........................127
3rd (6700)............................97
2nd (6700)............................70
1st (6700)............................47

FUEL ECONOMY

Normal driving, mpg 13.0
Cruising range, mi (1-gal. res) 385

HANDLING

Lateral accel, 100-ft radius, g ...0.858
Speed thru 700-ft slalom, mph ...62.7

BRAKES

Minimum stopping distances, ft:
From 60 mph 156
From 80 mph 270
Control in panic stop...........very good
Pedal effort for 0.5g stop, lb 22
Fade: percent increase in pedal effort to maintain 0.5g deceleration in 6 stops from 60 mph.....................nil
Parking: hold 30% grade? ....yes
Overall brake rating..............very good

INTERIOR NOISE

Idle in neutral, dBA 65
Maximum, 1st gear 87
Constant 30 mph 72
50 mph..............................79
70 mph..............................79
90 mph..............................84

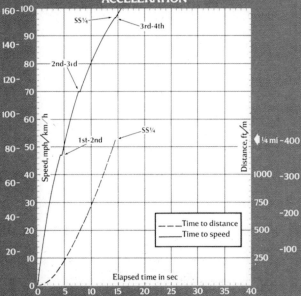

ACCELERATION

H&B BMW M635CSi

The classic business suit bulges with more muscle

THE 6-SERIES BMW, in U.S.-legal form, has always been just a bit on the sedate, understated side, with less power than its substantial chassis and beautiful body would call for. The original 630CSi appeared in mid-1976; as a 1977 model for the U.S. it produced 176 bhp from an L-Jetronic 3.0-liter six. With emissions standards tightening, the extra 224 cc of the 633CSi gave it just one more horsepower in 1979 and another four by 1982, as BMW refined its U.S. plumbing. The 6-series was no slouch, but hard-driving BMW enthusiasts were tantalized by the European 635CSi, which had been putting out

218 *Pferdstärke* since 1978, not to mention the mid-engine M[...] with a twin-overhead-camshaft, 24-valve version of the six pr[...] ducing 277 bhp. The latter car was brought in as a gray-mark[...] item for awhile; it's now history, but its formidable engine n[...] sits at the front of the well-known coupe. Giving it, at last, t[...] muscles to fill out the suit.

The 24-valve coupe is known as the M635CSi. M is f[...] Motorsports, the *Rennabteilung* that has churned out Tourin[...] Formula 2 and Formula 1 victories for the marque, as well as t[...] M1 in its own special series. The 6 stands for the body type, [...] course, the 35 indicates the 3.5-liter (actually 3453-cc) displac[...] ment, and the Coupe-Sport-injected letters have been on t[...] U.S. cars all along. But the engine is even stronger than t[...] original M1's; with Bosch Motronic injection, a higher compre[...] sion ratio (up to 10.0:1 from 9.0:1) and new induction and e[...] haust systems, this greatest of all contemporary inline-6s p[...] out a whopping 286 bhp DIN, equal to approximately 281 SA[...] and an estimated 251 lb-ft of torque. Now that it has all t[...] power a sane person can ask for, what does it do with it?

Just about everything a sane person can ask for. You probab[...] already know that an M635CSi did 154.6 mph in our Worl[...] Fastest Cars exercise (R&T, September 1984). Our current te[...] car, a 1984 model made EPA and DOT-legal by H&B of Berk[...]

PHOTOS BY JOHN LAMM

ey, California, and further enhanced by H&B chassis, wheel, ody and interior equipment, is an exhilarating performer. Once ou get to 3000 rpm, the acceleration becomes explosive, yet he car's refinement allows it to charge downfield without rip- ing out a single shoulder seam. Clearly a matter of having your teak and eating it too. Stay off the throttle, and the M635CSi is he comfortable, if slightly stiff and bulky coupe you've always nown; get on it and you'll have the full attention of every traf- c enforcement officer in your state. In making the engine emis- ions-legal, H&B doesn't seem to have lost any of the power, lthough at the top—6000 rpm to redline—the six seems just a ny bit less willing than the one we ran in Europe in 1984. The earbox, a strengthened 5-speed, is mated to a 3.73:1 final drive compared with 3.45 for the regular factory 635CSi) and gives etter dig off the line if a slightly lower maximum speed. The hifting is notchy when the box is cold, but effortless after that.

H&B's chassis kit includes special springs front and rear, uned to the factory-installed Bilstein shocks, and adjustable nti-roll bars. The wheels are 3-piece H&B 8 x 16-in. alloy, nounting 225/50VR-16 Yokohama A-008 tires. The body and nterior options are mostly appearance oriented, although the xtra gauges (oil pressure, oil temperature, voltmeter), four lella quartz halogen headlights and aerodynamic side skirts are →

AT A GLANCE	H&B BMW M635CSi	Ferrari Mondial Cabriolet	Porsche 928S
Price, base/ as tested	$48,207 $57,382	$65,000 $66,180	$50,000 $50,000
Curb weight, lb	3350	3545	3425
Engine/drive	inline-6/rwd	V-8/rwd	V-8/rwd
Transmission	5-sp M	5-sp M	5-sp M
0–60 mph, sec	6.4	7.6	5.9
Standing ¼ mi, sec @ mph	15.0 @ 95.5	16.0 @ 87.0	14.2 @ 101.5
Stopping distance from 60 mph, ft	141	153	145
Lateral acceleration, g	0.826	0.808	0.820
Slalom speed, mph	58.8	60.3	57.9
Fuel economy, mpg	16.5	13.5	est 17.0

	Pro	Con
M635 CSi:	responsive and powerful en- gine, excellent brakes, superb handling and room for four	high price, Teutonic interior ap- pointments not for everybody, sparse parts availability
Mondial Cabriolet: tested 5-84	good overall performance, Ital- ian charm, exciting sounds	limited rear-seat room, weight, modest acceleration in class, difficult folding top, price
928S: tested 4-85	excellent power and handling, high-quality finish, adequate luggage room	poor outward vision, weight, limited rear-seat room

ROAD & TRACK
R&T
ROAD TEST

functional (at the extreme ends of the performance spectrum, at least). The result of all this equipment (besides adding more than $9000 to the already hefty $48,207 asking price) is superb comportment in all but the tightest places (parking lot jockeys may never know how good this particular Bimmer is). The lateral acceleration figure is 0.826g, slalom speed is 58.8 mph (remember, this a big car), and the brakes are absolutely splendid, pulling the 3485-lb car down to nought from 60 mph in just 141

ft, from 80 in 249, and with excellent ABS control at all tim With brakes like these, you can go incredibly fast with full con dence. The H&B suspension modifications give a tauter ride a less body roll, but without undue harshness.

The interior is all business, of course, in the usual BMW ult authoritative way, with fairly stiff seats (uncomfortably narr for larger persons and shy on head room with the sunroof) a little design "warmth." That's okay if you're all business, but that's the intent, then we can nitpick a bit: The steering whe adjustment could be improved, the shift lever ought to be a lit closer, and the instrument lighting could be better for those wi older, less adapting eyesight. But the coupe's rational body sty gives space and outward vision of the kind you just can't get the mid-engine exotics with which you normally associate th level of performance.

In short, the H&B M635CSi is the BMW coupe that enthu asts have been wanting for nearly nine years. When the 630C first arrived, we missed the agility of the preceding 3.0CS; n this bigger, tougher car has the power and handling to cope wi any situation. It strongly impressed every member of the sta including those of less competitive bent. After all, it can slowly very well, too. Just not very often.

PRICE

List price, San Francisco	$48,207
Price as tested	$57,382

Price as tested includes std equip. (elect. window lifts, trip computer, central door locking), H&B alloy wheels and Yokohama A-008 tires ($2716), air cond ($1484), H&B suspension group ($1469), elect. sunroof ($743), leather int ($679), AM/FM stereo/cassette ($599), metallic paint ($411), H&B instrument group ($394), security alarm ($222), striping ($216), elect. antenna ($149), tinted glass ($84), warning triangle ($9)

ENGINE

Type	dohc 4-valve inline-6
Bore x stroke, in./mm	3.68 x 3.31....93.4 x 84.0
Displacement, cu in./cc	211......3453
Compression ratio	10.5:1
Bhp @ rpm, SAE net/kW	est 281/210 @ 6500
Torque @ rpm, lb-ft/Nm	est 251/340 @ 4500
Fuel injection	Bosch Motronic
Fuel requirement	premium unleaded, 92 pump octane

DRIVETRAIN

Transmission	5-sp manual
Gear ratios: 5th (0.81)	3.02:1
4th (1.00)	3.73:1
3rd (1.35)	5.04:1
2nd (2.08)	7.76:1
1st (3.51)	13.09:1
Final drive ratio	3.73:1

GENERAL

Curb weight, lb/kg	3350	1521
Test weight	3485	1582
Weight dist (with driver), f/r, %	55/45	
Wheelbase, in./mm	103.3	2625
Track, front/rear	55.9/58.3	1420/1480
Length	187.2	4755
Width	67.9	1725
Height	53.3	1354
Trunk space, cu ft/liters	15.7	445
Fuel capacity, U.S. gal./liters	18.5	70

CHASSIS & BODY

Layout	front engine/rear drive
Body/frame	unit steel
Brake system	11.2-in. (284-mm) vented discs front, 11.2-in. (284-mm) discs rear; ABS; vacuum assisted
Wheels	cast alloy, 16 x 8
Tires	Yokohama A-008, 225/50VR-16
Steering type	recirculating ball, power assisted
Turns, lock-to-lock	3.5
Suspension, front/rear:	MacPherson struts, double-pivot lower links, coil springs, tube shocks, anti-roll bar/modified semi-trailing arms, coil springs, tube shocks, anti-roll bar

CALCULATED DATA

Lb/bhp (test weight)	12.4
Mph/1000 rpm (5th gear)	24.0
Engine revs/mi (60 mph)	2500
R&T steering index	1.35
Brake swept area, sq in./ton	220

ROAD TEST RESULTS

ACCELERATION

Time to distance, sec:

0–100 ft	3.2
0–50u ft	8.2
0–1320 ft (¼ mi)	15.0
Speed at end of ¼ mi, mph	95.5

Time to speed, sec:

0–30 mph	2.4
0–50 mph	4.9
0–60 mph	6.4
0–70 mph	8.5
0–80 mph	10.7
0–100 mph	16.9

HANDLING

Lateral accel, 100-ft radius, g	0.826
Speed thru 700-ft slalom, mph	58.8

FUEL ECONOMY

Normal driving, mpg	16.5

BRAKES

Minimum stopping distances, ft:

From 60 mph	141
From 80 mph	249
Control in panic stop	excellent
Pedal effort for 0.5g stop, lb	20
Fade: percent increase in pedal effort to maintain 0.5g deceleration in 6 stops from 60 mph	nil
Overall brake rating	excellent

SPEEDS IN GEARS

5th gear (6100 rpm)	est 145
4th (6500)	129
3rd (6500)	97
2nd (6500)	65
1st (6500)	38

INTERIOR NOISE

Constant 30 mph, dBA	63
50 mph	66
70 mph	75

ACCELERATION

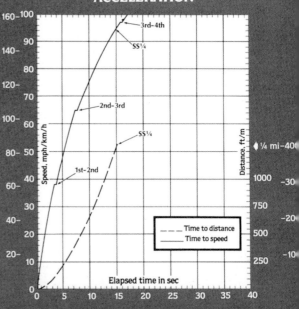

MUNICH MUSCLE

A 5-series BMW for the terminally impatient

BY PAUL FRERE

PHOTOS BY JEFFREY R. ZWART

BMW's SECOND-SERIES M535i is not exactly the answer to Mercedes' 16-valve hot shot; that will come later. But it is an answer to those who complain that BMWs are losing their sporting image.

Basically, the M535i is a 528i in which the 184-bhp DIN 2.8-liter 6-cylinder is replaced by the 218-bhp 3.4-liter inline-6. The package includes a beefier 5-speed gearbox, 25-percent limited-slip differential, more sporting suspension with Bilstein gas-pressurized shock absorbers, Michelin 220/55VR-390 TRX tires on alloy wheels and various spoilers that lower the normal model's uninspiring 0.40 drag coefficient to a claimed 0.37. Add Recaro bucket seats and a smaller steering wheel and there is your M535i. ABS anti-lock brakes are standard, as is the overdrive gearbox, but you can also order the car with a close-ratio 5-speed or BMW's 4-speed automatic with lockup torque converter.

To understand the significance of the M535i, it is necessary to consider two new Mercedes. First came the 16-valve 190, and to answer that BMW is developing a 16-valve, 4-cylinder 323i. The M323i will receive two-thirds of the 3.4-liter M1 engine as used in the M635CSi coupe. More recently Mercedes-Benz has introduced the new 300E, which has the aerodynamics to be much faster than anything BMW could offer in this price class. That is the car BMW has aimed at with the M535i. Normally the M prefix indicates that the car was developed by BMW Motorsport, the subsidiary responsible for racing activities. But the M535i is assembled on the regular assembly line of the Dingolfing factory with the other 5-series cars, because BMW Motorsport wouldn't be able to meet the expected demand.

The car I took out for a day during a visit to Munich was a standard one with the wide-ratio overdrive gearbox, and the first thing I did was gather performance figures. The factory's claim of 143-mph top speed is perfectly justified as I obtained a 2-way average of 143.5 mph in 4th gear at 6000 rpm. Shifting to 5th drops the speed to about 140 mph at 4750 rpm. As the close-ratio box is doubtlessly more in line with the sporting character of the car, I must say that for use on non-restricted German motorways, the overdrive 5th has something to commend it.

Acceleration is a match for top speed. I measured a 0 to 60 mph time of 7.1 seconds, a 0–100 mph time of 19.0 sec and 0–125 mph in 35.3 sec. The standing-start kilometer took 27.8 sec.

On the back roads of the Danude valley, the car's handling qualities were put into perspective. Here the BMW was a real joy to drive, displaying minimal roll and a neutral feel up to the limit, when easily controlled oversteer arrives. Lifting off accentuates the tendency, but never in an embarrassing way. In the lower gears power oversteer can be easily fed to the car with the limited-slip differential and excellent power assisted steering providing good feel under all circumstances. In fact, all the controls work beautifully, from gearchange to heater controls, and the pedals are ideally arranged for heel-and-toeing. This 4-door is, in fact, as much fun to drive as most real sports cars, while ride comfort has suffered very little from the suspension modifications.

Though the M535i is not a light car

(3050 lb with 17 gal. of fuel) and in spite of only indifferent aerodynamics, it is certainly no gas guzzler. In a day's hard driving, including performance tests, it returned 15.2 mpg.

Of course, BMW could do even better. If the 3.4-liter fits, so will the twincam, 24-valve M1 engine producing 289 bhp. Wouldn't that be a good project for BMW Motorsport?

Letter from Europe

BY PAUL FRERE

THE M5

Driving impressions of BMW's road-scorcher

CAN APPEARANCES BE deceiving? You bet! And that's particularly true for BMW's new M5. Nothing about its sedate exterior bespeaks its remarkable performance. Nor is it distinguished essentially from its Bavarian brethren except by diminutive M badges front and rear. Yet this latest Bimmer is undoubtedly today's fastest 4-door sedan by a major manufacturer.

The figures I achieved speak for themselves: a maximum 2-way speed of 151 mph (the factory says my run was not quite long enough as it claims 152), 0 to 60 mph in 6.2 seconds, a standing quarter mile in 14.4 and a standing kilometer in a rousing 26.2, just before changing up into 5th at 125 mph.

So where does the secret to all this oomph lie? Under the hood and in the wheel arches. There's that wonderful straight-6, 24-valve 3.5-liter directly derived from the engine that powered the BMW coupes to victory in America's IMSA series, and later, in production form, was the heart beat of the M1 sports coupe. For the M5 and the M635CSi sister model, it was further improved by the fully eleetronic Bosch Motronic engine management system that raised its power from 277 to 286 bhp while making it even more tractable and economical.

This engine is matched to a 5-speed gearbox similar to that of the 528i and 535i models but with taller-geared 1st, 2nd and 3rd ratios. Direct 4th and 0.81:1 5th are retained. But in contrast to standard models, 5th gear, despite the step-up, has no overdrive character as the final-drive ratio is raised numerically from 3.07 to 3.73:1, and maximum speed very near-

PHOTO BY R. GAFFRON

ly coincides with the 6500 peak revolutions in 5th. The clutch is also matched to the higher power of the engine—most apparent when you push the pedal—even though its action is helped by an over-center spring.

Other modifications that differentiate the M5 from lesser Bimmers involve the running gear. The car is lowered, the springs and anti-roll bars are stiffer, the shock absorbers are gas-pressurized Bilsteins, and larger brakes with 4-piston calipers at the front wheels are fitted. Then there are the huge 220/55VR-390 TRX tires and braking by Bosch ABS. BMW's excellent power assisted steering is standard, of course, providing very good feel at speed while being reasonably light for parking maneuvers, even though the special 3-spoke steering wheel is comparatively small as befits a sports sedan.

The sporting character is emphasized further by BMW's own bucket seats, normally upholstered in cloth, but leather in the test car, and adjustable for height and rake plus thigh support. The seats provide a wonderful hold that is essential because of the high lateral forces the car can generate under hard cornering.

This car, you see, despite its external appearance and generous accommodation for four or even five passengers and their luggage, is the next best thing to a full-blood sports car. It handles like one and certainly goes like one. On any road, a competent driver at the wheel can keep up with anything he is likely to encounter.

But the real charm of this car is that it is just as happy being driven leisurely or in dense city traffic. Even though it develops a healthy 83 bhp/liter, the 24-valve engine will pull smoothly from less than 1000 rpm in 5th and very strongly from less than 4000 or so.

Good as this low-speed performance is, however, it's not what the M5 is meant for. It begs to be pushed, to be cornered fast; and with that precise gear change and an engine that revels in being revved, it's almost impossible to resist the temptation.

So, go ahead. Let yourself be tempted, but don't be surprised if the engine is not as quiet as Jaguar's V-12. You can't expect a 24-valver revving to 7000 rpm to be unobtrusive, but the sound is music to the enthusiast's ears.

Cornering is another pleasure. Except in downhill hairpins, there is never a trace of unwelcome understeer, even though the front-end geometry and settings are almost identical with that of other 5-series BMWs. Lift off in mid-corner and the car closes its line, but—surely due to the stiffer springs and dampers and to the standard limited-slip differential—transition from the almost neutral attitude to oversteer is less brutal than in other BMWs.

With the available power, it is possible to powerslide the car around a bend, even on a dry road, in 2nd or 3rd. On wet or damp surfaces, of course, it's the easiest thing to do and—again thanks to the limited-slip differential—the car can easily be steered with the accelerator. The high-geared steering (16.5:1 overall) allows the driver to keep perfect control.

The only real criticism, from a sporting driver's point of view, is the large gap between 2nd and 3rd gear. The former allows just 62 mph before the cutout intervenes, while 3rd is good for 95 mph. This means it is useless to drop into 2nd unless the speed has dropped to 50 mph and the engine speed to a little over 3500 rpm. Because of the engine's good flexibility, this is perfectly acceptable under any normal conditions but frustrating if you try to extract the last ounce from the car.

As long as you remain aware of its power, the M5 is essentially a safe car. Even in the wet, the big Michelins hang on stubbornly. To get an idea of the car's potential I recently left Herrenberg, near Stuttgart, at 2:30 p.m., drove through pouring rain, stopped for dinner and still reached Nice, 720 miles away, at 10:45 that night. Most of the distance was covered by motorways, but it included 25 miles on traffic-infested German roads and a tour through Freiburg. It also included three refueling and several tollgate stops. Nevertheless, as I was coming into Nice the onboard computer indicated a trip average of exactly 92 mph. I cruised at 125 mph and more wherever possible (darkness and heavy rain discouraged police from coming out with their radar) and got 12.8 mpg, quite good considering the speed and the less than state-of-the-art aerodynamics. And even in the worst of the downpours, the big car could be driven at 125 mph without aquaplaning.

At nearly 85,000 Deutsche Mark ($35,105), the M5 is an expensive car. It is spacious, fast, safe and great fun to drive. It is also luxuriously appointed and beautifully finished. Knowledgeable gas-station attendants will always offer to check the oil just to have a look at the engine, a delight to behold.

But any car is a compromise, and you may ask what has to be sacrificed, aside from your bank account. There are two things: some luggage space (because the big battery is moved from the front end to the luggage compartment, where it is contained in a well finished box covered in the same quality fabric) and some low-speed ride comfort. The space taken by the battery is not significant as the stowage area is large anyway. And the initial harshness is quickly forgotten as the faster you drive, the more comfortable the ride becomes. Although comfort will never be the model's strong point, it would certainly be unfair to complain because the excellent seats and the M5's dynamic qualities make it superb. Imagine what that car would be if it were based on a well shaped, modern aerodynamic body.

PHOTOS BY BRIAN BLADES

BMW

M3 & 325is

Breeding improves the racing

THE OLD DICTUM that racing improves the breed has always been part of the creed of all motorsports enthusiasts. It is sometimes difficult to show how a technology trickles down from the likes of an Indy or an IMSA GTP car; but when the racing hardware is similar to what is sold for the street, an immediate benefit for the consumer is more believable. But how much of a racing sedan actually finds its way to a street machine? Usually, precious little; there are virtually no market pressures to apply racing technology. At best, a bit of the image rubs off.

Enter the Federation Internationale de l'Automobile (FIA) and its rules for Group A racers. To qualify a car for Group A, a manufacturer must produce at least 5000 cars of that type in any given 12-month period. The cars must have a minimum of four seats. Minimum weight is related to engine displacement, but the cylinders may not be bored out more than 0.6 mm to reach the displacement limit for that weight class; similarly for sleeving down engines too large for the desired weight class.

Individual components may be modified, polished, lightened, machined, etched or heat treated, but not replaced by parts stemming from other sources. The original fuel injection system must be retained, but may be modified. The camshaft is free, as is its timing. Suspension pickup points must remain unchanged. Wheels and tires must be contained within the original bodywork; they aren't allowed to stick out. Add-on aerodynamic aids beyond the car's original road-going equipment are not allowed.

The result of all this is that cars not immediately associated with racing are used to good effect in this predominantly European class. Victory Lane at the Nürburgring or Spa has in years past been occupied by the likes of Volvo and Rover; the 1985 Class 1 (over 2.5 liters) was won by Volvo, closely followed by Rover with BMW a distant 3rd. In Class 2 (1.6–2.5 liters) Alfa Romeo beat out BMW. In 1986 BMW won both Class 1 and 2, against competition from Mercedes-Benz (190E 2.3) and Rover (Vitesse, aka the 3500).

The manufacturers were begin-ning to get serious about touring cars, fielding teams both above and below board. Back in 1987 there were several racing series for Group A cars, including the then-new World Touring Car Championship, coinciding with the European Touring Car Championship except for four races in Australia and New Zealand. Track successes mean more dealer sales. To achieve its own unfair advantage, BMW decided to enter Group A in a big way—by laying on a series of 5000 cars for the road

designed solely to field similar cars on the track. A direct example of racing improving the breed—or, more correctly, the right breeding making racing possible. The car is called the M3 and is based on the familiar 3-series sports sedans. We compared this homologation special to its more civilized brother, the 325is, and the results are very interesting.

The M3 is a product of BMW Motorsport GmbH, but motorsport is not that group's sole business. Other M products include the Formula 1

When revved up high, little 4-cylinder makes almost as much power as its 6-cylinder cousin. Homologated racing doesn't hurt the breed.

engine and tuned street cars plus designer clothes and "Motorsport" dead pedals in designer colors. The M3 is the first BMW since the M1 to be built for homologation.

The M3 at first glance looks like a typical cafe racer. But on this car, all the add-ons have a purpose. It's all there because it needs to be there for racing. Remember, no spoiler on the road car means no spoiler on the racer, no add-on fender flares allowed. Not immediately noticeable is the greater rake to the M3's backlight, achieved by moving its bottom edge back and fairing it all in with a plastic cap over the C-pillars and the rear edge of the roof. The trunk lid was raised by installing a plastic molding to replace the normal metal lid. Spoilers, skirts, fat tires and boxy fender flares capable of covering wheels up to 10 in. wide (the largest allowed in its racing class) complete the zoomy kit. Despite, or perhaps better said, *because* of all the add-ons, BMW claims a C_X of 0.33.

Under the skin, more modifications have been made. The front suspension, for example, has altered pickup points. The front hub carrier is different, giving the M3 more caster than the "civilian" versions for better high-speed stability and more steering feel. The power-assisted steering has been quickened. Lower control arms are aluminum instead of steel. The car has been lowered, and rising-rate springs have been installed at the rear. Spring, shock, anti-roll bar and rubber-bushing calibrations have been changed. The brakes have been upgraded to those used on the 6- and 7-series cars. A 25-percent limited-slip differential and ABS brakes are standard.

The shift lever of the U.S. market car displays a conventional shift pattern, in contrast to the European model that has 1st to the left and back. Gear ratios, too, are different. The U.S. car is geared significantly lower in 1st and 2nd, for better acceleration in the lower gears. Ratios in the remaining gears are similar but not identical.

The engine bay is also heavily modified. The engine is surprisingly not the newer, lighter, aluminum M20 inline-6 used in other cars of the 3-series, but rather the S14 inline-4, derived from the old M10 that also spawned the F1 powerplant. The M3 engine develops 192 bhp at 6750 rpm and 170 lb-ft of torque at 4750 rpm. In contrast to its 4-cylinder older brothers in the BMW family, the M3's engine has siamesed cylinders that also serve to stiffen the block. Why the step backward, to a four? The shorter, forged crankshaft of the four is stiffer, more resistant to torsional vibrations, and can be revved higher; the new six was designed for low weight and easy, cost-effective assembly and is not as strong as the older design. Also no 4-valve head is readily available for the new six, while the old four had 4-valve heads as long ago as 1966.

Note that the new six is not to be confused with the bigger six used in the larger 5-, 6-, and 7-series cars and the 4-valve M1 powerplant now used in the M635CSi and M5.

The M3 engine features two chain-driven cams and a cast-iron block, while the 325is has a single belt-driven cam. By a wide margin, the M3 has greater power potential than the new six and can rev higher in racing trim; BMW claims a boost up to 10,000 rpm is possible. The in-

R O A D T E S T D A T A

M3

List price, all POE **$34,950**
Price as tested **$34,950**
Price as tested includes std equip. (ABS, air cond, AM/FM stereo/cassette, elect. sunroof, leather int, trip computer, elect. window lifts, elect. adj mirrors, central locking)

CHASSIS & BODY

Layout .... front engine/rear drive
Body/frame ....steel & plastic/
unit steel
Brake system, f/r ....11.0-in. vented discs/11.1-in. vented discs, vacuum assist, ABS
Wheels ....cast alloy, 15 x 7J
Tires .....Pirelli P600, 205/55VR-15
Steering type .... rack & pinion, power assist
Turns, lock to lock 3.6
Turning circle, ft 36.4
Suspension, f/r: MacPherson struts, lower A-arms, coil springs, tube shocks, anti-roll bar/semi-trailing arms, coil springs, tube shocks, anti-roll bar

GENERAL

Curb weight, lb **2865**
Test weight.....................**3005**
Wt dist (w/driver), f/r, % **52/48**
Wheelbase, in. **101.0**
Track, f/r **55.6/56.1**
Length **171.1**
Width **66.1**
Height **53.9**
Trunk space, cu ft **14.8**
Fuel capacity, U.S. gal. **14.5**

ENGINE

Type ....dohc 4-valve inline-4
Bore x stroke, mm ..... **93.4 x 84.0**
Displacement, cc **2302**
Compression ratio **10.5:1**
Bhp @ rpm, SAE net ...**192 @ 6750**
Torque @ rpm, lb-ft.....**170 @ 4750**
Fuel injection ....elect.
Fuel requirement .... unleaded, 91-pump oct

DRIVETRAIN

Transmission ....**5-sp manual**
Gear ratios: 5th (0.81) **3.32:1**
4th (1.00) **4.10:1**
3rd (1.40)................**5.74:1**
2nd (2.20) **9.02:1**
1st (3.83)................**15.70:1**
Final-drive ratio **4.10:1**

ACCELERATION

Time to distance, sec:
0–100 ft.....................**3.1**
0–500 ft.....................**8.2**
0–1320 ft (¼ mi) **15.4**
Speed at end of ¼ mi, mph....**91.0**
Time to speed, sec:
0–30 mph **2.2**
0–40 mph **3.6**
0–50 mph **5.1**
0–60 mph **7.1**
0–70 mph **9.2**
0–80 mph **11.7**
0–90 mph **15.0**
0–100 mph.............. est **20.0**

BRAKING

Minimum stopping distances, ft:
From 60 mph **135**
From 80 mph **239**
Control in panic stop ....**excellent**
Overall brake rating ....**very good**

HANDLING

Lateral accel, 100-ft radius, g.. **0.82**
Speed thru 700-ft slalom, mph **64.7**

SPEEDS IN GEARS

Maximum engine rpm **7250**
5th gear (rpm) mph est **(5410)** 143
4th, est (7250) **125**
3rd (7250) **90**
2nd (7250).......................**57**
1st (7250) **33**

CALCULATED DATA

Lb/bhp (test weight) **15.7**
Bhp/liter **83.4**
Engine revs @ 60 mph in 5th gear **2270**
R&T steering index............ **1.31**

INTERIOR NOISE

Idle in neutral, dBA.................**59**
Maximum, 1st gear **79**
Constant 70 mph **75**

FUEL ECONOMY

Normal driving, mpg............ **20.5**

duction system uses a Bosch Motronic III and four throttle butterflies to reduce lag, one per cylinder. A larger cast-aluminum oil pan, with windage tray and baffles, holds the greater quantity of oil required on the race track.

The interior of the car has the familiar, excellent BMW ergonomics. Subtle changes tell the driver that this is an extraordinary coupe; the speedometer goes to 160 mph, the tach to 8000 with a 7250-rpm redline, and the fuel economy gauge in the speedometer has been replaced by an oil-temperature gauge. Although the M3 is intended to provide a basis for a race car, it comes fully equipped with sunroof, electric window lifts, central locking, sound system and air conditioning. About the only option is metallic paint. Automatic transmission is not available.

What shall we use as a yardstick? A good candidate is the BMW 325is. The 325 family features the 2.5-liter inline-6, which develops 168 bhp at 5800 rpm and 164 lb-ft at 4300. Compare these figures to the M3; although power is less, torque is similar and is developed at lower revs. That's significant, as we'll soon see. In comparison to the M3, the gearing is taller all across the board, which should hurt the 325is in acceleration. The 325is has a limited-slip differential, sport suspension with twin-tube shocks similar to the M3, sport seats, front air dam and small body-color rear lip spoiler and a

number of detail changes compared with the 1987 model.

Seat time. The first impression upon entering the M3 is how well everything is laid out for serious driving. The steering wheel fits the hands; the gauges are where they should be. The grippy seats, among the best to be found anywhere, are adjustable for rake, reach, height and thigh support, thankfully without any electric motors. The ventila-

tion system works well. Materials and workmanship in the interior are excellent.

On the road, the handling of the M3 has a typical BMW trace of oversteer at the limit, useful when mastered. Cornering performance of the M3 is spirited, with little lean. The car feels tossable. The pedals are easy to heel and toe, and the shifter has a somewhat notchy but accurate feel. Smooth, quick shifts are easily

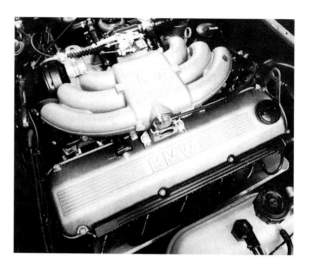

BMW has persisted with its straight-6, refining it successfully in a world of V-6s. It has replaced 4-cylinder Bimmers as the norm.

mastered. Steering is light but precise with nice feedback, allowing control of that oversteer. The suspension is not as hard as one might expect. The ABS brakes are, as always, simply wonderful, with a nice, hard pedal.

Now the down side. The unfortunate thing is the engine. It is the logical choice for BMW's motorsport activities, in view of its power potential; but under most driving conditions one is likely to encounter without need of a helmet, it is harsh, rough, buzzy and boomy. There's lots of valve-train noise, thanks to the chain-driven overhead cams. There is a lack of power off the line, but BMW wisely chose super-low gearing for the first two gears. It's useful around town but long-legged if need be. The engine comes on the cam at 4500 rpm or so.

By comparison, the 325is engine is quiet. Although not as noiseless as, say, the prime mover of the Acura Legend or the bigger BMWs, it is certainly one of the smoother engines around. A wee bit of valve-train noise can be heard, but it's more of the well-oiled machinery variety and not an annoyance to the enthusiast.

One staffer summed it all up by asking, "Who needs the M3's 4-cylinder peakiness with this car's smooth, torquey, very tractable quick six?"

All of this is forgotten when the M3 is driven quickly on a mountain road. Preferably with the windows down. All of that booming and buzzing around town suddenly seems insignificant; in fact, it's pleasant. *This is what it's all about.* The engine, when revved hard, shoots the car from turn to turn; the four butterflies make it a happy revver. The hard brake pedal and ABS allow braking deep into the turns, even in the face of guardrails and 500-ft drops, far past the point where prudence would have one back off in lesser cars. The shifter and clutch are quick and precise. The steering is precise; the driver is in control. Suddenly it all makes sense. This is as close as most owners will come to participatory motorsport, and after all, that is what this car was designed to do. Said one driver, "It seduces me despite my better judgment."

And how does the 325is fare under such driving? Not at all badly. Although breeding will tell, and the

325 is not race-bred, it does quite well. It, too, is a joy to drive under such conditions; it, too, has the foolproof braking and predictable handling. The difference is in degree; the brake pedal is a bit softer, the steering a mite less precise, the suspension a tad softer. Where the 325is shines is in all-around utility. The engine develops more torque at lower rpm than the M3, allowing spirited performance around town and away from stops, in spite of its gear-ratio handicap.

Which one to buy? The M3 is the choice for those who crave a car whose racing image is more than skin deep. This is a race car, make no mistake; every significant part on it justifies its presence on the racers. When pushed to its limits, it performs like a race car—fast and noisy.

For customers who don't need the motorsport image, who may feel a bit self-conscious about the M3's plastic body bits and spoilers, the more conservative 325 is a more logical choice. It's far more civilized and offers very nearly the same performance at a significantly lower cost.

—*Road & Track, February 1988*

R O A D   T E S T   D A T A

325is

List price, all POE **$28,950**
Price as tested **$28,950**
Price as tested includes std equip.: ABS, air cond, AM/FM stereo/cassette, elect. sunroof, leather int, trip computer, elect. window lifts, elect. adj mirrors, central locking

CHASSIS & BODY

Layout .... front engine/rear drive
Body/frame .... unit steel
Brake system, f/r .....10.2-in. vented discs/10.2-in. vented discs, vacuum assist, ABS
Wheels ....cast alloy, 15 x 6½JJ
Tires .... Uniroyal Rallye 340/65, 195/65VR-14
Steering type .... rack & pinion, power assist
Turns, lock to lock 3.9
Turning circle, ft 34.4
Suspension, f/r: MacPherson struts, lower A-arms, coil springs, tube shocks, anti-roll bar/semi-trailing arms, coil springs, tube shocks, anti-roll bar

GENERAL

Curb weight, lb **2825**
Test weight....................**2965**
Wt dist (w/driver), f/r, % **53/47**
Wheelbase, in. **101.2**
Track, f/r **55.4/55.7**
Length **175.2**
Width **64.8**
Height **54.3**
Trunk space, cu ft **14.3**
Fuel capacity, U.S. gal. **16.4**

ENGINE

Type ....**sohc inline-6**
Bore x stroke, mm ..... **84.0 x 75.0**
Displacement, cc **2494**
Compression ratio **8.8:1**
Bhp @ rpm, SAE net ...**168 @ 5800**
Torque @ rpm, lb-ft.....**164 @ 4300**
Fuel injection .... elect.
Fuel requirement .... unleaded, 87-pump oct

DRIVETRAIN

Transmission .... **5-sp manual**
Gear ratios: 5th (0.81) **3.02:1**
4th (1.00) **3.73:1**
3rd (1.40)................. **5.22:1**
2nd (2.20) **8.21:1**
1st (3.83)................**14.29:1**
Final-drive ratio **3.73:1**

ACCELERATION

Time to distance, sec:
0–100 ft **3.3**
0–500 ft **8.6**
0–1320 ft (¼ mi) **15.7**
Speed at end of ¼ mi, mph.... **88.5**
Time to speed, sec:
0–30 mph **2.5**
0–40 mph **3.8**
0–50 mph **5.6**
0–60 mph **7.5**
0–70 mph **9.6**
0–80 mph **12.3**
0–90 mph **16.2**
0–100 mph .... **est 21.5**

BRAKING

Minimum stopping distances, ft:
From 60 mph 152
From 80 mph 263
Control in panic stop ....**excellent**
Overall brake rating ....**very good**

HANDLING

Lateral accel, 100-ft radius, g.. **0.79**
Speed thru 700-ft slalom, mph **64.6**

SPEEDS IN GEARS

Maximum engine rpm **6200**
5th gear (rpm) mph, est **(5660) 133**
4th est (6200) **119**
3rd (6200) **85**
2nd (6200) **54**
1st (6200) **31**

CALCULATED DATA

Lb/bhp (test weight) **17.7**
Bhp/liter **67.4**
Engine revs @ 60 mph in 5th gear **2580**
R&T steering index............. **1.34**

INTERIOR NOISE

Idle in neutral, dBA.................**52**
Maximum, 1st gear **77**
Constant 70 mph **70**

FUEL ECONOMY

Normal driving, mpg............ **20.5**

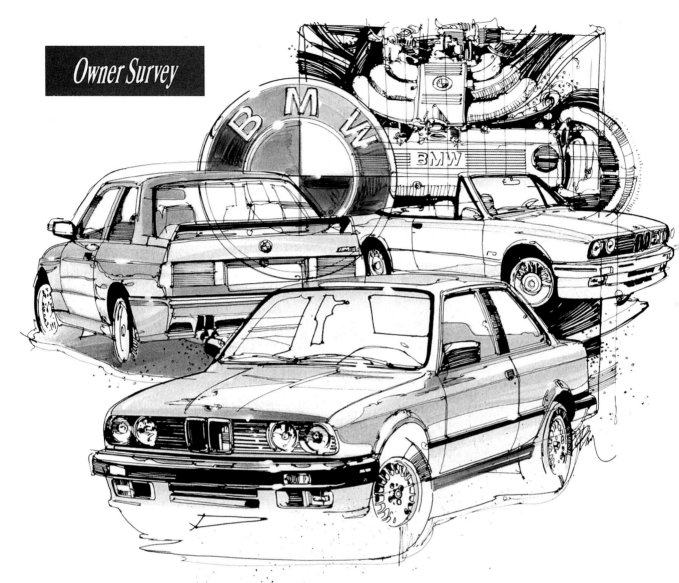

BMW 325 & M3 1984-1989

BY PETER BOHR
ILLUSTRATION BY DENNIS BROWN

"Car is super, service is great!"—1987 325is Owner

IT'S A TOUGH world out there. And for a high-end auto-maker like BMW, it's getting meaner all the time.

The Japanese, of course, are making a frontal assault on BMW's traditional turf with the Acura, Lexus and Infiniti. Then there are always those formidable cross-town rivals, Audi and Mercedes. And finally, there are the Americans with their new-and-improved Cadillacs, Lincolns and, eventually, Jaguars.

How will BMW fare? This *Road & Track* Owner Survey may provide a clue. In the future, say marketing experts, it won't be enough to offer an excellent product; the luxury-

car game will be won or lost in the dealerships' "back ends"—the service departments. And in this respect, judging from our Owner Survey, BMW is on a path to victory.

In all our Owner Surveys since 1975, no other auto-maker has garnered such a favorable response when it comes to service. Nearly three-quarters of the respondents to this survey rated their BMW dealers as good or excellent. That compares with a previous high of 67 percent for both Mazda dealers (1982 survey) and Toyota dealers (1987), and with an average for all of our surveys of only 59 percent. The owners' high regard for BMW's after-sale service is even more surprising because, as we shall see, not only is the cost of service anything but cheap, but also the BMWs covered in the survey are not without reliability problems.

"The engine in the 325i makes all the difference in the world—let the revs begin!" —1987 325is Owner

---

This survey includes the M3 and all 325 models—the "Baby Bimmers." Hold on now, because you'll need a scorecard to keep track of the various 325 permutations.

The 325 began simply enough in 1984 when BMW installed the 6-cylinder "eta" engine from the 528e into the 318i bodywork. Although the low-revving engine produced abundant torque and good fuel economy, it wasn't the most sporting of powerplants.

At first the 325e came only as a 2-door; a 4-door version came along in 1985. In 1986, BMW dropped the "e" from the name on the base version of the 325, even though the car still had the eta engine. The 4-door in luxury trim (leather upholstery, etc.) became the 325e, while the 2-door in sport trim (air dam, rear-deck spoiler, etc.) became the 325es.

■ Sluggish eta inline-6 gave way to this 168-bhp version in 1987.

In 1987, BMW replaced the eta engine with a higher-revving, higher-bhp powerplant, and the car became the 325i (luxury trim) and 325is (sport trim). The eta engine wasn't actually dropped entirely; the base 325 still carried the engine until 1989. In 1987 there was a body-style addition to the lineup as well: the 325i convertible.

So by 1988, the 3-Series included the base 325 with the eta engine in either 2- or 4-door version, the 325i, the 325is and the 325i convertible. Yet another 325 variation came along that year: the all-wheel-drive 2-door 325iX.

Got all that? Good, because there's more—the M3. This is a Motorsport-bred hot rod with aggressive spoilers, wide wheels and a 2.3-liter dohc 16-valve 4-cylinder engine.

Our survey comprises 46 1984 models, 76 1985 models, 125 1986 models, 163 1987 models, 121 1988 models and 10 1989 models—for a total of 541 cars. Of this total 68 are M3s. In general, responses from M3 owners

paralleled those from 325 owners; we'll note the important exceptions along the way.

Just 1 percent of the cars in the survey are 325iX models, while 8 percent are convertibles. Less than 20 percent of the cars have an automatic transmission. All the cars in the survey are well-equipped; even plain-wrapper 325s are chock-full of features like ABS (from 1986 on), electric window lifts, a sunroof and air conditioning.

As in previous Owner Surveys, we only tabulated questionnaires from people who had bought their cars new and had put at least 10,000 miles on the odometer. The typical car in the survey had been driven 31,357 miles.

"I wish people would drop the 'yuppie' association with BMW." —1985 325e Owner

---

We can't say for certain if they're young or upwardly mobile, but we do know that a solid 63 percent of the owners in our survey called themselves professionals or managers. Another 19 percent said they were business owners or entrepreneurs.

"My BMW is a sports car with room to take clients to lunch." —1987 325is Owner

---

The *raison d'être* of a sports sedan is its versatility. An overwhelming 87 percent of the owners use their 3-Series cars as daily transport. Thirty-nine percent use them for weekend jaunts and long trips as well. And 7 percent use them in various competitive events.

But it seems these BMW owners aren't lead-foots; only 14 percent say they drive their cars very hard.

"They're too common in Southern California." —1987 325i Convertible Owner

---

Yes, ragtop Bimmers are just the thing for hitting the California beaches in style. But the largest percentage (35) of our survey respondents hail from the Northeast. Midwesterners follow with 18 percent, Westerners with 16 percent and Southeasterners, 13 percent.

"High fun-per-gallon rating. My 2002 has gone 210,000 miles. Oh boy, 190,000 to go on my 325!" —1987 325 Owner

---

We asked the owners to check off five features that influenced their decision to buy a BMW 3-Series. Engineering, handling, performance/acceleration, workmanship, reliability/durability were tallied in that order.

Although they didn't end up among the top five, two attributes received notably high consideration from the BMW owners. Having a car that was built in Germany was very important to a fifth of them. And familiarity with the marque was important to more than a quarter of them; that is, they bought a 3-Series car after owning other BMWs. The car's exterior styling was a significant "buy" factor to only 19 percent of the owners—a low figure among our surveys. But for M3 owners alone, styling was important to 40 percent.

Then we asked the survey respondents to select their car's five best attributes "now that you've owned it for a while." The same five virtues topped the list again, indicating the owners' initial expectations were fulfilled.

We also wanted to hear some complaints. Though we asked for five, only four items appear statistically significant. Topping the complaint list was high insurance rates. Then came lack of interior room. The trauma of paying BMW's sticker prices was a definite downer as well.

"This car is a blast to drive and perfect for me. If only BMW dealers wouldn't look at you as an open wallet when it comes to service."
—1987 325i Owner

Then there was dealer service—specifically, the cost of it. Owners mentioned such prices as $300–$600 for routine service, $318 to repair a cruise control, $300 to remove the dashboard and fix a warning light, $40 to change sparkplugs, $300 for front-wheel bearings and $315 to replace worn brake pads. Altogether, a whopping 74 percent rated prices for parts and labor as expensive or very expensive. Taking figures from two recent surveys, we compared this with 47 and 46 percent for Honda CRX and for Corvette owners, respectively.

And yet 74 percent of the owners gave very high marks to BMW dealers. Why? We can only speculate that the majority of dealers provided courteous, competent service, so the owners were willing to forgive high prices. And, perhaps they recognized that such prices are part of the equation of owning an upmarket car. Furthermore, a number of owners mentioned that both the dealers and BMW of North America had gone to considerable lengths to back up their product, even to the point of no-cost repairs when cars were long out of warranty.

"Great driving car on dry roads. Poor in the rain. Dangerous in snow."—1986 325 Owner

---

Though it wasn't on our questionnaire, owners commented on the 3-Series' poor handling in wet or icy conditions. Some said they had to carry sandbags in the trunk for traction if they wanted to use their cars in the winter. Of course BMW has a solution—the 325iX.

The typical car in all our Owner Surveys since 1975 had a total of 11 problem areas reported by 5 percent or more of the survey respondents. Four of those problems on the typical car were serious enough to make it either inoperable or unsafe to drive.

The typical 3-Series BMW in this survey had nine prob-

lem areas, only one of them serious. So while these BMWs are better than average, they're far from trouble-free.

We consulted two specialists at either end of the BMW service spectrum. As a mechanic at a BMW dealership in Riverside, California, Cy Franke is in the trenches, so to speak. As technical manager for BMW of North America, Ralph Beir issues the service bulletins to which Cy and other dealer mechanics adhere.

"I'm surprised at the number of problems I've had with a car of BMW's quality."—1986 325es Owner

---

Electrical problems top the list. Like their counterparts at other automakers, BMW engineers have become enamored with high-tech doodads—like the "service indicator" on the 3-Series cars.

This is a group of little green lights that turn red when it's time for a visit to the mechanic. Unfortunately, the system has had its glitches, causing, among other things, intermittent tachometer failures and fluctuating temperature gauges. Another warning device, the "check engine light," has also been prone to erroneous displays.

More serious, many 3-Series cars built before 1987 had faulty idle-control units. When these failed, at best they would cause a fluctuating idle. At worst, they would send the BMW to the dealer on the end of a tow truck's hook. However, the units were replaced under warranty.

Faulty window lifts and central door locks are other ills. When they fail, the window lifts stick in the closed position. "Find the plug in the door panel for the window crank and slam the area around it with your fist," said Franke. That often provides a temporary, if inelegant, fix.

BMW dealers have had to replace a lot of batteries on 3-Series cars. According to Beir, the problems often arose because of inadequate maintenance before the cars were ever sold. But he adds that some aftermarket burglar alarms and telephones cause a heavy draw on batteries.

These 3-Series cars go through brake pads rapidly. However, BMW changed to a harder pad material in late 1987. But, unfortunately, the new pads seem to encourage warped rotors. "We're working on the problem," said Beir.

All the 3-Series engines appear to be remarkably robust—with the exception of gaskets. On the 6-cylinder engines, faulty head gaskets caused annoying oil leaks (but not coolant loss, a more serious matter). On the 4-cylinder M3 engines, there was a rash of bad intake manifold gaskets that would cause a lumpy idle.

It's now well known that modern BMW engines (and those from a number of other manufacturers, for that matter) are particularly sensitive to carbon buildup on the intake valves. In 1986 and 1987, BMW conducted an "engine campaign" to clean valves. At no cost to BMW owners, dealer mechanics blasted the valves with walnut shells. It's an expensive operation, taking about five hours of labor. To keep the valves and fuel-injection systems clean, BMW wants owners to use a gasoline with cleaning agents. "Or buy a gasoline without these agents and use an additive," said Beir. But he warns owners *not* to use both, or they may dilute the engine oil over time.

Though relatively few respondents had cars with automatic transmissions, BMW has had serious problems with them. "I wouldn't buy a BMW with an automatic unless I also bought an extended warranty," said Franke.

Our owners weren't fond of the 3-Series air conditioners. Aside from actual problems with the units—mostly bad evaporator units or inferior auxiliary fans—they don't seem to put out enough cool air even when they're working right. Beir suggests that when a car has been sitting in the sun, owners should open all the windows to let out the "super-heated" air, before turning on the air conditioner.

Finally, a significant number of owners complained of problems with body parts and trim, such as discolored exterior plastic strips and cracking leather. As for the leather, Beir said it's important to regularly treat it with a substance called Karneol, available at BMW dealers. And owners of 325i convertibles griped about poor weather sealing. "It's common for the door window glass to hit the top instead of the weatherstripping," said Franke. "But it can be adjusted."

"Would you buy another?" It's always the most telling question in our Owner Surveys. Altogether, 83 percent of our BMW owners said "yes!" That's a good 10 points above the average for our surveys.

But it's also well below the highest figures we've encountered—95 percent for Mazda RX-7 owners (1982) or 90 percent for Honda CRX owners (1989).

However, we should note that when the M3 owners were separated from the others, 94 percent of them said they'd buy another.

"This is my third BMW. I love the car, but I could not afford to buy a new one."
—1985 325e Owner

Given the enthusiasm 3-Series owners have for their cars, it's a good bet that the 83-percent buy-another figure would be higher if new BMWs weren't so expensive. Between 1984 and 1989, base 325 prices rose about 20 percent.

But according to Beir, BMW is at least making a serious attempt to reduce the cost of maintenance. "We are aware that prices are high," he said. "We have adjusted prices [downward] of certain items, and we have not reached the end of the program. We have entered a new era of consumer service, and we're determined to be the best."

It's this attitude that may just keep current BMW owners coming back into BMW showrooms despite sticker shock. After all, as the owner of a 325i convertible put it, "The price of admission is high, but well worth it."

FIVE ATTRIBUTES OWNERS EXPECTED

Engineering
Handling
Performance/acceleration
Workmanship
Reliability/durability

FIVE BEST ATTRIBUTES OWNERS FOUND

Handling
Engineering
Performance/acceleration
Workmanship
Reliability/durability

FIVE WORST ATTRIBUTES OWNERS FOUND

Insurance rating
Interior room
Good value/price
Dealer service/parts availability
(no fifth worst)

RATING DEALER SERVICE

	BMW	Avg[1]
Excellent	41%	27%
Good	33%	32%
Fair	13%	21%
Poor	11%	20%
No response	4%	

[1]Average for all cars surveyed since 1975.

RATING DEALER PRICES FOR PARTS AND LABOR

Very reasonable	2%
Reasonable	19%
Expensive	48%
Very expensive	26%
No response	5%

NUMBER OF PROBLEM AREAS

	BMW	Avg[1]
Reported by 10% or more	2	6
Reported by 5–9%	7	5
Total	9	11
Reliability areas	1	4

[1]Average for all cars surveyed since 1975.

PROBLEM AREAS

Computer-controlled sensors/operating hardware[2] (11%)
Brake pads (11%)
Window lifts (8%)
Instruments (6%)
Central locking (6%)
Air conditioning (6%)
Exterior body parts (6%)
Brake rotors (5%)
Engine gaskets (5%)

[2]Reliability area.

BUY ANOTHER OF THE SAME MAKE?

	BMW	Avg[1]
Yes	83%	74%
No	7%	14%
Undecided	10%	12%

[1]Average for all cars surveyed since 1975.

BMW M5

One of the Ten Best Cars in the World, 1991
Also, Best Coupe/Sedan, more than $45,000

Bayerische Motoren Werke all but invented the proper state-of-the-art sports sedan, every car in its lineup being wonderfully exemplary of the genre. And the one that absolutely captivates our attention is the M5.

In recognizing the dual personality of this car, we're pleased to honor the BMW M5 as the Best Coupe/Sedan beyond $45,000 and also one of the Ten Best Cars in the World.

The M5 is a beautifully luxurious 4-door sedan, dare we emphasize even a practical one, but with the soul of a race car. A variant of its dohc 24-valve inline-6 achieved fame powering BMW's exotic M1, yet this engine can be as docile as you like. As one staff member put it, "The M5's personality is all under the control of your right foot." Accelerate to 60 mph in 6.4 sec. or motor routinely around town; the M5 lets you decide.

To call the M5 an "Ultimate Driving Machine" isn't just an advertising slogan; it's a simple statement of fact.

BMW M5

An exeeptional car for a select few

SOME 25 YEARS ago, Bayerische Motoren Werke popularized the idea of the medium-size, high-performance sports sedan. And there's a direct lineage from the 1800 TIs of those days through the 2500s, the Bavarias and the first-generation 5-Series BMWs to the car you see here, the M5.

Nor is its M heritage any less telling. In 1972, BMW Motorsport GmbH was formed, giving focus to the company's many competition interests. World Touring Car Championships and plenty of other honors followed, not to say some pretty potent automobiles. In 1978, for in-

stance, Motorsport brought forth the M1, a mid-engine Group 4/Group 5 racer whose obligatory 400-car production run for reasons of homologation gave us one of the all-time great exotics. (See September 1980 for our test of the M1—and remember its dohc 24-valve engine.) Others earning the red, blue and purple BMW Motorsport insignia include the M635CSi (September 1984), the M535i (May 1985), the first-generation M5 (April 1986) and the M3 (February 1988).

BMW Motorsport keeps busy.

So when the latest 5-Series BMW showed up a couple of years ago, we hoped its M variant wasn't far off.

And here's that very car, available to a select few North Americans as a 1991 model.

At first glance, only the cognoscenti will distinguish an M5 from its 535i sibling; and the M5 driver probably wouldn't want it any other way. A revised air dam up front, different bumper contours, subtle sidesills and 0.8-in. less ride height all contribute to retaining the 535i's 0.32 C_X, despite the M5's greater intake of cooling air and the increased frontal projection of its wide, super-low-profile 235/45ZR-17s mounted on 8-in. wheels.

These wheels, by the way, generated our only M5 style controversy.

31

Actually 5-spoke skeletal structures with bolt-on magnesium inserts, the latter have concentric rotor blades that cool the M5's oversize ABS-augmented brakes. What's more, the wheels' asymmetric rim design improves run-flat capability.

Elegant engineering, yes; but, as one driver said, "The wheels look too delicate and effeminate for the car's image. Plus, their rims and openings combine to give the appearance of tall-profile whitewalls."

No one objected to other aspects of the M5's suspension, though. Compared with the 535i's, its springs and shocks are stiffened. A limited-slip differential is fitted. Front and rear anti-roll bars are enlarged, the latter just a tad more than proportionally to bring the M5's fore/aft balance a bit closer to neutral.

"Taut but supple," noted one driver, "and at least one Japanese manufacturer could take lessons here in jiggle-avoidance."

"What wonderful pointability," said another, in his admiration of the M5's willingness to be placed pre-cisely with throttle and steering, seemingly regardless of road surface.

Exemplary though the handling is, what characterizes the M5 best is its marvelous powerplant. This in-line-6 has double overhead camshafts, 24 valves, a 10.0:1 compression ratio, Bosch Digital Motor Electronics engine management—and a mere, slight, tiny edge of mechanical harshness. Remember that BMW M1 exotic? This engine is a direct descendant of its powerplant. And as it burbles with just a bit of lumpiness at idle or wails like a banshee to its 7200-rpm redline, there's no mistaking its sporting heritage.

Refinements along the way include the Bosch DME combining ignition and fuel control, whereas the original M1 engine had mechanical injection. Also, new to our M5 are a forged crankshaft giving increased stroke and 3535-cc displacement, hitherto 3453 cc, as well as a lightened flywheel, revised camshaft profiles and resonance-charged intake passages and exhaust ducting.

Its resulting 310 bhp and 265 lb.-ft. of torque are produced with no loss of tractability in the sort of driving most of us do most of the time. Yet the M5 is capable of reaching 60 mph in 6.4 seconds, the quarter-mile marker in 15.0 sec. at 96.0 mph and, ultimately, a top speed (155 mph) limited solely by a consensus of German government and industry. Not bad for a luxurious 4-door sedan.

And luxurious the M5 is, in a Bavarian manner that's not as austere as Mercedes-Benz' philosophy, but still unmistakably Germanic. The interior is composed of subtly interacting surfaces, none of the organic wholeness typifying the latest of Japanese design. The driver faces an array of analog dials, black on white, and an airbag-fitted steering wheel. His or her passenger gets a glovebox whose ample volume rivals that of many apartment closets. Between them is a center console canted toward the driver and housing controls for climate (split left/right) and sound system.

Leather upholstery is standard, with exactly four seating positions defined,

■ Without glancing under the hood at Motorsport's twincam inline-6 or spending some time behind the M5's airbag-equipped wheel, most would never know this sleeper packs 310 rear-drive bhp.

the rear pair separated by a fixed center console enclosing a slide-out tray for cassette tapes and the like.

The overall feeling is that of a 4-place cockpit: functional and comfortable, if not particularly spacious.

Apart from its not being the preferred conveyance for four basketball players, why wouldn't just about anyone else absolutely lust for the BMW M5?

"The car's personality comes through loud and clear," said one staff member, "but there are some annoying aspects. Despite all the electric adjustments, I still can't find a decent driving position. The seat has too much lumbar support and the steering wheel is too high, excessively horizontal and not adjustable. Before airbags, BMW had an adjustable wheel, and others with airbags still do."

"The shifter," noted another, "took BMW's characteristically notchy, long-throw feeling to an extreme, especially in 1st–2nd actuation."

The point, of course, is that the M5 isn't a car for everyone. It hasn't been "clinic-ed" to mass acceptability or, worse, to mediocrity. Rather, it's a rolling tribute to BMW confidence, designed by Bavarian engineers who are damned sure of what they know. The M5 works splendidly for some and, we recognize, it just doesn't work at all for others (especially at the price).

Is it worth $56,600? Certainly to a select few. And to the rest, it can still serve as a comforting example of continuity: Considering that the Bavarians all but invented the sports sedan, is it any wonder they continue to do it so well and with such personality? ⊠

BMW M5

0–60 mph	6.4 sec
0–¼ mi	15.0 sec
Top speed	est 155 mph
Skidpad	0.80g
Slalom	61.4 mph
Brake rating	excellent

PRICE

List price, all POE .... **$56,600**   Price as tested **$59,655**
Price as tested includes standard equip. (air cond, AM/FM stereo/cassette, ABS, leather interior, cruise control, electric window lifts, sunroof, central locking & adjustable mirrors), gas-guzzler tax ($1850), cellular telephone ($1205).

ENGINE

Type	4-valve/cyl dohc **inline-6**
Displacement	216 cu in./3535 cc
Bore x stroke	3.68 x 3.39 in./ 93.4 x 86.0 mm
Compression ratio	10.0:1
Horsepower (SAE)	**310 bhp @ 6900 rpm**
Torque	**265 lb-ft @ 4750 rpm**
Maximum engine speed	7200 rpm
Fuel injection	Bosch Motronic elect. port
Fuel	prem unleaded, 91 pump oct

GENERAL DATA

Curb weight	**3950 lb**
Test weight	**4060 lb**
Weight dist, f/r, %	**50/50**
Wheelbase	108.7 in.
Track, f/r	58.0 in./58.9 in.
Length	185.8 in.
Width	68.9 in.
Height	55.4 in.
Trunk space	17.5 cu ft

DRIVETRAIN

Transmission .... **5-sp manual**

Gear	Ratio	Overall ratio	(Rpm) Mph
1st	3.51:1	13.72:1	37
2nd	2.08:1	8.13:1	62
3rd	1.35:1	5.28:1	96
4th	1.00:1	3.91:1	130
5th	0.81:1	3.17:1	est (7070) 155

Final drive ratio 3.91:1
Engine rpm @ 60 mph in 5th 2740

CHASSIS & BODY

Layout	**front engine/rear drive**
Body/frame	unit steel
Brakes, f/r	**12.4-in. vented discs/ 11.8-in. discs;** vacuum assist, ABS
Wheels	forged alloy, **17 x 8J**
Tires	Michelin MXX2, **235/45ZR-17**
Steering	**recirculating ball**, power assist
Turns, lock to lock	3.3
Suspension, f/r:	**MacPherson struts,** lower lateral links, compliance struts, coil springs, tube shocks, anti-roll bar/**semi-trailing arms,** coil springs, tube shocks, anti-roll bar

ACCELERATION

Time to speed	Seconds
0–30 mph	2.5
0–60 mph	6.4
0–80 mph	10.7
Time to distance	
0–100 ft	3.2
0–500 ft	8.3
0–1320 ft (¼ mi)	15.0 @ 96.0 mph

BRAKING

Minimum stopping distance	
From 60 mph	127 ft
From 80 mph	231 ft
Control	excellent
Pedal effort for 0.5g stop	14 lb
Fade, effort after six 0.5g stops from 60 mph	19 lb
Brake feel	excellent
Overall brake rating	excellent

FUEL ECONOMY

Normal driving	15.5 mpg
EPA city/highway	11/20 mpg
Fuel capacity	23.8 gal.

INTERIOR NOISE

Idle in neutral	58 dBA
Constant 70 mph	68 dBA

HANDLING

Lateral accel (200-ft skidpad)	0.80g
Balance	mild understeer
Speed thru 700-ft slalom	61.4 mph
Balance	mild understeer

Subjective ratings consist of excellent, very good, good, average, poor.

▼ Test Notes . . .

■ The M5 has that rare quality of being not only fast, but also able to accelerate to high speeds with absolutely no drama. In fact, it can be so quiet and smooth that you can hardly believe the speedometer.

■ Our handling measures of grip and control—lateral acceleration and slalom speed—indicate only average road qualities. However, subjectively, the M5 is remarkably well balanced, with agile handling and rewarding steering feel.

BMW M3

PHOTOS BY DAVID W. BIRD II

Throughout Europe, touring car championships provide a venue for manufacturers to strut their production-based stuff. In separate racing series in England, Germany and Italy, BMW M3s repeatedly speed to victory against Ford Sierra RS500s, Mercedes-Benz 190s and Alfa Romeo 75 Evoluziones. It's unfortunate that we Americans don't get to see the likes of Johnny Cecotto and Roberto Ravaglia putting the racing M3 through its paces here. However, we are fortunate to receive an essential part of the BMW Motorsport program: the production version of the M3.

Essential because, according to FIA rules for Group A, the racing cars must be based on models that have a production run of 5000 for any given 12-month period. So, to answer the cry of Group-A competition, BMW has essentially made a racing car out of its 3-Series, and is building it in sufficient numbers to field a competitive car for the track. We gladly accept this byproduct of the company's competitive drive, but what is it that makes the

34

M3 different?

Most visible is the changed body, with its blister-style fender flares, rocker skirts, integrated front air dam and plastic winged trunk lid. Also there, but harder to see, is a more steeply raked rear window that helps bring the C_X down from 0.39 to 0.33.

But the changes that bring the most fun are beneath that bold body, which has been lowered with the use of shorter springs. Along with bigger tires and new front hub carriers that allow for more caster, the M3 has altered front suspension pickup points, a quicker steering rack, aluminum lower control arms, monstrous 11-in. discs with ABS (from the 6- and 7-Series) and different calibration for the anti-roll bars, shocks and rubber bushings.

Strangely, the M3 is not powered by an inline-6, as one might expect, but by a twincam 2.3-liter inline-4. Called the S14, the engine is a far cry from the anemic 4-cylinder that moved the 318i. The M3's engine puts out 192 bhp at 6750 rpm and is more closely related to BMW's Motorsport Formula 1 engine. At idle, the engine has a beautiful burbly note that implies serious camshafts. Then up around 3500-4000 rpm, the suspicion is confirmed as the engine pulls strongly all the way to redline and the driver is pushed back into his seat as he rows through the 5-speed. The low gear ratios in 1st and 2nd gears make spritely driving around town a joy; 60 mph is reached in a scant 7.1 seconds.

Inside, the M3 has the gauges needed to keep track of the potent powerplant, including an oil temperature gauge, an 8000-rpm tach and a 160-mph speedometer. Apart from that, the interior has all the niceties of the 3-Series: supportive leather seats, a/c, stereo, sunroof, electric window lifts and even cruise control.

The essence of the M3, though, is acute performance. With its good power and forgiving yet fun handling, it's no wonder that Skip Barber has chosen it as the workhorse for his advanced driving school.

—*Andrew Bornhop*

CLASH
OF THE
TEUTONS

Three cracks of rolling thunder from Germany

PHOTOS BY JOHN LAMM

THE GERMAN TOWN of Hockenheim is perfect for comparison tests. In addition to having one of R&T European Editor Paul Frère's favorite Greek restaurants—essential for discussing the cars after a good day of driving—it also affords access to the freedom of *Autobahnen*, the beauty of country roads and the majesty of Hockenheimring, a world-class race circuit nestled in the woods.

From Ingolstadt, Munich and Stuttgart we gathered an Audi Coupe S2, a BMW M3 Sport Evolution and a Mercedes-Benz 190E 2.5-16 Evolution II and lined them up, toe to toe and tire to tire, in and around Hockenheim. There could be no more fitting a place for these three makes to square off than Hockenheim. After all, full-on race versions of the BMW M3, Mercedes 190E 2.5-16 and Audi V8 have been chasing each other around Hockenheimring, Nürburgring and other tracks and street circuits all year in pursuit of the victor's trophy in the Group A German Touring Car Championship.

Each of the three cars in our test is a sort of hybrid machine, its spirit placed somewhere between that of a road car and that of a race car. Each is significant as it represents the forefront of its maker's technological abilities,

from computerized engine-management systems to aerodynamics. Each is also a limited-production car that may or may not ever see American roads deserving of its talent. And so it was that we traveled to Germany and assembled three of the best and brightest "something-extra" cars that the country has to offer. We poked, prodded, tested and pushed them on a race track, experienced them flat-out on the last public frontier of high-speed driving—the German *Autobahn*—and enjoyed them on the lovely secondary and tertiary roads in the southern province of Baden-Württemberg.

The spiritual essences of the three cars are, of course, their engines. Motivation for our Teutonic trio is supplied by two normally aspirated dohc 16-valve 2.5-liter 4-cylinder powerplants (in the M-B and BMW) and one turbocharged dohc 20-valve 2.2-liter inline-5 (naturally belonging to the Audi).

The journey that a stock 190E 2.5-16 engine takes on its way to becoming an Evolution II engine is a short but meticulous one. Slight modifications in compression ratio, valve lift and timing, intake porting, combustion chambers, catalytic converters and computer chips combine to contribute more muscle to the Mercedes. At the end of the day, the Evolution II puts out 232 bhp DIN and 181 lb.-ft. of torque compared with the stock 2.5-16's 195 bhp and 170 lb.-ft. of torque, and the tachometer allows 500 rpm more reach before redlining at 7700.

As if to match its Group A rival in Stuttgart, BMW bored and stroked the stock M3's 2.3-liter four into a 2.5, bringing its volume to within a few capfuls of the Mercedes engine. Thus stretched, the new BMW M3 Evolution engine produces 238 bhp DIN and 177 lb.-ft. of torque.

Comparisons of the 2.5-liter powerplants came naturally to the drivers: "The Mercedes' engine seems slightly less aggressive than the BMW's (keeping in mind that the M-B is more than 300 lb. heavier)," began one entry in the Evo II's notebook, "but it is exceptionally smooth for a big four right up to its 7700-rpm limit."

Another driver contrasted the two engines this way: "The BMW's en-

gine, which is not quite as smooth as the Mercedes', has fair midrange torque and revs beautifully, if loudly, to the upper limits."

Moving up in piston count, but deceptively down in horsepower is the Audi Coupe S2. Ingolstadt is justifiably proud of the S2's deep-breathing, intercooled 220-bhp DIN

straight-5, which descended from the Sport Quattro's 306-bhp competition engine. Although it came up about 250 cc and a few bhp shy of its 2.5-liter competitors, the S2 engine was far from being the runt of our test litter. You see, if the Audi couldn't win the horsepower numbers war, its race-bred 2.2-liter turbocharged

■ All three of these strapping Germans smirk at the challenge of sustained high-speed driving on the *Autobahn*. Both the Mercedes and BMW receive their propulsive urge from 16-valve 2.5-liter inline-4 engines. Audi, the same company that brought us inside-caliper brakes on the V8 sedan, seems to take pleasure in doing things just a bit differently—power for the S2 comes from a turbocharged 20-valve 2.2-liter straight-5 (below).

engine—with ignition program re-mapped and turbo boost boosted—still approaches that magic 100-bhp-per-liter benchmark. And the S2 engine's torque characteristics—a significant 228-lb.-ft. cranked at an appreciably low 1950 rpm—slammed the door on the two Evolution cars.

"I suspect that the Audi's per-formance is quite deceptive," wrote one perceptive editor. "It has the smoothest and torquiest engine, with very good turbo response."

The Coupe S2 complied with that editor's impressions by posting a 6.0-second 0-to-60-mph time—fully a half-second quicker than the BMW and 0.9 sec. more fleet than the Mer-

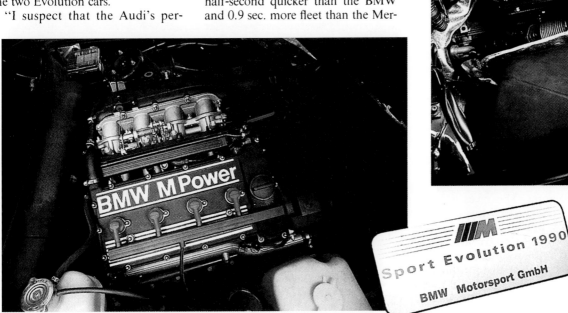

cedes. The Audi proved itself adept not only as a sprinter, but as a quarter-miler as well, once again besting the competition with a 14.6-sec. run.

The power created by each of the 4-wheeled lions in our test was transmitted through a 5-speed manual transmission. The Audi's shift pattern is the familiar one, but the Mercedes and BMW gearboxes come with a racing shift configuration. First gear is down and to the left and the other four forward gears make up the "H" pattern. The gate for reverse is at the upper left, above 1st.

And it was in this transmission realm that we discovered one of the few areas where all three cars shuffled their feet.

"The Mercedes' gearbox is too notchy," complained one notebook entry. "The M3's gearbox is quick, but slightly notchy," said another. Even the S2 couldn't escape some criticism: "In hard driving, the shifter's notchiness is magnified. The gearbox has a rubbery feel to it, with imprecise gates."

Despite our dissatisfaction with the feel and action of the three gearboxes, we agreed that the ratios were well matched with their respective engines.

Because of the exacting nature of much of the driving we were doing, we paid a lot of attention to how well the cars reacted to steering inputs and how well the feedback through the steering wheel was connecting us to the roads. Power-assisted steering systems—rack-and-pinion on the S2 and the M3, recirculating-ball on the Mercedes Evo II—appealed to us in varying degrees, but as a general rule, the surest way of receiving our praise was by not getting in the way of our driving. This is where the Audi Coupe S2 received some of its most stern criticism: "The Audi's boosted steering is much too light. The boost is speed-sensitive, but the effort remains too light throughout the spectrum. This gives a disconnected feeling to the driver, one step further away from the road than I am comfortable with, especially at higher speeds on sweeping corners."

The two Evolution cars, on the other hand, were praised for the excellence of their steering feel and turn-in, with the BMW coming out as the favorite: "The M3's power

PRICE			
	Audi Coupe S2	BMW M3 Sport Evolution	Mercedes-Benz 190E 2.5-16 Evolution II
Base price	$45,700	$56,700	$72,960

GENERAL DATA			
Curb weight, est	3130 lb	2650 lb	2955 lb
Test weight, est	3280 lb	2800 lb	3105 lb
Wheelbase	100.4 in.	101.0 in.	104.9 in.
Track, f/r	56.9 in./56.6 in.	55.8 in./56.3 in.	58.1 in./58.1 in.
Length	173.3 in.	471.1 in.	178.9 in.
Width	67.6 in.	66.1 in.	67.7 in.
Height	54.1 in.	53.9 in.	52.2 in.

ENGINE			
Type	turbo dohc inline-5	dohc inline-4	dohc inline-4
Displacement	136 cu in./2226 cc	151 cu in./2467 cc	150 cu in./2463 cc
Bore x stroke	3.19 x 3.40 in./ 81.0 x 86.4 mm	3.74 x 3.43 in./ 95.0 x 87.0 mm	3.83 x 3.26 in./ 97.3 x 82.8 mm
Compression ratio	9.3:1	10.2:1	9.7:1
Horsepower (DIN)	220 bhp @ 5900 rpm	238 bhp @ 7000 rpm	232 bhp @ 7200 rpm
Torque	228 lb-ft @ 1950 rpm	177 lb-ft @ 4750 rpm	181 lb-ft @ 5000 rpm
Maximum engine speed	7100 rpm	7300 rpm	7700 rpm
Fuel injection	Bosch elect. port	Bosch elect. port	Bosch mech port
Fuel	prem unleaded, 91 pump oct	prem unleaded, 91 pump oct	prem unleaded, 91 pump oct

ACCOMMODATIONS			
Seating capacity	5	5	5
Head room, f/r	35.0 in./35.5 in.	38.0 in./34.5 in.	37.0 in./34.5 in.
Seat width, f/r	2 x 19.5 in./52.5 in.	na	2 x 20.5 in./51.0 in.
Front leg room	42.0 in.	42.5 in.	na
Rear knee room	na	23.5 in.	na
Trunk space	9.0 + 6.6 cu ft	14.8 cu ft	12.9 cu ft

INTERIOR NOISE			
Idle in neutral	49 dBA	54 dBA	47 dBA
Constant 70 mph	68 dBA	71 dBA	67 dBA

CHASSIS & BODY			
Layout	front engine/awd	front engine/rwd	front engine/rwd
Body/frame	unit steel	unit steel	unit steel
Brakes, f/r	10.9-in. vented discs/ 9.6-in. discs; power assist, ABS	11.0-in. vented discs/ 11.1-in. vented discs; power assist, ABS	11.8-in. vented discs/ 10.9-in. vented discs; power assist, ABS
Wheels	cast alloy, 16 x 7J	cast alloy, 16 x 7J	cast alloy, 17 x 8¼
Tires	Kleber G 551 Z, 205/55ZR-16	Pirelli P700-Z, 225/45ZR-16	Dunlop SP Sport D40 M 245/40ZR-17
Steering	rack & pinion, power assist	rack & pinion, power assist	recirculating ball, power assist
Overall ratio	16.8:1	19.6:1	na
Suspension, f/r	MacPherson struts, lower A-arms, coil springs, tube shocks, anti-roll bar/Chapman struts, lower A-arms, coil springs, tube shocks, anti-roll bar	MacPherson struts, lower A-arms, coil springs, tube shocks, anti-roll bar/semi-trailing arms, coil springs, tube shocks, anti-roll bar	modified MacPherson struts, lower A-arms, coil springs, tube shocks, anti-roll bar, adj ride height/ 5-link, coil springs, tube shocks, anti-roll bar, adj ride height

DRIVETRAIN

	Audi Coupe S2	BMW M3 Sport Evolution	Mercedes-Benz 190E 2.5-16 Evolution II
Transmission	5-sp manual	5-sp manual	5-sp manual
Gear: Ratio/Overall/(Rpm) Mph			
1st, :1	3.50/14.39/(7100) 35	3.29/10.36/(7300) 39	3.25/12.51/(7700) 36
2nd, :1	1.84/7.57/(7100) 67	2.08/6.55/(7300) 62	1.90/7.33/(7700) 61
3rd, :1	1.22/5.02/(7100) 101	1.45/4.57/(7300) 89	1.32/5.09/(7700) 88
4th, :1	0.90/3.71/(7100) 137	1.04/3.28/(7300) 123	0.98/3.75/(7700) 119
5th, :1	0.71/2.94/(6300) 154	0.72/2.27/(6315) 154	0.71/2.74/(7235) 154
Final drive ratio	4.11:1	3.15:1	3.85:1
Engine rpm @ 60 mph in 5th	2460	2450	2820

ACCELERATION

	Audi	Seconds	BMW Seconds	Mercedes Seconds
Time to speed				
0–30 mph	2.0		2.6	2.5
0–60 mph	6.0		6.5	6.9
0–90 mph	13.1		12.9	14.3
Time to distance				
0–100 ft	2.9		3.2	3.2
0–500 ft	7.8		8.2	8.4
0–1320 ft (¼ mi)	14.6 @ 96.5 mph		14.8 @ 95.5 mph	15.3 @ 93.5 mph

BRAKING

	Audi	BMW	Mercedes
Minimum stopping distance			
From 60 mph	144 ft	137 ft	140 ft
From 80 mph	247 ft	242 ft	240 ft
Control	excellent	excellent	excellent
Pedal effort for 0.5g stop	22 lb	13 lb	14 lb
Fade: effort after six 0.5g stops from 60 mph	22 lb	13 lb	14 lb
Brake feel	excellent	excellent	excellent
Overall brake rating	excellent	excellent	excellent

HANDLING

	Audi	BMW	Mercedes
Lateral accel (200-ft skidpad):	na	na	na
Speed thru 700-ft slalom	61.0 mph	64.5 mph	62.3 mph
Balance	moderate understeer	neutral	neutral

FUEL ECONOMY

	Audi	BMW	Mercedes
Normal driving	19.0 mpg	20.5 mpg	18.0 mpg
Fuel capacity	18.5 gal.	18.5 gal.	18.0 gal.

Test Notes . . .

■ The S2's awd grip off the line and excellent mid-rpm torque made it the group's surprising drag-race winner. Tossed through the slalom, its awd also gave it most-benign honors, though considerable body roll and the group's narrowest tires prevented another victory.

■ The BMW's firm ride may become tiresome on the road, but at the track it makes the M3 the fastest-reacting and easiest to drive of the three. And though potent near redline, the M3's engine is thin on torque at lower revs, requiring constant attention to proper gear selection.

■ The Evo II takes some getting used to, but with familiarity, you realize there's plenty of potential here. Oddly, its best handling is delivered with the suspension's adjustable ride height left in the high position. When lowered, abrupt cornering causes the suspension to hit hard against its bump stops.

Subjective ratings consist of excellent, very good, good, average, poor; na means information is not available.

steering is the best of the group. It is nicely weighted, has good feel and is quick around center."

Modifying the stock suspension setups of the Mercedes 190E, the Audi Coupe and the BMW M3 for the competition versions of each was anything but a complicated matter of redesigning components or re-thinking layouts for the race track. The course of action chosen by all three manufacturers was, instead, a relatively simple one of adding more girth to the cars' already athletic suspension muscle, spring and sinew.

Throughout the two-year history of its sports-minded Evolution models, Mercedes-Benz has generally left the stock 190E 2.5-16 front suspension of modified MacPherson struts, lower A-arms, springs, shocks, anti-roll bars and hydropneumatic leveling in place. The primary suspension build-up on both last year's Evolution I and our Evolution II test car involves a strengthened version of the standard sedan's multilink rear suspension. And just to even things out, as it were, the Evo II's suspension system is also equipped with a hydropneumatic self-leveling control system.

Tested and finalized at the Nürburgring, the Audi Coupe S2's upgraded suspension features stiffer springs and shocks, and thicker anti-roll bars. For added chassis rigidity, a cross-brace has been installed between the front shock towers.

In creating an Evolution model of the M3, BMW has addressed one of our chief reservations about the M3 models currently zooming around in the U.S.: namely, handling-versus-ride. The "sport suspension tuning" version on the standard M3 (recalibrated springs, shocks, anti-roll bars and bushings at both ends with MacPherson struts and lower A-arms in front, semi-trailing arms at the rear) is great for spirited driving, but a tad too stiff for comfortable everyday use. In response to this problem, Munich has endowed the M3 Sport Evolution with EDC (Electronic Damping Control), BMW's version of cockpit-adjustable shocks. Just select your current mood from the rotary dial on the center console—Comfort, Normal or Sport—and you're off, ready for sport or pleasure, a point not missed by at least one driver: "The adjustable suspension on the BMW transforms it. I don't like the M3 we have in the U.S., but this car is really different, much better. And the adjustable suspension has a lot to do with it. The Normal setting is best, with just a little body roll and still a lot of handling."

Other editors were even more effusive in their praise of the BMW's sportiness. "The tires grip like spikes, and the chassis is well-nigh impossible to upset. The M3's stability, handling and road feel remind me more of a race car than of a street

■ Green seat fabric, matching diagonally striped door-panel inserts and a fat-rim 3-spoke steering wheel are tip-offs to the S2's seriously sporting nature. A closer inspection reveals off-white gauge faces.

car set up for extra-urban activities. The Mercedes, on the other hand, feels like a luxury sedan resisting the transformation from street car to track car."

Drivers who preferred the Mercedes appreciated its ride/handling balance and its tendency to be less temperamental than the BMW: "Drop-throttle tuck-in is just right for an average driver and sufficient for an expert. The BMW has more tuck, which makes it better for an expert driver."

Although there isn't any mention of Audi's full-time all-wheel-drive system in the proper name of the Coupe S2, the car is definitely a Quattro, with all of the best and worst traits that go along with that.

The first entry in the Quattro's credit column is the extra stability and peace of mind that come with having four wheels pulling for you instead of just two. The Quattro system features a Torsen center differential and a rear differential that can be locked manually from inside the car by pressing a button.

The S2's Quattro edge was instrumental in enabling it to keep up with the BMW and Mercedes on snakey, twisting roads, the awd making up for the rear-wheel-drive cars' advantage in rubber: The Audi gave pursuit on 205/55ZR-16 tires, while the BMW rode on 225/45ZR-16s, and the M-B was hoofing on 17-in. wheels shod with 245/40ZR-17 tires.

So what price does the Audi Coupe S2 have to pay for its four-footed stability? Well, all-wheel-drive cars, from the Subaru Justy to the Porsche 911 Carrera 4, understeer and the S2 is no exception. "Although the Coupe S2 is very forgiving and easy to drive at speed (it has a fair amount of body roll), it understeers—almost to the point of being frustrating at times," lamented one of the editors.

The added weight of the Quattro system aggravated the condition, and the Audi ended up behind the BMW and Mercedes (which exhibited better balance and more poise) in high-speed transitional maneuvers like our slalom testing.

As far as top-speed runs go, we managed to find a few rare miles of *Autobahn* that weren't overcrowded, so we were able to stretch the cars' legs a bit. Our three coursers were all so smooth and tracked so steadily at their preset limits—154 mph for the Audi, BMW and the Mercedes (manufacturers in Germany have agreed upon a limited top speed of about 155 mph for their sedans)—that it almost made the thrill of speed without legal limits seem common. The kick was in how each car got there: the Coupe S2's turbo whining and reaching out for more power; the Evolution II's engine building toward a peak as the revs increased; and the M3 Sport Evolution's engine pulling relentlessly up through its wide powerband.

Braking is a crucial aspect for cars of this caliber, so it pleases us to report that the stopping characteristics of all three competitors were excellent. The Mercedes and BMW (both sporting beefier disc brakes than their non-race-ordained counterparts) were nearly parallel performers, while the Audi had to give up a few feet to its lighter rivals. ABS, fitted to all three cars, takes the variable of driver skill out of the equation for quick stops. Only the Audi, however, offers the added option of an ABS override button for drivers who like to take threshold braking into their own hands.

Our notebooks contained laudatory remarks for the braking of all three cars, but it was track driving that really allowed us to test the mettle of the cars' braking systems:

"The Audi's brakes got a bit spongy after a track session with some fairly hard braking."

"The Mercedes' brakes are excellent: I experienced no fade after 20 consecutive fast laps on Hockenheim's short circuit."

As any peacock will tell you, being voted top bird in the aviary isn't everything—how you show off your feathers counts for a lot. By the same token, the Mercedes-Benz 190E 2.5-16 Evolution II didn't garner any winning votes in the performance category. But it attracted more attention than the other two "birds" combined. Being a 4-door sedan had a little to do with it: The Evo II is slightly longer, wider and lower than either the 2-door BMW or the Audi Coupe. But what really pushes the Mercedes over the top as far as looks go is its sensational, trunk-mounted

rear spoiler. No other aerodynamic piece on the car can even approach it. The snarling fender blisters, adjustable front air dam and aero rear bumper play functional second fiddle to the most outrageous wing since the Plymouth Superbird.

The BMW's adjustable rear wing looks half-hearted by comparison. Munich lowered the M3's nose by about a half-inch while creating the Sport Evolution, and it flared the fenders even more to accommodate the SE's wider-than-stock-M3 tires.

■ The M3 Evolution's seats hold you in place with the firmness of a father's hand. Gauges are standard-issue BMW, and a switch controlling shock damping (below) sprouts from the console.

But the BMW is still no match for the Mercedes in the double-take department, although most of us agreed that the overall appearance of the BMW was more integrated and less tacked-on-looking than its Evolution counterpart from Stuttgart.

Then again, it's hard to argue with the M-B's 0.30 coefficient of drag (the BMW's is 0.35). A ride-height adjustment switch, located on the dash, allows the Mercedes to hunker even closer to the ground for a little extra aerodynamic advantage.

■ It's odd that the Mercedes, with its shout-for-attention bodywork, has the most staid interior. Plaid inserts spice things up a bit, as does the floor-mounted fire extinguisher.

Another important part of the Evolution II's air management is an opaque plastic deflector fitted over the upper portion of the rear window. This piece was a constant source of complaints because it reduced the driver's rearward vision dramatically. We understand that we are not alone in our frustration with the deflector because at least one M-B project engineer has cut out a large section from it on his personal Evolution II.

The Audi Coupe S2 is distinguished from other Audi Coupes principally by its new front-end treatment (based on the V8 model), special 5-spoke alloy wheels and S2 badges placed front and rear.

One would be hard pressed to find a better mix of sporting-yet-comfortable interiors than in these three cars. The Audi was generally looked upon as the comfort leader and the BMW as the race driver's choice, but all three boasted snug, supportive seats, grippy steering wheels and big, readable gauges.

The Mercedes' interior is characterized by the feeling of businesslike austerity that German cars are known for. That isn't a complaint, just an observation. One editor, in fact, could have stood with a little less opulence in favor of lightening the car's load: "Comfort is quite acceptable for a car in which handling is a priority," he noted, "although I would prefer a car not so burdened with weighty gimmicks such as air conditioning and electric windows."

Such restraint was shown in the BMW, which, while it did have air conditioning, had manual-crank windows. There is an air of race readiness about the M3 Sport Evolution's cockpit. The tactile sensation of the steering wheel wrapped in brushed black leather is enough to get one itching to do hot laps. The distinctive BMW Motorsport blue and red, stitched into the upholstery of the M3's superb seats, adds to the effect.

In the Audi, the stitching says "Quattro," and the seats are just as nice. Our Coupe S2's seats were done up in a green fabric that was designed to complement the lush, deep green color of the car's exterior paint. The Audi's elevated comfort level was noted by all. Its light gray-faced gauges made an impression on us as well, earning praise from some, while others thought they looked gimmicky.

Our final tally found the editors evenly divided between the BMW M3 Sport Evolution and the Audi Coupe S2 as the sports car of preference.

"I was astonished that the Audi was my choice as the winner among the three cars," confessed one driver. "I liked it best because of the all-wheel drive, and I thought it was the best all-around car. It would be a great skier's car, for instance, and it's easy to drive every day as well. If I had to buy one car from the bunch, it would be the Audi."

"For me, the M3 Sport Evolution is the easiest to drive of the three cars in this test," responded a second editor. "Whether I was running it around Hockenheimring, tooling through the city, or opening it up on the *Autobahn*, the BMW felt right at home. With just enough gear selected, the power rolls on beautifully, and the engine pulls like a demon."

A third editor put the debate into perspective by saying, "The Audi is the most civilized of the trio, but the M3 is the greatest fun of the group."

And the Mercedes-Benz 190E 2.5-16 Evolution II—still a knockout performer—got stuck somewhere in the middle, playing bridesmaid to one car that was a better road automobile and to another that was a better Evolution.

The gap between the Mercedes and the other two cars is widened even further when price is taken into consideration. At $72,960, the Evolution II is easily the most expensive car in the group, followed by the M3 Sport Evolution at $56,700. The quick and comfy Coupe S2 stands out as the bargain of the field tagged at $45,700. True, the Audi is a bit less exclusive than the other two contenders—Mercedes is only building 500 Evo IIs (and all are spoken for), BMW is drawing the line at about 600 Sport Evolution M3s—but it also has the best chance of finding its way to North America.

Until then, we can take comfort in our memories of the race track in the woods, Baden-Württemberg's back roads, the fleeting wonder of the *Autobahnen* and the excellence displayed by our three favorite traveling companions. ◉

Dinan
BMW 5-SERIES

Performance without sacrifice

BY JOE RUSZ
PHOTOS BY DEAN SIRACUSA

I N THE GOOD old days, or at least in the Sixties, the road to high performance was a simple two-lane. You'd bolt on a bigger carburetor, stick in a hotter camshaft and perhaps some high-compression pistons and *voilà:* instant horsepower. Crisp handling—for those who also wanted their car to negotiate turns smartly—was achieved in similarly simple fashion: namely, by adding beefy springs, stiff shocks and fat tires.

Times have changed and nowadays the road to high performance is more like a freeway. Most engines are fuel-injected, electronically controlled and factory-sealed, so unless you have a degree from MIT, about the only component you're likely to recognize under the hood is the dipstick. And, knowledgeable or not, you are strongly discouraged from enhancing output (by swapping microchips, for example) by the authorities.

Fortunately, modifying suspension is not illegal (although, given some of the cars we've driven, perhaps it should be), and most time-honored methods still apply. However, in the sophisticat-

ed Nineties, any high-performance suspension worth its lateral g-forces must deliver a tolerably smooth ride—not unlike that of a Dinan BMW, which also has a legally modified engine and is exactly what the modern-day specialty sedan should be.

To understand how the Dinan came to be, you should know something about the man behind the machine, Steve Dinan. As a teenage musclecar enthusiast with an electrical engineer for a father, the St. Louis native grew up with a thorough understanding of both hot-rodding techniques and electronics. Although his dad and the United States Air Force believed he had an aptitude for the latter, Steve preferred automobiles, and after his tour of duty as a radar technician was over, he got a job as a foreign-car mechanic.

Gravitating toward BMWs because he "liked the way they were put together," Dinan opened his own BMW tuning facility, Bavarian Performance, in 1979. Among other things, he resuscitated baby Bimmers by installing a turbocharging system he had developed for the 320i back in 1977. Unfortunately, aftermarket turbo installations fell out of favor among enthusiasts, and, in 1985, Dinan decided to manufacture and sell BMW suspension kits—while preparing a variety of racing cars for numerous Northern California drivers.

When BMW began building sedans with large-displacement, 4-valve engines, Dinan turned his attention back to tuning and developed kits for both the sohc and twincam sixes. For a variety of reasons (basic engine design, cost, reliability), Steve used different means to enhance the BMW's 2- and 4-valve powerplants: turbocharging for the 535i; increased displacement and a higher compression ratio for the normally aspirated M5. He also went

about modifying each car's suspension differently, as we shall see.

But wait a minute! If BMW is "The ultimate driving machine," why would anyone need a Dinan? To be different. But more important, to go faster and more sure-footedly than the rest of the crowd. Compare the numbers of the Dinan M5 and 535i Turbo with those of the stock Bimmer 4-doors, and you'll find that the modified M5 and Turbo are about 1 and 2 seconds quicker, respectively. In fact, with nearly identical 0-to-60-mph times of 5.6 and 5.7 sec., the Dinans are in league with fast company that includes the Acura NSX, Corvette LT1 and ZR-1, and Porsche 968.

And yet, despite their similar acceleration times, the Dinan 535i Turbo and M5 are two different animals. The 535i is very much a family sedan, with subdued engine and moderately firm ride. The M5, although still a family 4-door, is the sporty Bimmer with a lively engine and taut suspension that gives away a tiny bit of ride quality for a whole lot of handling.

The Dinan 535i Turbo, which begins life as the more sedate Bimmer, gets the lion's share of attention. Dinan technicians take apart the engine, replace the stock 9:1 pistons with 8:1

■ BMW engine bays have always been orderly, but Dinan's craftsmanship makes them shine–note 535i Turbo's neatly fabricated and polished intercooler and lots of expertly applied wrinkle-finish paint.

slugs and reassemble the powerplant to stock specs. Then they install high-flow injectors, a recalibrated airflow meter, special exhaust headers, heavy-duty clutch and reengineered Bosch Motronic while adding an air-to-air intercooler with an air intake in the front bumper.

Turning their attention to the chassis and body, Dinan technicians fit the 535i with larger-diameter front brakes, 17 x 9-in. wheels shod with Yokohama AVS tires and install the Stage 4 suspension package comprising stiffer springs, shocks and (adjustable) front and rear anti-roll bars. Camber plates up front dial in negative camber, while a special Dinan crossmember at the rear gives the back wheels some positive camber—to offset the negative rear camber that occurs as a result of lowering the car. All of these components, plus a $700 gauge option, tack about $29,000 onto the price of a 535i, which costs $44,350 new.

Dinan's Turbo costs about $3500 less than its M5 because a stock 535i, having less content than the stock M5, is less expensive. Truth is, most of the money spent on the Turbo is in the engine, which costs $19,500 versus $9995 for the aspro powerplant. But 20 grand buys you 405 bhp, plus an axle-wrenching 438 lb.-ft. of torque, that gets the Turbo off the mark and on its way in rapid fashion—to 60 mph in 5.7 sec., to the quarter mile in 13.9.

Dinan's normally aspirated M5 is

the enthusiast's Bimmer. Its bored and stroked 3800-cc (vs. 3430-cc) engine is blueprinted and balanced, and sports a billet crankshaft, higher-compression forged pistons and a reprogrammed Bosch Motronic. It loves to be toyed with, and like most 4-valves, it thrives on high revs. Although it develops "only" 382 bhp and 343 lb.-ft. of torque, it's actually quicker than the Turbo from 0 to 60 mph, this despite the M5's 290 lb. greater weight.

Except for the 535i's Dinan camber-adjusting rear subframe, which it doesn't have or need, the Dinan M5 uses the same suspension components as the Turbo. And because its stock brakes are more than adequate, the M5 does without the Turbo's 13-inchers although it does use the same wheels and tires.

Special exhaust plumbing and reduced-restriction mufflers (with stock converters) are fitted to the Turbo. (Dinan says this is a more effective method of boosting horsepower than larger catalytic converters.) Common to 535i and M5 is the modified speed-control circuitry that allows the Dinans to reach their true top speed (160 mph for both), rather than the artificial 155-mph limit agreed upon by German sedan builders.

Although both Dinans expand the 5-Series' performance envelope, each car has its own personality. The Turbo feels as if it accelerates quicker because there's more torque. And that inimitable boot in the butt that occurs when the compressor spools up only reinforces this perception. In fact, with 405 bhp, there's no need for a lot of shift work. Simply step on the gas and motor away in silent, effortless style.

Like the powerplant, the Turbo's handling and ride are also more subdued. The Dinan 535i suspension feels more compliant, and the car rolls more and tends to understeer, especially on the skidpad where even throttle liftoff fails to induce oversteer. Nevertheless, the Turbo gets around the skidpad quicker than the stiffer M5, aided in part by its camber-compensating rear subframe that keeps the back wheels planted flatly against the surface. Unfortunately, compliance and positive camber inducement have their downsides, and in the abrupt, side-to-side motion of the slalom, the Turbo exhibits a rubbery feel that unsettles both the car's and the driver's composure. That said, I should point out that at 61.5 mph, the Dinan Turbo is 3.5 mph quicker through the pylons than a stock 535i.

Compared with the Turbo, the M5

feels more lively. The twincam engine makes better mechanical sounds and has that deep-breather induction roar that's missing in the Turbo. And, although it's flexible and torquey enough to pull strongly at low revs, the Dinan 4-valve really comes alive above 4500 rpm as it quickly (and willingly) spins to its 7300-rpm redline.

The stock M5 gearbox works nicely with the increased-displacement Dinan engine whose performance characteristics (as tracked by its power and torque curves) parallel those of the factory M5 powerplant. However, shift, clutch and steering effort seem greater, and even if the M5 wasn't almost 300 lb. heavier than the 535i, you'd think so because of the feel of these controls.

And yet the Dinan M5 is light on its feet, despite its meaty 255/40-series tires that measure a healthy 10 in. across. Unlike the Turbo, M5's handling is nearly neutral with mild un-

Dinan BMW 535i Turbo

PRICE

Base price	$44,350
Price as tested	$73,490

Price as tested includes BMW std equip. (air cond, AM/FM stereo/cassette, ABS, cruise control, central locking; elect. window lifts, door locks, mirrors), plus Dinan high-performance engine with turbocharger system ($19,500), Stage 4 suspension ($2800), 3-piece alloy wheels and hubs ($3100), Yokohama AVS tires ($1000), brakes ($2040), gauges ($700).

ENGINE

Type	turbo sohc inline-6
Displacement	209 cu in./3430 cc
Bore x stroke	3.62 x 3.39 in./ 92.0 x 86.0 mm
Compression ratio	8.0:1
Horsepower (SAE)	405 bhp @ 5500 rpm
Torque	438 lb-ft @ 4500 rpm
Maximum engine speed	6400 rpm
Fuel injection	elect. sequential port
Fuel	prem unleaded, 92 pump octane

CHASSIS & BODY

Layout	front engine/rear drive
Body/frame	unit steel
Brakes	
Front	13.0-in. vented discs
Rear	11.8-in. discs
Assist type	vacuum, ABS
Wheels	cast alloy, 17 x 9J
Tires	Yokohama AVS, 255/40ZR-17
Steering	recirc ball, variable power assist
Overall ratio	16.2
Turns, lock to lock	3.5
Turning circle	37.7 ft
Suspension	
Front	MacPherson struts, lower lateral links, compliance struts, coil springs, tube shocks, anti-roll bar
Rear	semi-trailing arms, coil springs, tube shocks, anti-roll bar

GENERAL DATA

Curb weight	3660 lb
Test weight	3815 lb
Weight dist (with driver), f/r, %	50/50
Wheelbase	108.7 in.
Track, f/r	58.2 in./59.0 in.
Length	185.8 in.
Width	68.9 in.
Height	54.7 in.

ACCELERATION

Time to speed	Seconds
0–30 mph	2.2
0–40 mph	3.3
0–50 mph	4.2
0–60 mph	5.7
0–70 mph	7.1
0–80 mph	8.6
0–90 mph	10.4
0–100 mph	12.9
Time to distance	
0–100 ft	3.1
0–500 ft	7.7
0–1320 ft (¼ mi)	13.9 @ 104.0 mph

FUEL ECONOMY

Normal driving	15.0 mpg
Fuel capacity	21.1 gal.

BRAKING

Minimum stopping distance	
From 60 mph	119 ft
From 80 mph	221 ft
Control	excellent
Brake feel	excellent
Overall brake rating	excellent

HANDLING

Lateral accel (200-ft skidpad)	0.89g
Balance	mild understeer
Speed thru 700-ft slalom	61.5 mph
Balance	mild understeer

DRIVETRAIN

Transmission	5-sp manual

Gear	Ratio	Overall ratio	(Rpm)	Mph
1st	3.83:1	13.21:1	(6400)	34
2nd	2.20:1	7.59:1	(6400)	59
3rd	1.40:1	4.83:1	(6400)	93
4th	1.00:1	3.45:1	(6400)	130
5th	0.81:1	2.79:1	est (6400)	160

Final drive ratio	3.45:1
Engine rpm @ 60 mph in 5th	2400

Subjective ratings consist of excellent, very good, good, average, poor.

dersteer that can be controlled through throttle application. In fact, because of the chassis' balance and the engine's responsiveness, it's possible to position the car by this means, as our road tester did in the slalom where the M5 schussed its way through the cones at an impressive 63.1 mph, nearly 2 mph faster than the stock M5 we tested in the August 1990 issue. The skidpad told a subtly different story, with the Dinan M5's lateral acceleration of

■ **M5 has the more aggressive suspension tuning; Turbo's detonation-warning LEDs are neatly done.**

Dinan BMW M5

PRICE

Base price	**$60,700**
Price as tested	**$77,045**

Price as tested includes BMW std equip. (air cond, AM/FM stereo/cassette, ABS, cruise control, central locking; elect. window lifts, door locks, mirrors), plus Dinan high-performance 3.8-liter engine ($9995), Stage 3 suspension ($2250), 3-piece alloy wheels and hubs ($3100), Yokohama AVS tires ($1000).

ENGINE

Type	4-valve/cyl dohc **inline-6**
Displacement	232 cu in./3800 cc
Bore x stroke	3.69 x 3.62 in./ 93.8 x 92.0 mm
Compression ratio	10.2:1
Horsepower (SAE)	**382 bhp @ 6500 rpm**
Torque	**343 lb-ft @ 5500 rpm**
Maximum engine speed	7300 rpm
Fuel injection	Bosch Motronic elect. sequential port
Fuel	prem unleaded, 92 pump octane

CHASSIS & BODY

Layout	**front engine/rear drive**
Body/frame	unit steel
Brakes	
Front	**12.4-in. vented discs**
Rear	**11.8-in. discs**
Assist type	vacuum, ABS
Wheels	cast alloy, 17 x 9J
Tires	Yokohama AVS, **255/40ZR-17**
Steering	**recirc ball**, variable power assist
Overall ratio	15.6
Turns, lock to lock	3.5
Turning circle	38.6 ft
Suspension	
Front	**MacPherson struts, lower lateral links, compliance struts,** coil springs, tube shocks, anti-roll bar
Rear	**semi-trailing arms,** coil springs, tube shocks, anti-roll bar

GENERAL DATA

Curb weight	**3950 lb**
Test weight	4100 lb
Weight dist (with driver), f/r, %	50/50
Wheelbase	108.7 in.
Track, f/r	58.2 in./59.0 in.
Length	**185.8 in.**
Width	**68.9 in.**
Height	**54.7 in.**

ACCELERATION

Time to speed	Seconds
0–30 mph	2.2
0–40 mph	3.4
0–50 mph	4.5
0–60 mph	5.6
0–70 mph	7.5
0–80 mph	9.3
0–90 mph	11.0
0–100 mph	13.7
Time to distance	
0–100 ft	3.1
0–500 ft	7.9
0–1320 ft (¼ mi)	14.1 @ 102.5 mph

FUEL ECONOMY

Normal driving	14.0 mpg
Fuel capacity	21.1 gal.

BRAKING

Minimum stopping distance	
From 60 mph	122 ft
From 80 mph	216 ft
Control	excellent
Brake feel	excellent
Overall brake rating	excellent

HANDLING

Lateral accel (200-ft skidpad)	0.87g
Balance	mild understeer
Speed thru 700-ft slalom	63.1 mph
Balance	mild understeer

DRIVETRAIN

Transmission	5-sp manual

Gear	Ratio	Overall ratio	(Rpm)	Mph
1st	3.51:1	13.72:1	(7300)	37
2nd	2.08:1	8.13:1	(7300)	63
3rd	1.35:1	5.28:1	(7300)	96
4th	1.00:1	3.91:1	(7300)	130
5th	0.81:1	3.17:1	est (7300)	160

Final drive ratio	3.91:1
Engine rpm @ 60 mph in 5th	2740

Subjective ratings consist of excellent, very good, good, average, poor.

0.87g being slightly less than the Turbo's 0.89g, we suspect because the Turbo's powerband allowed its rear tires to be worked slightly harder.

Of course, if you're the sort of person who gets off strictly on numbers, you're missing the point made by cars such as the Dinan BMWs, which offer a blend of performance, ride and comfort. "If we cross the line where the car is peaky or nasty, we back it off a notch," says Steve Dinan, whose philosophy is that his cars should be spirited, run 125,000 miles and retain the civility of a BMW. To ensure that they do, Dinan follows factory maintenance intervals and validates his work with his own 3-year/36,000-mile warranty. But the most heartening news is that turbocharged and normally aspirated Dinan powerplants are approved for highway use in all 50 states.

Although Dinan Engineering can build you a complete car and has begun supplying selected BMW dealerships with 5-Series sedans equipped with modified suspensions and other bolt-ons, the company's mainstay is sales of components. These can be fitted to existing BMWs by dealers or by the Dinan service department whose 12 employees also work on Acura, Infiniti, Lexus and Mercedes-Benz automobiles. And Dinan's BMW line is not restricted to the 5-Series. In fact, the company has a line of high-performance products for all late-model Bimmers, including an emissions-legal, twin-turbo V-12 for the 750i and 850i.

For BMW owners with a penchant for performance, that's good news. ◉

FIRST DRIVE

BMW M3

Bargain *bahn*stormer from BMW's performance emporium

BY RON SESSIONS

BMW OF NORTH America President Victor Doolan could hardly contain his enthusiasm. An all-new iteration of the Group A Touring Car Championship-inspired BMW M3, gone from these shores for more than two years now, will be in U.S. showrooms this spring.

Exhibit A is the $35,900 1994 M3, which, by the way, is the same price the previous-generation 4-cylinder M3 sold for when last seen here in 1991. Based on the ever-popular 325is Coupe, the new M3 is a more mature sports coupe that's gone to finishing school. Gone is the cafe-racer look of the 1988–1991 model. The new M3 forgoes the jumbo wheel blisters and bigger-than-life, pedestal-mounted rear wing of the emeritus model for an understated performance look.

BMW watchers will note the more pronounced, body-color front air dam and ground-effect side cladding, the wheel-well-popping 17-in. alloy rims with Z-rated rubber, stanchion-mounted side mirrors, and, of course, the emblematic M3 decklid badge. Otherwise, this M is a bit of a Q-ship, drawing little attention to itself until called upon to do so.

Slip behind the wheel of the new M3, strap yourself into the specially bolstered, form-fitting bucket seat, key the engine to life and instead of the frenetic vibrato of a very busy 4-holer, you're serenaded by the siren of six silken cylinders. In U.S. trim, the new M3 is empowered by a bored and stroked version of the 325's dohc 24-valve inline-6. At 2990 cc, the M3 engine pumps out an attention-getting 240 bhp at 6000 rpm, a 25-percent increase over the 325 powerplant. Also, torque is emboldened some 22 percent to 225 lb.-ft., and more important, peak torque occurs lower in the rev range (4250 vs. 4700 rpm) where American drivers can use it to best advantage. Mated to BMW's excellent close-ratio 5-speed, the M3 can doze along in almost any gear, thanks to the broad power band.

Dozing was the last thing on my mind, however, as I ran a U.S.-spec M3 up through the gears, exited pit lane and nosed through the apex of the sharp right-hand Turn 1 on the Nürburgring Grand Prix circuit at a recent BMW press gathering. For comparison purposes at the track, BMW assembled an impressive entourage of its best sports sedans and coupes (current M5, 1991 M3 4-cylinder, 635CSi, Euro-spec 286-bhp 1993 M3 and a baseline 325is).

The U.S.-spec M3 shares its chassis pieces and grippy 235/40ZR-17 tires with the European-market model. As such, it's hunkered down 1.2 in. lower and sports a stance 2.0 in. wider than a stock 325is. Spring rates are raised and shock valving increased to handle spirited driving, but not to the jiggly levels of the previous-generation M3. At the very enjoyable limit, the M3 exhibits mild understeer that can be coaxed into line-tightening oversteer with judicious use of the throttle. A natural athlete with 50/50 weight distribution, the M3 gives excellent turn-in response and is crisp in transitions. Dive, squat and roll are exiled to another province.

When it comes time to scrub off *Autobahn* levels of speed in a hurry, the M3 drops anchor with linear-feeling, easy-to-modulate 4-wheel discs with anti-lock. Always poised. Balanced. Fun.

Only on the long straights did I miss the 286 bhp and 7000-rpm redline of the considerably more expensive (and non-U.S.-emissions-certified) Euro-spec M3. However, a series of impromptu drag races between the U.S. and Euro-spec M3s bore out BMW's claims of comparable low-speed performance; the two clocked off nearly identical 6-second 0–60-mph runs.

If modern-day BMWs have always been drivers' cars, then BMW Motorsports M-series offerings have been street cars of exceptional desire and outstanding ability. BMW's Vic Doolan promises an enticing series of new M-brand models will be arriving at BMW stores over the next few months and years. An M3 with automatic transmission is on the horizon, and the upcoming South Carolina-built BMW sports car will likely have an M-application. So what we have to look forward to is a performance-car emporium in the making. Now that's enough to put a smile on any enthusiast's face.

BMW

850 CSi

Earthquakes, torrential rain, and a $108,450 Bavarian flagship in a 4-wheel computer-aided drift

BY DENNIS SIMANAITIS
PHOTOS BY GUY SPANGENBERG

WHAT WITH FIRESTORMS, earthquakes, mud slides and, as I begin this report, torrential rains, flooding and even a tornado, Southern California has hardly been a boring place of late. I know that the rest of the country has suffered through an absolutely terrible winter as well. You would think we should all be lusting after AM General HUMMERS and not bucks-up European exotics.

But I've just driven our BMW 850CSi test car to the office through this latest cruel onslaught of Mother Nature (and hasn't she been a cruel mother). Not only did I arrive just fine, thanks, but I had a super-neat driving experience as well, with one recurring thought: This is what it must feel like to drive a Formula 1 car of the 1993 vintage.

You may think I've been out overly long in the weather (Southern Califor-

nians reserve this word "weather" only for the anomalies), but let me amplify. Like its 850i predecessor—and a 1993 F1 car—this car is dense with electronically controlled driver aids. Plus, in its CSi trim—and like the F1 car—this BMW coupe exhibits gobs of performance in just about every dynamic area. Driven in decent conditions—as for our track testing and photography, for instance—its acceleration, braking and handling are superlative. Driven in horrid conditions, its powerplant, brakes and suspension are equally superlative—but now you realize the important role played by the car's electronic gadgetry.

Before we continue, though, let's put the BMW 8-Series lineup in perspective. At $108,450 (gulp; and to think I was drifting it in the rain), the CSi is the company flagship, its V-12 powerplant bored and stroked by BMW M GmbH, the renamed BMW Motorsport. Think of this car as the firm's M8, in limited production of 200 examples over two years (and, sorry, you're already too late for the first year's run). Most 8-Series coupes will be in 840i form ($73,140), propelled by Bayerische Motoren Werke's lovely V-8 mated to its state-of-the-art 5-speed automatic. Between these is the 850Ci ($94,150), essentially the car we tested back in June 1991.

The arithmetically advantaged will recognize that healthy pieces of change separate these cars, so it's not unkind to ask what sets the CSi at the pinnacle.

The most important, and costly, difference is the car's V-12 powerplant. Its displacement of 5576 cc is 12 percent larger than the Ci's, but its 372 bhp is 26 percent greater, a compression ratio bumped to 9.8:1 being part of this analysis. Torque increases to 402 lb.-ft. from a measly 332.

Apart from cylinder count, the CSi's powerplant is a conservative one, a single overhead camshaft per bank actuating a bare minimum of two valves per cylinder. In fact, several of our staff members thought the powerplant performed too conservatively as well. There's plenty of power, mind, but it's satiny-smooth. And, except for the wonderful Spitfire whine of the starter, the powerplant's mechanical sounds are subtle, or to put it rather less kindly, they're without character.

No one is looking for a calico-ripping snarl here. Nor would anyone be offended by a little audible reminder of the V-12 once it's running.

■ Pretty but precarious: a scant 3.9 in. between air dam and asphalt.

■ Stop and go: 12.8-in. vented discs and 372 smooth bhp.

THE COMPETITION

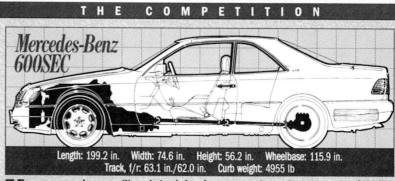

Mercedes-Benz 600SEC

Length: 199.2 in.   Width: 74.6 in.   Height: 56.2 in.   Wheelbase: 115.9 in.
Track, f/r: 63.1 in./62.0 in.   Curb weight: 4955 lb

■ These cars may be competitors, but only in price, performance and luxury. In what really matters, each has a special spirit unto itself. The SEC is big, heavy, sturdy; a storming bank vault and proud of it. Its three-pointed star carries more prestige than any automotive symbol south of the Rolls-Royce Spirit of Ecstasy. It isn't the sports/GT that the Porsche 928 is, but its V-12 can be docile or violent; your right foot decides. And, unlike the other two, it has rear seats that might even hold real people. (Tested: 4/93)

Current list price	$132,000
Engine	dohc 6.0-liter V-12
Horsepower	389 bhp @ 5200 rpm
Torque	420 lb-ft @ 3800 rpm
Transmission	4-speed automatic
0–60 mph	6.6 sec
Braking, 60–0 mph	125 ft
Lateral accel (200-ft skidpad)	0.75g
EPA city/highway	15/19 mpg

Porsche 928 GTS

Length: 178.1 in.   Width: 74.4 in.   Height: 50.5 in.   Wheelbase: 98.4 in.
Track, f/r: 61.1 in./63.6 in.   Curb weight: 3595 lb

■ The GTS iteration of the Porsche 928 has more power, more tire, more wheel, more brakes and more amenities than ever before in the car's 17-year (!) history. Then why has the 928 been glued to the dealership floor? The only reason I can fathom is that its "proper Porsche" 911 siblings attract attention of those lusting after Zuffenhausen products, thus leaving this perfectly capable car to be the perfectly rational choice for someone desiring a little exclusivity in this world. (First Drive: 7/92)

Current list price	$85,260
Engine	dohc 5.4-liter V-8
Horsepower	345 bhp @ 5700 rpm
Torque	369 lb-ft @ 4250 rpm
Transmission	5-speed manual
0–60 mph	est 5.5 sec
Braking, 60–0 mph	na
Lateral accel (200-ft skidpad)	na
EPA city/highway	12/19 mpg

1994 BMW 850CSi

IMPORTER

BMW of North America, Inc.
P.O. Box 1227
Westwood, N.J. 07675-1227

PRICE

List price	$98,500
Price as tested	$108,450

Price as tested includes std equip. (dual airbags, ABS, All Season Traction control, air cond, leather interior, AM/FM stereo/cassette, cruise control; pwr windows, seats, mirrors, sunroof and central locking; 6-disc CD player/changer, cellular phone), luxury tax ($6950), gas-guzzler tax ($3000).

0–60 mph	5.9 sec
0–¼ mi	14.4 sec
Top speed	155 mph*
Skidpad	0.89g
Slalom	62.0 mph
Brake rating	excellent

TEST CONDITIONS

Temperature	75° F
Wind	calm
Humidity	60%
Elevation	350 ft

SCALE: 10 in.(254mm) DIVISIONS
DRAWING BY BILL DOBSON

ENGINE

Type.... aluminum block & heads, **V-12**
Valvetrain.......... sohc 2-valve/cyl
Displacement .... 340 cu in./5576 cc
Bore x stroke .... 3.39 x 3.15 in./
86.0 x 80.0 mm
Compression ratio.............. 9.8:1
Horsepower
(SAE)........ **372 bhp @ 5300 rpm**
Bhp/liter......................... 66.7
Torque........ **402 lb-ft @ 4000 rpm**
Maximum engine speed.... 6400 rpm/
gear dependent
Fuel injection: dual Bosch MH-Motronic
Fuel .... prem unleaded, 91 pump oct

CHASSIS & BODY

Layout .... **front engine/rear drive**
Body/frame .... unit steel
Brakes
Front........ **12.8-in. vented discs**
Rear................ **12.8-in. discs**
Assist type.......... hydraulic, ABS
Total swept area........ 605 sq in.
Swept area/ton........ 278 sq in.
Wheels................ forged alloy;
17 x 8J f, 17 x 9J r
Tires......... Michelin Pilot SC MXX3;
235/45ZR-17 f, 265/40ZR-17 r
Steering... **recirc ball**, vari power assist
Overall ratio................ 15.4:1
Turns, lock to lock.............. 3.3
Turning circle................ 37.7 ft
Suspension
Front .... **MacPherson struts,
double-pivot lower arms**, coil
springs, tube shocks, anti-roll bar
Rear.......... **multilink**, coil springs,
tube shocks, anti-roll bar

DRIVETRAIN

Transmission			6-sp manual
Gear	Ratio	Overall ratio	(Rpm) Mph
1st	4.25:1	12.45:1	(6400) 37
2nd	2.53:1	7.41:1	(6400) 63
3rd	1.68:1	4.92:1	(6200) 92
4th	1.24:1	3.63:1	(6100) 123
5th	1.00:1	2.93:1	(6000) 149
6th	0.83:1	2.43:1	(5150) 155*
Final drive ratio			4.27:1

Engine rpm @ 60 mph in 6th 2000
* Electronically limited

GENERAL DATA

Curb weight	4240 lb
Test weight	4355 lb
Weight dist (with driver), f/r, %	51/49
Wheelbase	105.7 in.
Track, f/r	61.2 in./61.5 in.
Length	188.2 in.
Width	73.0 in.
Height	52.8 in.
Ground clearance	3.9 in.
Trunk space	11.0 cu ft

MAINTENANCE

Oil/filter change	7500 mi/7500 mi
Tuneup	30,000 mi/use-dependent
Basic warranty	48 mo/50,000 mi

ACCOMMODATIONS

Seating capacity	2+2
Head room, f/r	38.0 in./34.5 in.
Seat width, f/r:	2 x 19.5 in./2 x 20.0 in.
Front-seat leg room	42.5 in.
Rear-seat knee room	19.0 in.
Seatback adjustment	35 deg
Seat travel	6.5 in.

INTERIOR NOISE

Idle in neutral	52 dBA
Maximum in 1st gear	74 dBA
Constant 50 mph	64 dBA
70 mph	67 dBA

INSTRUMENTATION

190-mph speedometer, 8000-rpm tach, coolant temp, fuel level

ACCELERATION

Time to speed	Seconds
0–30 mph	2.3
0–40 mph	3.6
0–50 mph	4.7
0–60 mph	5.9
0–70 mph	7.9
0–80 mph	9.6
0–90 mph	11.5
0–100 mph	14.3
Time to distance	
0–100 ft	3.1
0–500 ft	8.0
0–1320 ft (¼ mi):14.4 sec @ 100.5 mph	

FUEL ECONOMY

Normal driving	est 13.0 mpg
EPA city/highway	12/20 mpg
Cruise range	est 296 miles
Fuel capacity	23.8 gal.

BRAKING

Minimum stopping distance	
From 60 mph	135 ft
From 80 mph	220 ft
Control	excellent
Pedal effort for 0.5g stop	20 lb
Fade, effort after six 0.5g stops from 60 mph	20 lb
Brake feel	excellent
Overall brake rating	excellent

HANDLING

Lateral accel (200-ft skidpad)	0.89g
Balance	mild understeer
Speed thru 700-ft slalom	62.0 mph
Balance	mild understeer
Lateral seat support	excellent

Subjective ratings consist of excellent, very good, good, average, poor; na means information is not available.

Test Notes...

■ Through the slalom, the 850CSi spun its wheels too easily in 3rd gear, but didn't have quite enough response in 4th—despite having six gears to choose from.

■ Switch off the traction control, and the 850CSi is transformed from a mild understeerer into a tossable delight. Controllable power oversteer is immediately available.

■ The 850CSi's engine is powerful; a 4240-lb. car that can reach 60 mph in under 6 seconds is impressive. But the BMW V-12's refinement almost goes too far; perhaps a rawer edge would satisfy more.

There's reminder aplenty once you depress that pedal on the right. Sixty mph arrives as quickly as 5.9 seconds (versus 7.3 for the Ci). And, owing to the car's Variable Throttle Linkage, it comes up in a suitably complex manner: There's a console switch marked S for Sport and K for Comfort. (And, contrary to Mark Twain's view, I believe foreigners actually pronounce better than they spell.) Anyway, Sport invokes a more aggressive actuation of throttle hardware; Comfort, a smoother, softer control.

A gimmick? I'd certainly keep it on Komfort when weather arrives, all the better to feather into that torque.

Or, returning to my F1 fantasy, occasionally I tried just planting my foot to the floor and letting the All Season Traction electronics do its stuff. (Don't try this at home, kids; remember, I'm a professional.) In fact, ASC+T, as it's also known, modulates power through spark timing and throttle and, if needed, applies one or the other rear brake until a negligible degree of slip is achieved. It's fun in the wet, and I would guess uncanny on ice or snow.

And, no, we haven't had sleet in Newport Beach just yet.

Even with something as simple as full-grip acceleration in a straight line, there's electronic wizardry at work. The CSi's redline is variously 6400 rpm (in 1st and 2nd gear), 6200 (for 3rd), 6100 (4th), 6000 (5th) and 5150 (6th); this last one, by our own calculation as the car's top speed is electronically limited to a Deutsche *politischkorrekt* 155 mph. And isn't *that* the kind of PC thinking you could buy into?

There's good logic in these variable revs: An enthusiast is unlikely to bounce off the limiter for long in the lower gears; but one might stay in 4th, say, through some handling transition. What's more, like a lot of the CSi's electronics, the variable rev limiter is transparent under all but the most extreme conditions.

Other CSi characteristics that are less transparent include its front air dam and rear skirt with diffuser, its 17-in. M-styled forged alloy wheels

and fore/aft-specific rubber. Front tires are 235/45ZRs; rears, 265/40ZRs. The suspension is M-modified as well, its ride height reduced to the point that care must be taken to avoid damage to the air dam's rubber protection strip. (We managed to ruin one.)

It's a low car and it's a large one as well; some would say too large for what's essentially a 2-seater. (Though there are belts back there, think of the rear area as upholstered niches for extra things, not extra people.) The front is certainly a comfortable, secure place for driver and passenger. A multiplicity of colors and textures, and gathered Nappa leather and yew hardwood,

The 850's seats feature integral seatbelt retractors, "floating" headrests.

give the CSi's interior rather more warmth than is common in lesser BMWs. And I particularly like the stylish reminder of its heritage: a subtle stitching on the leather-wrapped steering wheel, three-toned in M Motorsport red, blue and mauve.

The CSi's dynamic capabilities remind me of this heritage as well. Note, for instance, the car's laudably quick slalom speed of 62.0 mph, right up there with nimble little front-wheel-drivers that ordinarily excel in this exercise. Indeed, our Road Test Editor Kim Reynolds found the car very controllable in its transitions from gate to gate, hampered only a bit by gearing that gave him too much throttle sensitivity in 3rd and too little in 4th. And the CSi circled our skidpad at a steady-state 0.89g, not bad at all for a car with a test weight of 4355 lb. Reynolds reported mild understeer,

very good controllability and a high fun factor. (Apparently he found this big coupe as tossable in the dry as I did in the wet.) Both of Kim's evaluations, by the way, were done with All Season Traction in its off position.

Braking gave no such option and none required, what with the CSi's ABS performing splendidly: Kim's "panic" stops were utterly misnamed in this case, 60–0 mph in 135 ft. and 80–0 in 220, with the least bit of drama imaginable. And, despite the car's healthy test weight, the brakes exhibited no fade whatsoever in our extremely rigorous six-stops-from-60 routine. In our road experiences, the brakes were equally superlative, with or without weather.

So what sets the CSi apart from other European supercoupes? The Mercedes-Benz 600SEC and Porsche 928 GTS might be thought of as competitors, and some accompanying comments amplify on this.

On the other hand, cars of this level are acquired and should be appreciated for their unique spirits, not for their comparable features of performance, luxury or style. The 850CSi is, first and foremost, a BMW. Sporty and capable, like a Porsche. Luxurious and capable, like a Mercedes-Benz. Yet unlike either of these.

Maybe its most serious competitors are others in the BMW 8-Series line. When we evaluated the original 850i back in June 1991, we said it was up to someone to take its canvas and to paint in dazzling reds and sunburst yellows. It's a bit more subtle, but what we have here in the CSi is BMW M's red, blue and mauve. ⊚

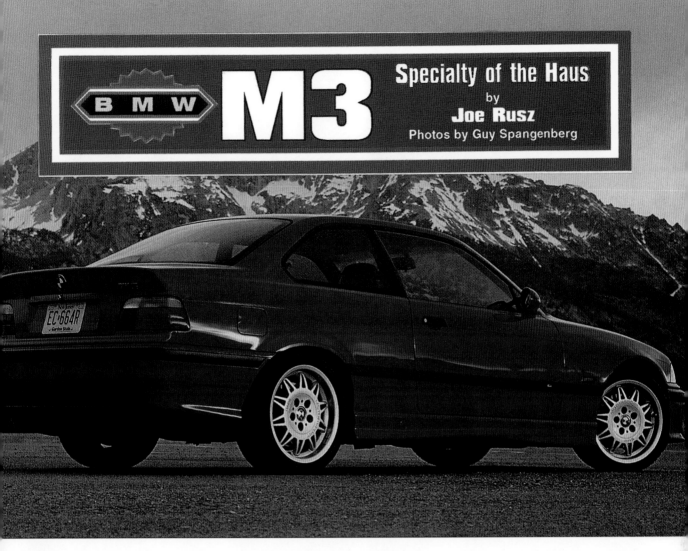

BMW M3

Specialty of the Haus

by **Joe Rusz**

Photos by Guy Spangenberg

You hear a lot about tuner cars these days. Production automobiles modified for high performance by independent specialists such as AMG, Alpina, Callaway, Doug Rippie, Ruf and TWR (Tom Walkinshaw Racing). Mercs, Bimmers, Vettes and Camaros, Porsche 911s and a variety of Jags, tweaked to mechanical perfection and sold as specials by their builders—usually at premium prices.

Then there's the BMW M3, an exciting sport coupe that could easily pass itself off as a tuner car because of its looks (terrific) and its performance (ditto). You could pay plenty for a car like this and not even have a warranty to go with it. But thanks to the forward-thinking management at BMW, this hot little 3-Series can be yours for just $3000 more than a "normal" BMW, namely, the 325is.

How can they do that?

Simple. Unlike a tuner car that's assembled piecemeal and in limited numbers by a handful of workers, the M3 is built in BMW's sprawling Munich factory alongside other 3-Series models. And while it's not as exclu-

> *It'll outrun a Camaro Z28 or a Mustang Cobra and give a Porsche 968 a run for its money.*

sive as, say, an Alpina BMW, that M moniker means that the design and engineering of the car was executed at BMW Motorsport, the same facility that performs to-order modifications (engine swaps, suspension improvements, custom painting, etc) to customer-owned Bimmers.

Not by accident is this operation called BMW Motorsport: The company racing cars are built there. So is the 600-bhp, 6.0-liter V-12 that powers the legendary McLaren F1, claimed to be the world's fastest (and most expensive) exotic. And so was the original M3 (built from 1988 to 1991), a so-called homologation special whose bulbous fenders and aero aids (including a trunk-mounted rear spoiler) gave it a cafe-racer look that was shunned by those who preferred their BMWs on the understated side.

With acceleration times that were only marginally quicker than those of the normal 325 (0 to 60 mph in 7.1 sec, 0 to the 1/4-mile in 15.4 sec), the first-edition M3 was all but ignored by performance buffs, who expected a lot more from a car that cost nearly $6000 more than the already pricey ($29,000) 325is. Thus, when the decision was made to build an

M3 successor, BMW made certain that the car would be tastefully styled, quick and attractively priced. And so it is—on all counts.

Beginning with looks, which are distinctive without being garish. Although the front air dam, with its central air intake flanked by brake-cooling ducts, is certainly very businesslike in appearance, the M3's other aerodynamic aids (flared side skirts, deeper rear lower surround with built-in air diffusor that accommodates the polished exhaust tips, cantilevered side mirrors) are a bit more sedately styled. In fact those who insist on being noticed should forego mundane colors such as black, white or silver and order something more arresting—like Dakar Yellow or Mugello Red.

Performance is pleasantly exhila-

rating, even amazing for a car powered by a relatively small displacement, normally aspirated engine. With 0–60 and quarter-mile times of 6.0 and 14.6 sec respectively, the 1995 M3 is quicker than all but the hottest sports cars and turbocharged coupes. It'll outrun a Camaro Z28 or a Mustang Cobra and give a Porsche 968 a run for its money—using nothing more exotic than BMW's standard-issue dohc inline-6, bored (2.0 mm) and stroked (10.8 mm) to 3.0 liters. This increased displacement improves low- and mid-range torque, which is further enhanced by a special exhaust system and by a recalibration of the same variable valve-timing setup used by the 325is.

To keep costs down, the U.S.-spec M3 engine uses the same 24-valve cylinder head and single-throttle intake system as the 325is (and 525i) powerplant, in contrast to the European and Canadian M3s that get a more exotic (spelled "expensive") head with individual throttle butterflies. No need to worry, however, because with 240 bhp on tap, the domestic M3 engine is perfectly suited to American driv-

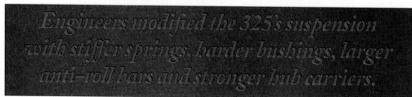

Engineers modified the 325's suspension with stiffer springs, harder bushings, larger anti-roll bars and stronger hub carriers.

ing styles, which favor brisk acceleration over pure top speed.

What the original M3 lacked in performance it made up for in handling, which was the car's strong suit—impressive, even by today's standards. But still not as good as the new M3's. To achieve this level, BMW chassis engineers modified the 325's suspension by fitting shorter,

stiffer springs, harder bushings, larger anti-roll bars and stronger hub carriers. Larger-diameter M-design alloy wheels and Z-rated tires bolt to reinforced hub carriers that sport 1-in.-larger-diameter vented disc brakes—with ABS, of course.

The M3 is based on the 325is, so its interior is already chock full of features. That hasn't stopped BMW from

adding those extra M-touches—sports seats with broad side bolsters (covered in Nappa Leather or suede-trimmed cloth emblazoned with M-Series signature magenta/purple/blue stripes), leather-rimmed M-Technic steering wheel, and M-Series instruments, including a 160-mph speedometer and 8000-rpm tach.

It's all very tasteful, very understated, in a European elegance kind of way. In fact, if your idea of a tuner car is cantilevered wings and other appendages doused with Kandy Apple paint and a dyed-leather interior with phony wood (don't forget the megawatt stereo and cellular phone), you'll be disappointed by the M3. Metaphorically speaking BMW's version walks softly and carries a big stick.

Climb aboard, fire it up, ease on through the gears and it feels just like another BMW, silky smooth, tractable, quiet. Tip into the throttle, however, and feel the power build—from a lazy 1000 rpm where the M3 can cruise comfortably, to maximum revs (6800 in 1st and 2nd, 6500 in the top three gears). Although the M-powerplant comes on strong at 4000 rpm, its broad torque band enables it to perform more than adequately at lower engine speeds. That's good news for those of us who do most of our driving in urban areas, often in heavy traffic.

Though there's no need to overexercise the M3's shifter, it's certainly reassuring to know that when the red mist rises, the Bimmer's buttery-smooth linkage almost seems to anticipate your command by slipping firmly into the proper gate.

Psychic, you could call it, much like the rest of the car, which seems to respond to your very thoughts—especially when it comes to handling. A flick of the steering wheel places the M3 exactly where some subliminal voice hinted it should be.

Actually, the M3 is not so much an Amazing Kreskin as a Harry Houdini, deftly getting you out of tight spots of your own devising, thanks to BMW's variable-assist, variable-ratio steering, which provides extra boost when parking, and quick response (with proportionately less boost) during high-speed cornering. That aforementioned Motorsport-tuned suspension embues the M3 with a balanced feel (mild understeer with a touch of trailing-throttle oversteer) with a pool-table-flat stance and minimal body roll. And a ride that is compliant without being mushy.

Nor have the Motorsports folks overlooked brakes—at 12 in. plus the M3's discs are bigger than the Corvette LT1's. Fade-free, their ability is enhanced by reprogrammed ABS to accommodate the higher pedal pressures associated with intense late braking.

While enjoying such high levels of performance, it's easy to overlook the fact that the M3 is a sedan, and a luxury one at that. Although rear leg room is dependent on the size of the front occupants, the M3 is quite capable of hauling four people plus luggage, which can be stowed in the Bimmer's roomy trunk.

It's also easy to overlook the fact that the M3 is a true White and Blue BMW, not just a tuner's one-off. Of course, there's a down side to all of this: Although there may be only a handful of specials, some 2500 M3s will reach American shores, which means that yours may not be the only M-Series on the block. On the other hand, you'll like what you see—a handsome sport coupe. Driven by a person of discriminating taste with an eye for a tuner-car bargain.

BMW

M3

PRICE

List price, all POE	$35,800
Price as tested	$39,483

Price as tested includes std equip. (ABS, dual airbags, air cond, lim-slip diff, leather int, AM/FM-stereo/cassette, pwr windows & mirrors, central locking), pwr sunroof ($1120), cruise control & foglights ($455), luxury tax ($638), dest charge ($470).

ENGINE

Type	dohc 24-valve inline-6
Displacement	2989 cc
Bore x stroke	86.0 x 85.8 mm
Compression ratio	10.5:1
Horsepower, SAE net	240 bhp @ 6000 rpm
Torque	225 lb-ft @ 4250 rpm
Maximum engine speed	6500 rpm[1]
Fuel injection	Bosch HFM-Motronic
Fuel requirement	premium unleaded

GENERAL DATA

Curb weight	3180 lb
Weight distribution, f/r, %	50/50
Wheelbase	106.3 in.
Track, f/r	56.0/56.9 in.
Length	174.5 in.
Width	67.3 in.
Height	52.6 in.
Trunk space	14.5 + 6.0 cu ft

CHASSIS & BODY

Layout	front engine/rear drive
Body/frame	unit steel
Brakes, f/r	12.4-in. vented discs/12.3-in. vented discs, vacuum assist, ABS
Wheels	cast-alloy, 17 x 7.5J
Tires	235/40ZR-17
Steering	rack & pinion, power assist
Turns, lock to lock	3.0
Suspension, f/r	MacPherson struts, double-pivot lower arms, coil springs, tube shocks, anti-roll bar/multi-link, coil springs, tube shocks, anti-roll bar

DRIVETRAIN

Transmission			5-sp manual	
Gear	Ratio	Overall Ratio	(Rpm)	Mph
1st	4.20:1	13.23:1	(6800)	36
2nd	2.49:1	7.84:1	(6800)	60
3rd	1.66:1	5.23:1	(6500)	86
4th	1.24:1	3.91:1	(6500)	115
5th	1.00:1	3.15:1	(6250)	137[2]
Final-drive ratio				3.15:1

Engine rpm @ 60 mph, top gear ..... 2725 rpm

ACCELERATION

Time to speed	seconds
0-30 mph	2.2
0-40 mph	3.4
0-50 mph	4.7
0-60 mph	6.0
0-70 mph	8.3
0-80 mph	10.3
0-90 mph	13.0
0-100 mph	16.0
Time to distance	
0-100 ft	3.1
0-500 ft	8.0
0-1320 ft (1/4 mile)	14.6 sec @ 96.0 mph

BRAKING

Minimum stopping distance	
From 60 mph	120 ft
From 80 mph	217 ft
Control	excellent
Overall brake rating	excellent

HANDLING

Lateral accel (200-ft skidpad)	0.87g
Speed thru 700-ft slalom	62.8 mph

FUEL ECONOMY

Normal driving	24.6 mpg
Fuel economy (EPA city/highway)	19/27 mpg
Fuel capacity	17.2 gal.

[1]6800 rpm in 1st & 2nd gear
[2]top speed electronically limited
est estimated
na means information not available

BMW

M3

meets

AMG tweaks make the C36 shriek, but is the car a match for BMW's M3?

BY RICHARD HOMAN
PHOTOS BY JOHN KONKAL

MERCEDES-BENZ C36

WOW. WOW IS plenty dramatic. But as a complete Road Test, let alone a Comparison Test, it strikes even me, the lonely writer hurtling headlong toward his deadline, as woefully inadequate. Wow is not only not a contender for the Ken Purdy Award for Excellence in Automotive Journalism, it's a one-way ticket out of the business. Just ask my editor.

But I remember the first time I saddled up a 1994 BMW M3 and spurred the throttle: The half-moon grin on my face was preceded by an exclamation that could not be mistaken for anything but praise. And this afternoon, Senior Editor Joe Rusz got back from an apparently spirited lunchtime workout in the new-to-the-U.S. Mercedes-Benz C36. His first time in it. I asked Joe what he thought of the car, and he was kind enough to write my lead for me: "Wow," he said.

I nodded. I knew what he meant, having driven the pilot European C36 a little more than a year ago in Germany (see "Autobahn Aristocrats" in our December 1993 issue). And readers of our August 1994 issue will remember our being wowed by the BMW M3 in a Road Test. Here were two top German carmakers, each seeing the other as primary competition, each bringing to the North American market a showcase performance car constructed from the best of its bread-and-butter automobiles (the M3 is based on the 325is Coupe, the C36 on the C280 sedan) and each casting a distinct image in our minds—"Mercedes-like" and "BMW-like" are certainly part of any enthusiast's vocabulary.

The U.S. introduction of the Mercedes-Benz C36 presented us with an ideal opportunity to put both cars under the harsh light of scrutiny and see which one, if either, blinked.

Our favorite performance laboratory for such scrutiny is the clinical research facility known as Willow Springs International Raceway, particularly the 1.3-mile asphalt snake known as the Streets of Willow. It was on this miniature road course that our two cars distinguished themselves (in general as well as from each other).

The BMW appeared to be having the most fun out at the track, but just barely. From its razor-sharp, variable-assist/variable-ratio rack-and-pinion steering and multilink suspension right down to its 40-series tires, the M3 chatted up a storm, keeping its driver in touch with every nuance of the road, responding to every steering input. The more nimble of the two cars, the BMW, was also the more exacting, with a penchant for oversteer. But the payoff for keeping tail dancing to a minimum was high. Any reasonable com-

■ The styled 17-in. aluminum wheels, the leather-wrapped steering wheel and shift knob, the instrument cluster and, of course, the 268-bhp twincam inline-6 all bear the performance promise of the AMG logo. The Mercedes-Benz C36 never misses a beat as the E500 for buyers on a budget.

bination of steering, throttle and concentration went a long way toward turning in the most gratifying laps.

It's a bit harder to get into a rhythm in the Mercedes C36. The inputs aren't quite as keen as in the BMW; the steering is not as quick. The suspension isn't set up to be as taut as the BMW's, giving, instead, a nod to ride comfort. In its understeering nature, the C36 shows considerable bias toward its wider rear tires. In corners, it will tuck in reluctantly if you drop the throttle. But the fast way around in the C36 is to go deep into a corner, taking full advantage of the powerful brakes, repoint and then let the engine's immense low-end thrust fire you off toward the next transition. A different kind of driving than in the BMW M3, but just as effective, pro-

viding a pleasant surprise at the track. As I learned at the C36's introduction in Germany, this is a car best appreciated at high speeds, most effective in creating the shortest distance between two points.

Both cars appear to be getting the absolute best out of their respective inline-6 engines. There isn't a dull spot in either car's wide power band, and while the BMW may not have the operatic torque of the Mercedes, it balances the equation by playing its 5-speed manual gearbox (and lighter weight) to the Benz's 4-speed automatic. A pure driver's setup, the M3's pedal placement is ideal for heel-and-toe shifting. And while both cars can call up substantial power from anywhere in the rev range, the trip from 60 to 100 mph in the Mercedes is one of the best

9.0-second vacations we know of.

And you may ask yourself: How did they get here?

In a sense, both the C36 and the M3 are pioneer projects for their German parent companies. Mercedes has collaborated with famed tuner AMG to create the C36. For better than two decades, "Mercedes" and "AMG" have been coming off the lips of enthusiasts in the same breath, as though the companies were one and the same. In truth, however, AMG spent most of its time acting as a sort of personal trainer for M-B models, developing super-Benzes like the 300E-sedan-based "Hammer" (a 6.0-liter V-8, 365-bhp helping of Wow) and enlisting to help out with Mercedes' German Touring Car Championship efforts. The C36 is the first car acknowledged

as a joint effort by both M-B and AMG. As such, the yearly output of 1200 C36 models—including about 400 for the U.S.A.—will carry an AMG badge and be sold throughout the world by Mercedes-Benz dealers.

The journey from mild-mannered C-class to C36 begins at Mercedes' Bremen factory in northern Germany. At Bremen, the essence of a C280 sedan comes together along the C-class assembly line; however, the future C36 gets special treatment from the Mercedes workers, who fit a sturdier final drive, the larger vented front discs

of the SL600, the larger rears of the E420, stiffer front and rear anti-roll bars, shorter springs (to hunker the car down) and a quicker-ratio steering box. Before the C36-to-be leaves Bremen, the factory also mounts the 17-in. AMG wheels and damn-wide, low-profile Bridgestone Expedia S-01 tires (full-size spare included), and front fenders that have been modified on the inside to accommodate the broader rubber. Now the car, sans bumpers and skirts, is ready to head south to AMG.

It is at AMG's headquarters/work-

shops in Affalterbach, near Stuttgart, that the C36 meets its performance destiny. Special gas-pressure shocks are installed, and finishing bodywork— plastic rear bumper, side skirts and front bumper/apron—is attached. Besides adding to the C36's visual form, the front apron is also functional, incorporating a set of foglights and ducting air to the car's massive—bigger than a Ferrari 512TR's—front brakes, which, as mentioned, were spirited from the SL600 roadster.

The interior, swaddled in leather, is highlighted by electrically adjustable

sport seats (sporty, yes, but also kind to long-distance travelers), a Bose sound system, and an AMG instrument panel, two-tone steering wheel and shift knob to remind the lucky driver just how lucky he is. The faux carbon-fiber console trim of the European C36 gives way to the American expectations of a Mercedes—burled walnut—although the Schmevlar Kevlar is still used to set off the U.S. car's B-pillars.

None of this hard work would mean much if the engine wasn't a showcase piece. Not to worry. As soon as the car arrives at AMG's facility, Affalterbach's finest remove the drivetrain and begin the modifications. In the process, one dohc 24-valve inline-6 (2.8 liters, 194 bhp, 199 lb.-ft. of torque) comes out of the engine bay, and another, bored and stroked to 3.6 liters, is dropped in to take its place.

The AMG-altered six features a higher compression ratio and modifications to the cylinder head, block and engine-management computer. Taking it from the top, the engine gets these performance enhancers: a larger-diameter, variable-length intake manifold, enlarged cylinder-head ports, a new high-lift intake cam and revised variable intake-valve timing, and revised exhaust cam timing. The significant performance boost necessitates the use of forged-aluminum pistons, modified rods and a new crankshaft. Additional oil-spray jets are also installed in the engine block. At the purge end, a new low-noise, freer-flowing exhaust system

sends emissions through two ceramic catalytic converters and out the dual, chrome-tipped pipes.

And at the end of the day, the C36's normally aspirated engine rings the bell at 268 bhp and a 280-lb.-ft. wallop of peak torque delivered at 4000 rpm. For a transmission, AMG scanned the three-pointed stars on the horizon and sourced the 4-speed automatic used in the V-8 E420 and E500 sedans. Driving absolutists, note: There is no manual gearbox anywhere on that horizon.

On the BMW side, the second-generation M3 is another kind of first. The Bavarian company's high-performance subsidiary, BMW Motorsport (newly baptized "BMW M"), not only is responsible for continuing to engineer (in some cases, build) the heat-seeking "M" cars, but also is in charge of the boutique business, BMW Individual. You say you want your 740i to come in Amethyst with a Forest Green leather interior, bird's-eye maple trim, a fax machine, color TV and a special mount for your golf clubs? No problem. BMW M can do that. M can also build an M5 Touring. Or provide a V-12 for McLaren's F1 supercar.

The M3 comes packed with individuality. At the leading edge is a revised, body-color front air dam that feeds air to the engine and front brakes. The aerodynamic side skirts, also done in body color, groove themselves pleas-

antly into one's memory, while the smallish side-view mirrors. which look suspect *and* limit the rearward view, do just the opposite. Inside the M3, leather-covered BMW M sport seats hold the driver and front-seat passenger firmly, while tasteful reminders of the blue/purple/red BMW M tricolor are planted in the seats, the shift knob, the stitching of the leather-covered steering wheel, and the gauges (recalibrated to reflect what this car is all about). If all this styling discretion goes against your enthusiast grain, you can substitute M3 cloth and suede upholstery (a no-cost option) and add a trunk-mounted spoiler (sorry, this one costs extra).

As is the case with the Mercedes C36, the core of the BMW's sublimely polished apple is its engine. When Munich decided to tailor a second-generation M3 specifically for the U.S., it was correctly confident that the 325is's dohc 24-valve inline-6—already plenty willing and able with 189 bhp and 181 lb.-ft. of torque—provided an excellent fabric to work with.

Enlarging the engine's displacement to 3.0 liters gives low- and midrange torque a shot in the arm, while a recalibration of the electronically controlled valve timing gives a booster shot to the upper-rpm range. Finish things off with a special large-diameter exhaust system, and the patient leaves the operating table healthier than ever, sounding better than ever and putting out 240 bhp and 225 lb.-ft. of torque.

PRICE

	BMW M3	Mercedes-Benz C36
Base price	$35,800	est $50,000
Price as tested	$38,407	est $55,815

Both cars include std equip. (dual airbags, ABS, leather int, air cond, AM/FM stereo/cassette; pwr windows, mirrors and door locks). **For M3:** pwr sunroof ($1120), cruise control ($455), luxury tax ($582), dest charge ($450). **For C36:** C1 Value Package (traction control, headlamp washer/wipers, heated front seats) $2835, retractable rear-seat headrests ($340), luxury tax ($2165), dest charge ($475).

GENERAL DATA

	BMW M3	Mercedes-Benz C36
Curb weight	3145 lb	3430 lb
Test weight	3295 lb	3585 lb
Weight dist, f/r, %	50/50	54/46
Wheelbase	106.3 in.	105.9 in.
Track, f/r	56.0 in./56.9 in.	58.9 in./58.2 in.
Length	174.5 in.	177.4 in.
Width	67.3 in.	67.7 in.
Height	52.6 in.	55.6 in.

ENGINE

	BMW M3	Mercedes-Benz C36
Type	dohc 24-valve inline-6	dohc 24-valve inline-6
Displacement	182 cu in./2990 cc	220 cu in./3606 cc
Bore x stroke	3.39 x 3.38 in./ 86.0 x 85.8 mm	3.58 x 3.64 in./ 91.0 x 92.4 mm
Compression ratio	10.5:1	10.5:1
Horsepower (SAE)	240 bhp @ 6000 rpm	268 bhp @ 5750 rpm
Torque	225 lb-ft @ 4250 rpm	280 lb-ft @ 4000 rpm
Maximum engine speed:	6800 rpm in 1st and 2nd, 6500 rpm in 3rd and 4th	6400 rpm
Fuel injection	dual Bosch HFM-Motronic	modified Bosch HFM-Motronic
Fuel	prem unleaded, 91 pump oct	prem unleaded, 91 pump oct

CHASSIS & BODY

	BMW M3	Mercedes-Benz C36
Layout	front engine/rear drive	front engine/rear drive
Body/frame	unit steel	unit steel
Brakes, f/r	12.4-in. vented discs/12.3-in. vented discs; vacuum assist, ABS	12.6-in. vented discs/10.9-in. vented discs; vacuum assist, ABS
Wheels	cast alloy, 17 x 7½J	cast alloy; 17 x 7½J f, 17 x 8½J r
Tires	Michelin Pilot SX MXX3, 235/40ZR-17	Bridgestone Expedia S-01; 225/45ZR-17 f, 245/40ZR-17 r
Steering	rack & pinion, power assist	recirculating ball, power assist
Turns, lock to lock	3.0	3.1
Turning circle	38.0 ft	35.2 ft
Suspension, f/r	MacPherson struts, double-pivot lower arms, coil springs, tube shocks, anti-roll bar/multilink, coil springs, tube shocks, anti-roll bar	upper & lower control arms, coil springs, tube shocks, anti-roll bar/ 5-link, coil springs, tube shocks, anti-roll bar

DRIVETRAIN

	BMW M3				Mercedes-Benz C36			
Transmission	5-speed manual				4-speed automatic			
Gear	Ratio	Overall ratio	(Rpm)	Mph	Ratio	Overall ratio	(Rpm)	Mph
1st, :1	4.20	13.23	(6800)	36	3.87	11.11	(6100)	36
2nd, :1	2.49	7.84	(6800)	60	2.25	6.46	(6400)	66
3rd, :1	1.66	5.23	(6500)	86	1.44	4.13	(6400)	103
4th, :1	1.24	3.91	(6500)	115	1.00	2.87	est (6400)	148
5th, :1	1.00	3.15	est (6230)	137*				
Final drive ratio				3.15:1	2.87:1			
Engine rpm @ 60 mph in top gear				2725	2625			

*Electronically limited.

ACCOMMODATIONS

	BMW M3	Mercedes-Benz C36
Seating capacity	4	5
Head room, f/r	38.0 in./34.0 in.	36.5 in./35.5 in.
Seat width, f/r	2 x 19.0 in./52.5 in.	2 x 16.5 in./50.5 in.
Front-seat leg room	43.5 in.	45.5 in.
Luggage space	9.2 cu ft	11.6 cu ft

FUEL ECONOMY

	BMW M3	Mercedes-Benz C36
Normal driving	24.5 mpg	25.0 mpg
EPA city/highway	19/27 mpg	18/22 mpg
Fuel capacity	17.2 gal.	16.4 gal.

INTERIOR NOISE

	BMW M3	Mercedes-Benz C36
Idle in neutral	40 dBA	44 dBA
Maximum, 1st gear	72 dBA	73 dBA
Constant 70 mph	69 dBA	72 dBA

HANDLING

	BMW M3	Mercedes-Benz C36
Lateral accel (200-ft skidpad)	0.90g	0.86g
Balance	mild understeer	moderate understeer
Speed thru 700-ft slalom	62.6 mph	62.2 mph
Balance	mild understeer	mild understeer

ACCELERATION

Time to speed	BMW M3 Seconds	Mercedes-Benz C36 Seconds
0–30 mph	1.9	2.3
0–40 mph	3.0	3.3
0–50 mph	4.1	4.6
0–60 mph	5.4	6.0
0–70 mph	7.2	7.7
0–80 mph	9.1	9.9
0–90 mph	11.4	12.2
0–100 mph	14.1	15.1
Time to distance		
0–100 ft	2.9	3.1
0–500 ft	7.7	8.0
0–1320 ft (¼ mi)	14.1 @ 99.5 mph	14.5 @ 98.5 mph

BRAKING

	BMW M3	Mercedes-Benz C36
Minimum stopping distance		
From 60 mph	122 ft	120 ft
From 80 mph	212 ft	210 ft
Control	excellent	excellent
Pedal effort for 0.5g stop	14 lb	12 lb
Fade, effort after six 0.5g stops		
from 60 mph	16 lb	17 lb
Brake feel	excellent	excellent
Overall brake rating	excellent	excellent

Subjective ratings consist of excellent, very good, good, average, poor; na means information is not available.

■ Take a look at two of the world's finest work stations: the BMW M3's interior—straight-faced, spare and brilliantly efficient—and its 240-bhp engine, the first 6-cylinder M3 ever.

///M3

BMW M employs a ZF 5-speed manual transmission to relay this power to the M3's rear wheels, through a 25-percent limited-slip differential.

Having the spirited balance of the 325is platform to build on is a blessing in that the 3-Series already has one of the sportiest suspension setups available in the under-$30,000 league. BMW M wisely chose to eschew any unnecessary gestures, opting instead to simply lower the car and add heft to the heroics already present in the BMW suspension.

As on the M-B C36, more car means bigger brakes, and the M3 delivers with thicker vented rotors front and rear. Those brakes are tucked neatly inside 17-in. BMW Motorsport (BMW M) wheels. And those wheels, in turn, are surrounded by supercar-low-profile 235/40ZR-17 Michelins.

Mercedes refuses to allow that the C36 spells competition for the BMW M3, and its four doors, automatic transmission and $50,000 price tag (versus two doors, a 5-speed manual and relatively painless $35,800 for the M3) would tend to bear this out. BMW may not have gotten M-B's "We come in peace" message, however. Munich showed a 4-door M3 at last year's Paris auto show, and an automatic transmission is also on the way (as is a convertible).

Strictly speaking, however, this isn't really a Comparison Test—A versus B—it's a Distinction Test. True, both cars are tops in quality and appointments, both feature hotted-up twin-cam inline-6s and game suspensions. (And both enjoy full manufacturer's warranties, no fine print.) But what they really are is the best of Benz and

BMW taken to performance extremes. The M3 feels light, sharp—a match for anything you're likely to meet on the road, priced to never grow moss on the showroom floor. Frankly, it's the best $36,000 an enthusiast can possibly spend on a BMW, and he'll still feel like he's getting a bargain. The Mercedes-Benz C36, on the completely other hand, establishes its credentials for opulence, quietness, bank-vault solidity and comfort, and then adds gobs of performance, courtesy of AMG. Its price puts the C36 in a more exclusive category, but it's also the smartest $50K that you can drop on a Mercedes today.

We Americans have a word for it. A short word that makes a decent lead for a Road Test and, for these two German thoroughbreds, a decent conclusion: Wow.

PHOTO BY GUY SPANGENBERG

BMW M3 Lightweight

An M3 for those serious about competition

BY SAM MITANI

"WE SHOULDN'T HAVE any problem getting arrested in that," photographer Guy Spangenberg said as I drove BMW's new M3 Lightweight into his driveway. An understandable reaction, considering the car's appearance: Its ground-licking front air dam, dynamic rear wing, flashy 17-in. alloy wheels and alpine white paint scheme with red/blue/purple checkers at the front and rear corners of the car turn heads on public roads like a swimsuit model in a penitentiary. But according to BMW officials, the M3 Lightweight's *raison d'être* is to race.

"Basically, the Lightweight was made in response to those who wanted to race the M3. Now, instead of tearing everything out (of the car), one can buy a car that's already partly prepared to run in an SCCA or IMSA event," Rob Mitchell, public relations manager of BMW of North America, said.

As the name implies, the M3 Lightweight is an M3 without the fat. BMW slashed roughly 200 lb. off the curb weight by deleting the air conditioning, stereo, sunroof, noise-reduction mats, tool kit, trunk lining, spare tire and even the jack. BMW also replaced the M3's doors with lighter aluminum ones. The result is a 50-state street-legal rocket that's a breath away from being show-

room-stock ready.

The output of the smooth-revving dohc inline-6 remains unchanged, producing 240 bhp at 6000 rpm and 225 lb.-ft. of torque at 4250, but the absence of sound deadening makes the growl of this wonderfully flexible 3.0-liter louder than ever.

Throw the shifter into 1st, stomp on the throttle and the Lightweight leaps into motion like a pouncing wildcat. The M3's 5-speed manual gearbox is one of the best in the business; its well-defined gates and short throws allow for quick flick-of-the-wrist shifts. And the clutch/brake/throttle pedals are aligned for simple heel-and-toeing—just roll your right foot over the brake pedal to blip the throttle.

Where the standard M3 accelerated impressively, the Lightweight is a half-step quicker, thanks to the car's reduced weight and a revised 3.23:1 final drive (from the standard M3's 3.15:1). It ran from zero to 60 mph in just 5.8 seconds, two tenths faster than the standard M3 (see our Road Test, August 1994).

Complementing this improvement in straight-line performance is the Lightweight's better handling. Engineers at BMW's M-Brand division lowered the M3 by a quarter inch and incorporated stiffer springs to the car's already taut suspension—MacPherson struts up front and a multilink setup at rear. They also added a strut brace to increase torsional rigidity at the car's front end. The result? More stability through corners and better overall balance—only a slight touch of understeer is detectable when the car is pushed to its limits. Turn-in response is crisp, thanks in part to the razorlike precision of its rack-and-pinion steering. And body roll is reduced.

Impressive as its roadholding ability is, the Lightweight's suspension is still significantly undersprung for competitive racing. Why didn't BMW incorporate a stiffer setup? "Because," explains Bernie Gobmeier, M-Brand manager, "we wanted a car that was still usable on the street. Serious racers can cus-

tomize their own Lightweights if they want to. We offer an aftermarket package that includes height-adjustable racing suspension, adjustable camber plates and cross-drilled brake rotors."

That explains the Lightweight's efficiency as a tourer. Ride quality is smooth, and the manually adjustable cloth-upholstered front seats are comfortable. After a multi-hour drive searching for photo locations, Spangenberg and I didn't feel the least bit tired.

However, we did notice a few problems when driving in traffic. The Lightweight's enormous rear wing blocks about 75 percent of the rear view. But perhaps most distressing of all was that every passing police officer seemed to greet us with a radar gun.

All things considered, the M3 Lightweight is for performance-car enthusiasts of every order…including image-hungry ones. The bad news is that not everyone can own one. BMW is importing only 85 Lightweights and selling them for $47,900, about $12,000 more than a standard M3. Is it worth it? It all depends on how serious you are about competition—whether it's on a racetrack, on a winding road or at your 10-year class reunion.

1997 BMW

M3

SEDAN

A sports sedan that defines the genre

BY ANDREW BORNHOP
PHOTOS BY RON PERRY

A MONGST THE AUTOMOTIV
press, this joke has been makir
the rounds for years: Why do
a chicken coop have only tw
doors? Because if it had four,
would be a chicken sedan! Regain yo
composure, please.

Now ponder a similar question, or
that BMW asked itself just a few yea
back: Why does the M3 have only tw
doors?

No need to answer this; BMW a
ready has. The new 4-door M3 Seda
is arriving in North America as yo
read this, just one year after its Euro
pean debut. And by no means is th
car a joke. Although we wish it can
with the European M3's 321-bhp ir
line-6 and optional sequential 6-spee
gearbox, the new 4-door for Americ
has proven itself to be a potent per
former, the fastest-accelerating 4-doo
we've tested in years.

With the traction control (standar
equipment for 1997) switched off
the Pomona drag strip, the M3 Seda
hit 60 mph in only 5.6 seconds an
streaked through the quarter mile i
14.2 sec. at 99.0 mph. What's mor
the rear-drive Sedan—which will like
ly account for more than half of th
6000 M3s BMW expects to sell i
1997—manages to pack all the sport
ing ability of the M3 Coupe into it
practical 4-door body.

No surprise here, because the M3 Sedan is essentially the same car as the Coupe—same engine, same gearbox, same wheels, same tires, same brakes, same suspension tuning, same wheelbase, same track...even the same overall length. About the only visible differences are the door count and the Sedan's slightly more upright windshield, which I prefer.

But inside the car, there is another difference: The M3 Sedan is fitted with BMW's standard sport seats, not

■ A perspective previously not possible in an M3: looking through a rear door opening, which reveals the standard BMW sport seats, a large-diameter steering wheel and the not-so-abundant rear-seat room. Not visible in this photo are small splashes of the BMW M colors that decorate various spots inside the M3. From the side, it's easy to see this is an M3 Sedan. From the driver's seat, however, it feels just like the Coupe.

the Coupe's aggressively bolstered seats from BMW M. Apparently, the smaller side bolsters of BMW's standard sport seats are needed to facilitate ingress and egress through the Sedan's smaller door openings. And one last point: The M3 Coupe comes exclusively with a manual gearbox, whereas the Sedan can be fitted with a 5-speed automatic as a $1200 option. Although we've experienced and enjoyed an M3 with that automatic, our Dakar Yellow II test car came fitted as God intended, with the 5-speed manual, a ZF gearbox whose linkage is satisfyingly crisp. Shifting it blindfolded, you could identify it as BMW's.

Bolted to the transmission is the M3's heart, a longitudinally mounted twin-cam inline-6 that for 1997 has grown from 3.0 to 3.2 liters, courtesy of a slightly larger bore and longer stroke

THE COMPETITION

Mercedes-Benz C36

Length: 177.4 in.　Width: 67.7 in.　Height: 56.1 in.　Wheelbase: 105.9 in.
Track, f/r: 58.9 in./58.2 in.　Curb weight: 3550 lb

■ BMW has its M Division; Mercedes has AMG. And this firm in Affalterbach, Germany, builds the potent C36, which has gained 8 bhp and 4 lb.-ft. of torque for 1997. According to Mercedes, this added power (plus a new 5-speed automatic transmission and a slightly lower final-drive ratio) should help knock a couple of tenths off the C36's 0–60 time. And though the heavier C36 still can't match the M3 Sedan at the drag strip—or in overall agility—it's a better 4-door because of its spacious back seat. (Tested: 2/95)

Current list price	$51,925
Engine	dohc 3.6-liter inline-6
Horsepower	276 bhp @ 5750 rpm
Torque	284 lb-ft @ 4000 rpm
Transmission	5-speed automatic
0–60 mph	6.0 sec
Braking, 60–0 mph	120 ft
Lateral accel (200-ft skidpad)	0.86g
EPA city/highway	18/24 mpg

(increased by almost 4 mm). Peak horsepower of this free-revving power-plant remains 240 bhp at 6000, but there's now 236 lb.-ft. of torque on tap at 3800 rpm, an increase of 11 lb.-ft. at 450 fewer rpm.

With the newfound torque and a curb weight of only 3150 lb. (just 5 lb. heavier than the M3 Coupe), we expected the Sedan to behave like the Coupe. It does. In everyday driving, there's the familiar get-down-to-business feel of a precision-crafted tool for the purpose of driving. The driving position is excellent, the view forward is unobstructed, and the car accelerates from a standstill like a cheetah. With the standard limited-slip differential's low 3.23:1 final-drive ratio (versus a standard 328i's 2.93:1), a quick burst of acceleration is just a dip of the accelerator away. As with the Coupe, the M3 Sedan's steering is also first-rate, nicely weighted and complemented by firm suspension tuning that gives the unit-body chassis a composed, well-planted feel in mid-corner. Playing an important role here is the Sedan's near-ideal weight distribution of 52/48, plus its sticky Michelin MXX3 Pilot tires mounted on the M3's unique 20-spoke alloy wheels.

In the slalom, the 4-door weaves through the pylons with ease, posting an outstanding 63.6-mph speed that's one mph faster than that of the M3 Coupe. Around our 200-ft.-diameter skidpad, the Sedan's 0.91g betters the Coupe's 0.90g. And in braking, the M3 Sedan's stopping distances—114 ft. from 60 mph and 204 from 80—are nothing short of excellent. Not only are they 8 ft. better than the M3 Coupe's from both speeds, but they ri-

val those of the Ferrari 550 Maranello, which is perhaps the best-braking car on the market today. Credit here goes to the M3's large disc brakes (12.4-in. front, 12.3-in. back) and the smooth-pulsing ABS hardware.

So, the new M3 Sedan is a great car, a worthy and practical companion to the M3 Coupe. It, however, is not without faults.

The brakes are a bit grabby on initial application, perhaps because of too much assist or an especially grippy pad compound. And although the M3's sideview mirrors look as if they might have won a design award, they need to be enlarged for improved vision. Moreover, those of us who like gauges wish the analog instrument panel had its fuel-economy readout replaced by an honest oil-pressure needle. Last, but not least, the M3 needs a 6-speed gearbox. The engine revs are too high for relaxed freeway cruising in 5th gear (at 70 mph, the engine is spinning at 3100 rpm). An overdrive 6th gear would further improve the M3's impressive EPA highway mileage figure of 28 mpg...not to mention the cabin's overall tranquility.

On another point, some critics say

■ Inline-6s are rare these days, and BMW's is a beauty. For 1997 it has grown to 3.2 liters, now an undersquare design that generates better low- and midrange torque. No smoothness has been lost, and the hit of power remains as satisfying as ever. With modern management and a few well-placed dress panels, the engine looks refreshingly uncomplicated.

the BMW 3-Series body is beginning to show its age. But to me it remains one of the best-looking sedans on the market. And as an M3 Coupe or Sedan it looks even better, with wheels and tires that offer a look of purposeful aggression. My only complaint concerning the body is the relative lack of rear-seat room. Though most people will find enough head room, leg room is barely adequate. And though there are seat-belts for three across the M3 Sedan's rear bench, it's practical for two adults.

While the M3 Sedan's rear seating isn't quite as spacious as that of a Toyota Camry, Nissan Maxima or C-class Mercedes-Benz, our enthusiasm remains intact. And though spy shots of the upcoming 3-Series reveal it to be a larger car with a better back seat, the current M3 Sedan is one of the few cars on the market that shines so brightly as a driver's car that it can be forgiven some minor flaws. For $40,000, we can't find a better combination of practicality and performance.

BMW's M Division—responsible for building the company's racing cars and highly regarded sedans such as the M5—has done it again. It has built a sports sedan that defines the genre. ◎

1997 BMW M3 SEDAN

IMPORTER

BMW of North America, Inc.
P.O. Box 1227
Westwood, N.J. 07675

PRICE

List price	$39,380
Price as tested	$40,266

Price as tested includes std equip. (ABS, traction control, limited-slip differential, dual airbags, leather upholstery, dual-zone automatic climate control, AM/FM stereo/cassette, central locking, foglights, heated mirrors, pwr windows & mirrors, rear-window defroster), luxury tax ($316), dest charge ($570).

0–60 mph	5.6 sec
0–¼ mi	14.2 sec
Top speed	137 mph*
Skidpad	0.91g
Slalom	63.6 mph
Brake rating	excellent

TEST CONDITIONS

Temperature	61° F
Wind	calm
Elevation	990 ft

SCALE: 10 in.(254mm) DIVISIONS
DRAWING BY BILL DOBSON

ENGINE

Type	cast-iron block, aluminum head, **inline-6**
Valvetrain	dohc 4 valve/cyl
Displacement	192 cu in./3152 cc
Bore x stroke	3.40 x 3.53 in./ 86.4 x 89.6 mm
Compression ratio	10.5:1

Horsepower

(SAE)	**240 bhp @ 6000 rpm**
Bhp/liter	76.1
Torque	**236 lb-ft @ 3800 rpm**
Maximum engine speed	6800 rpm
Fuel injection	elect. sequential port
Fuel	prem unleaded, 91 pump oct

CHASSIS & BODY

Layout	**front engine/rear drive**
Body/frame	unit steel

Brakes

Front	**12.4-in. vented discs**
Rear	**12.3-in. discs**
Assist type	vacuum; ABS
Total swept area	491 sq in.
Swept area/ton	296 sq in.
Wheels	cast alloy; **17 x 7½J f, 17 x 8½J r**
Tires	Michelin Pilot SX MXX3; **225/45ZR-17 f, 245/40ZR-17 r**
Steering	**rack & pinion**, pwr assist
Overall ratio	15.6:1
Turns, lock to lock	3.3
Turning circle	38.1 ft

Suspension

Front	**MacPherson struts, double-pivot lower arms,** coil springs, tube shocks, anti-roll bar
Rear	**multilink**, coil springs, tube shocks, anti-roll bar

DRIVETRAIN

Transmission .... **5-sp manual**

Gear	Ratio	Overall ratio	(Rpm) Mph
1st	4.20:1	13.57:1	(6800) 37
2nd	2.49:1	8.04:1	(6800) 62
3rd	1.66:1	5.36:1	(6800) 93
4th	1.24:1	4.01:1	(6800) 124
5th	1.00:1	3.23:1	(6050) 137*

Final drive ratio	3.23:1
Engine rpm @ 60 mph in 5th	2650

*Electronically limited.

GENERAL DATA

Curb weight	**3150 lb**
Test weight	3320 lb
Weight dist (with driver), f/r, %	52/48
Wheelbase	106.3 in.
Track, f/r	56.0 in./56.6 in.
Length	**174.5 in.**
Width	**66.9 in.**
Height	**53.7 in.**
Ground clearance	3.5 in.
Trunk space	15.0 cu ft

MAINTENANCE

Oil/filter change	7500 mi/7500 mi
Tuneup	30,000 mi
Basic warranty	48 mo/50,000 mi

ACCOMMODATIONS

Seating capacity	5
Head room, f/r	38.5 in./35.8 in.
Seat width, f/r	2 x 18.0 in./49.8 in.
Front-seat leg room	44.3 in.
Rear-seat knee room	23.3 in.
Seatback adjustment	50 deg
Seat travel	8.0 in.

INTERIOR NOISE

Idle in neutral	48 dBA
Maximum in 1st gear	79 dBA
Constant 50 mph	70 dBA
70 mph	73 dBA

INSTRUMENTATION

160-mph speedometer, 8000-rpm tach, coolant temp, fuel level, mpg

ACCELERATION

Time to speed	Seconds
0–30 mph	2.0
0–40 mph	3.2
0–50 mph	4.3
0–60 mph	5.6
0–70 mph	7.5
0–80 mph	9.2
0–90 mph	11.8
0–100 mph	14.5

Time to distance	
0–100 ft	3.0
0–500 ft	7.8
0–1320 ft (¼ mi):	14.2 @ 99.0 mph

FUEL ECONOMY

Normal driving	19.8 mpg
EPA city/highway	20/28 mpg
Cruise range	305 miles
Fuel capacity	16.4 gal.

BRAKING

Minimum stopping distance

From 60 mph	114 ft
From 80 mph	204 ft
Control	excellent
Pedal effort for 0.5g stop	10 lb
Fade, effort after six 0.5g stops from 60 mph	11 lb
Brake feel	excellent
Overall brake rating	excellent

HANDLING

Lateral accel (200-ft skidpad)	0.91g
Balance	mild understeer
Speed thru 700-ft slalom	63.6 mph
Balance	mild understeer
Lateral seat support	excellent

Test Notes...

■ In everyday driving, the M3's brakes feel grabby on initial application, but that sensation isn't apparent in our braking tests.

■ With its low gearing and an eagerness to rev, it's easy to accidentally hit the M3's rev limiter during acceleration runs.

■ In the slalom, the M3 Sedan certainly doesn't feel like a 4-door; it has the great balance and edgy aggression of the M3 Coupe.

Subjective ratings consist of excellent, very good, good, average, poor; na means information is not available.

STREET CIVIL, TRACK WORTHY

Whether on Streets of Willow or a favorite blue highway, Steve Dinan's muscle-bound M3s impress

BY DOUGLAS KOTT
PHOTOS BY GUY SPANGENBERG

POWERED!

ON A REMOTE, uphill stretch of the Antelope Valley Freeway, the meticulously waxed black BMW 535i jinked, feinted and jabbed through light traffic with the precision of Baron von Stockbroker from the Nigel Shiftright cartoon strip. As he whistled by, Bruno Magli loafer to firewall (and likely, cell phone to ear), and faded to a medium-size black speck in middle distance, I lost my typically stoic cruising composure and decided to reel him in.

Luckily, I had one of your better reels at my disposal: an Alpine White, hunkered-down, Dinan-modified BMW M3 whose 3.0-liter inline-6 is centrifugally supercharged to a 535i-eating 341 bhp. Now with my own Adidas Stan Smith to the floorboard, it was as if the black Bimmer were a crippled alien ship in a *Star Trek* episode, helplessly pulled toward my Bavarian mount by some invisible tractor beam. I eased off the throttle, let the gap open up again and repeated the process, the Dinan squirting forward in a seamless, torquey lunge to

within car-lengths of Von Stockbroker's rear bumper. Too easy. I disengaged, seeing as I'm kind of partial to my driver's license, air drag and gravity slowing the car noticeably without brake application. Back to impulse power, Scotty.

Later, puttering along Rosamond's main avenue on the way to Willow Springs racetrack for driving-impres-

sion laps and photos, I was struck by how well behaved this M3 was, and how small a toll in ride and driveability is exacted to allow this relatively upright, tidy 4-seater to accelerate, brake and corner with the likes of Ferrari F355s, Acura NSXs and fifth-generation Corvettes. No thigh-achingly-stiff clutch, no nervous steering that nibbles and hunts, no tire shoulders

squawking against fenderlips on every bump, no earth-tremor idle roughness—heck, our sound readings show it to be quieter than a stock M3 at both cruising speeds and under full-throttle acceleration in 1st gear. Dinan's motto is "Performance Without Sacrifice," and after experiencing this M3 (and two very fleet 5-Series cars in our May 1993 issue), I can attest it's

POWERED!

no hollow boast.

Now a standard BMW M3 is quite a piece of work in itself, and some would argue that efforts to improve it are sacrilege, tantamount to grafting a set of arms on the statue of Venus de Milo, or perhaps "touching up" the Mona Lisa's smile with a dab or two of acrylic. Steve Dinan, president and owner of Dinan Engineering, thinks otherwise, and has been fixing the unbroken in BMW circles for 18 years now. From his modest beginnings of offering a few suspension pieces to today employing 43 people in his Mountain View, California, shop, Dinan offers a full range of high-performance parts and services: everything from engine-management power chips to sky's-the-limit twin-turbo conversions—his catalog showcases a 606-bhp (!!) 850i thus endowed.

Evidently, BMW of North America thinks pretty highly of his modifications too, as it is now possible to order a Dinan BMW M3 or 850i (see sidebar) from any BMW dealership. The cars aren't assembled in Dinan's shop; rather, a set of Dinan pieces is sent to the dealership, to be installed on-site by certified BMW technicians, for a single package price that includes labor. Or the car can be done piecemeal, with labor charges calculated as you go. Moreover, the finished Dinan car will be covered, sort of, by BMW's new-car warranty, in some cases. You detect some hedging here, yes?

Well, it really depends on the level of tweaking. Order the blue M3 sedan in our story, which entails mostly chassis modifications, and BMW's 4-year, 50,000-mile basic warranty remains intact on any piece that's not Dinan-manufactured. Dinan matches this warranty on his springs, shocks, anti-roll bars and wheels. "It's done in a very seamless way," says Dinan, "where the customer gets his car fixed under warranty, gets the keys back and doesn't really know where the bill was sent."

Delve into the engine with Dinan camshafts or his supercharger kit—again installed by certified dealer technicians, or yourself if you feel a strong surge of mechanical aptitude coming on—and BMW's powertrain warranty (also 4 years/50,000 miles) is voided, replaced by Dinan's coverage of 2 years/unlimited mileage. It's important to note that all non-powertrain parts of the more heavily modified cars are still covered under BMW's 4-year warranty (or matched by Dinan's 4-year coverage).

Got that? No warranty covers damage from off-racetrack excursions, but we all behaved ourselves at the 1.3-mile Streets of Willow, a favorite test track nestled at the base of the Tehachapi Mountains near Lancaster, California. As well as reacquainting ourselves with the joys of power-on oversteer, we came away with six hours' worth of impressions of three increasingly powerful, eminently enjoyable Dinan M3s.

Blue M3 Sedan
Average lap time: 1:05.82

"IT LACKS THE raw edge of the cammed purple car or the over-the-top nature of the supercharged white car," opined our Online Editor Otis Meyer, "with midrange power that sweeps, rather than kicks into action." Disappointing? Hardly; it's just that the blue

■ Above, the Dinan M3's engine compartment appears relatively stock, save the polished aluminum strut-tower brace and the extra-thick ducting that leads to the airflow meter. Pop the dust cover off the strut's top (right) and subtleties are exposed—those camber plates are good for ½ degree of negative camber, as well as additional negative caster. A peek into the trunk reveals another chassis-stiffening brace, at the price of some utility.

M3, which represents what Dinan calls the "dealership package," pales in the light of the other cars' generous horsepower gains. In fact, if you peruse our performance data, you'll see that the blue car is a tenth or two slower to certain speeds than stock, likely because of our 20-degree-hotter test day at the Pomona Fairplex drag strip. The minor modifications to the powertrain (a low-restriction, cold-air induction system and a catalyst-back, aluminized-steel exhaust system) do give a claimed additional 17 bhp and an extra 9 lb.-ft. of torque (generated at 4,000 rpm, 200 higher than stock), but it's the extra exhaust and induction bark that really add to the sense of acceleration.

"Tasteful aggression" really sums up the appearance of the Dinans. Look elsewhere if outrageous bodywork kits, ground-scraping spoilers or towering wings are your thing. Dinan-spotters will recognize the slightly lower stance (by about 0.3 in.), the signature 5-spoke 3-piece modular wheels and the discreet chrome Dinan decklid badge, molded in the same factory-look beveled-edge letters. Wheel size is 17 x 8½ all around—the same size as stock in the rear, yet an inch wider than stock in front, so the buyer need purchase only two additional Michelin Pilot SX tires, size 245/40ZR-17. Suspension modifications consist of stiffer lowering springs, stiffer adjustable anti-roll bars tuned to reduce understeer, Koni rebound-adjustable shock absorbers and front-strut camber plates that, combined with the car's slight stock negative camber and camber gained by lowering the car, give a total

of 1.5 degrees negative. The showiest pieces are the front and rear strut-tower braces, done up in highly polished 6061-T6 aluminum, with inset ovals of carbon fiber.

And these components are far more than high-performance window dressing, the blue car negotiating our slalom like an asphalt-bound Franz Klammer at 65.8 mph, 2.2 mph quicker than stock, and circling our skidpad at 0.92g, a 0.01g improvement. Braking distances, though still excellent, were roughly 10 ft. longer, perhaps because additional negative camber doesn't give the ideal contact patch for straight-line braking. At the track, the blue sedan felt tidy, precise and secure, though it was the most eager at the limit to snap into oversteer when the throttle was lifted. The loosest of the three Dinans (the purple and white cars were fitted with ultra-sticky competition-compound Toyo tires), the blue car was also the most fun in some ways, as we were able to slide and drift it a bit more, giving a few more options of placement.

Purple M3 Coupe
Average lap time: 1:03.53

COME ABOUT 6,000 rpm, there's a Jekyll/Hyde transformation to this car's exhaust note, where the ascending throaty purr rips into a sharp, metallic honk that for all the world sounds like a Grand Prix racing motorcycle until the electronically extended rev limiter shuts things down at 7,000. Steve Dinan should make a digital recording of this sound and pipe it into his showroom with Dolby THX technology;

sales might triple.

Making this engine breathe was the prime directive, and Dinan accomplished it with a set of his high-lift/duration camshafts, a 4-mm-larger throttle body, a less restrictive airflow meter and cold-air induction system. On the exhaust side, the same big-bore, catalyst-back system is fitted. You might ask why an exhaust header isn't used, and Dinan admits that with the stock catalytic converter it might be good for about 4 bhp. It'd be a very expensive 4 bhp, though, as the header would be a difficult-to-construct insulated piece to conserve exhaust heat for quick converter light-off (those pesky emissions requirements do make it difficult for the aftermarket).

Without touching anything in the engine's bottom end, the changes make for a healthy 45-bhp increase and a torque boost of 31 lb.-ft., that extra twist felt very strongly in the useful 3,500–5,500-rpm range. Throttle response is lightning-quick, helped by a Sachs lightweight steel flywheel (13½ lb. lighter than the stock 44-lb. unit), and a pressure plate whose aluminum friction disc is coated with iron for durability. Even with this much mass taken out, the car moves away from rest in blessedly stock fashion, helped by a small bump in idle speed.

Suspension modifications are essentially the same as the blue sedan's, but this car uses a set of BMW M 17 x 8½ rear wheels on the front, with Toyo Proxes RA1 tires, size 235/45ZR-17, all around. Essentially a DOT-approved competition tire, the

■ At top left, Feature Editor Andrew Bornhop carves a nice opposite-lock arc through the Streets' left-hand sweeper. The blue sedan proved precise, and its stock Michelins conducive to luxurious power-on drifts. The purple coupe, piloted here by Associate Editor Sam Mitani, has a significantly more tenacious hold on the pavement, as well as more power through different camshafts and a

RA1s offer incredible grip under braking and through the slalom, and make this by far the easiest, most forgiving car to drive around the racetrack, quicker than the blue car by a full 2 seconds a lap. The combination of mild, predictable understeer and the fat midrange power—but not so much to upset the chassis—was ideally suited to the exits of the Streets' relatively sharp corners.

Perhaps Feature Editor Andrew Bornhop summed it up best: "I really love the cammy character of this engine...it has a nice, raw edge to it."

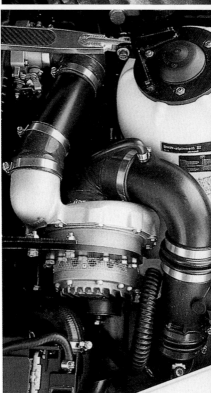

■ Key to the white coupe's scintillating power increase is Dinan's supercharger kit, which uses a neatly plumbed Powerdyne centrifugal blower whose lubrication-free ceramic bearings are cooled by a stream of ram-fed air; the heated air escapes through the screen-covered holes. Inside, Dinan prefers only discreet identification, the logo floormats being the only tip-off to the changes underhood.

White Supercharged M3 Coupe
Average lap time: 1:03.61

AS THE WHITE car drives up, you can hear its soft, slightly exotic whir. Inside the car, it's nearly inaudible without cupping a hand to your ear. But the compact Powerdyne centrifugal supercharger is what adds a quick-and-painless 101 bhp to this M3's 3.0-liter engine (the application for the 3.2-liter engine is being tested as we speak) and vaults the M3 into a select group of performance cars that can cover a standing-start quarter mile in the mid-13s.

Quiet operation was of the essence for the supercharger application, and

Dinan rejected many gear-drive centrifugal blowers for their excessive noise. The Powerdyne unit uses a Gilmer-type toothed belt and pulleys, and is unusual in its use of ceramic bearings, good for 40,000 rpm without lubrication. Dinan worked with Powerdyne to find these high-quality bearings and went as far as routing a ram-air tube to cool the housing's internals to 190 degrees Fahrenheit, well below the bearings' maximum operating temperature of 350.

The supercharger installation is a straightforward bolt-on, requiring no internal engine modifications.

Says Dinan: "We take a centrifugal blower that gains boost with rpm, and as the cylinder pressure falls off, we more or less prop it up; it remains relatively constant from middle revs all the way to redline. This is our way to work around the high 10.5:1 compression ratio."

Those weaned on the instant tip-in snap of a Roots blower may be slightly disappointed, but we think it dovetails perfectly with the high-revving character of the M3's engine. "The bottom end is perfectly tractable," says Engineering Editor Dennis Simanaitis. "You can drive all day long at 1,000–2,000 rpm with nary a stumble. But cross 4,500 rpm and you're in Porsche Turbo-eating territory." Senior Editor Joe Rusz echoed the sentiment: "Pulls like an Apollo booster (or is that pushes?), yet as docile as a lamb on Prozac."

Or as aggressive as a mongoose on the racetrack, where the white M3 felt the most like a race car. Chalk that up to the same springs, shocks, anti-roll bars and strut braces, plus what Dinan calls his Stage 4 suspension, with front strut plates that crank in a full 3 degrees of negative camber. More negative is dialed into the rear suspension as well through the factory adjustment provision, and a set of 255/40ZR-17 Toyo Proxes F1S tires, whose sticky compound is molded around a more compliant, street-oriented carcass than the Proxes RA1. "The white M3 is the dartiest of the three; it feels like it's the most on edge and I think for a really good driver it's the most fun," says Bornhop. "But it's also the hardest to drive well." This is reflected in our lap times too, as the supercharged car was

Supercharged Dinan M3

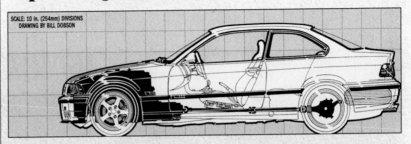

SCALE: 10 in. (254mm) DIVISIONS
DRAWING BY BILL DOBSON

TUNER

Dinan Engineering
150 South Whisman
Mountain View, Calif. 94041
(415) 962-9401

PRICE

List price, installed
(excluding stock BMW M3) **$17,800**
Price as tested includes centrifugal supercharger kit ($7000), high-flow catalyst-back exhaust system ($1300), high-flow throttle body ($400), Stage 4 performance suspension system (lowering springs, Koni rebound-adjustable shocks, adjustable anti-roll bars, 3.0-degree front negative camber plates) $1529, 3-piece Dinan wheels and Toyo Proxes F1S tires, 255/40ZR-17 ($4116), front strut-tower brace ($350), Dinan floormats ($150).

ENGINE

Type	cast-iron block, alum. head, supercharged **inline-6**
Valvetrain	dohc 4 valve/cyl
Displacement	182 cu in./2990 cc
Bore x stroke	3.39 x 3.38 in./ 86.0 x 85.8 mm
Compression ratio	10.5:1
Horsepower (SAE)	**341 bhp @ 6750 rpm**
Bhp/liter	114.0
Torque	**297 lb-ft @ 5000 rpm**
Maximum engine speed	7000 rpm
Fuel injection	elect. sequential port
Fuel	prem unleaded, 91 pump oct

CHASSIS & BODY

Layout	**front engine/rear drive**
Body/frame	unit steel
Brakes	
Front	**12.4-in. vented discs**
Rear	**12.3-in. discs**
Assist type	vacuum; ABS
Total swept area	491 sq in.
Swept area/ton	296 sq in.
Wheels	Dinan 3-piece modular, 17 x 8½
Tires	Toyo Proxes F1S, 255/40ZR-17
Steering	**rack & pinion**, power assist
Overall ratio	15.6:1
Turns, lock to lock	3.0
Turning circle	38.0 ft
Suspension	
Front	**MacPherson struts, double-pivot lower arms,** 3.0-degree negative camber plates, coil springs, Koni rebound-adjustable tube shocks, adjustable anti-roll bar
Rear	**multilink,** coil springs, rebound-adjustable Koni tube shocks, adjustable anti-roll bar

TEST CONDITIONS

Temperature	78° F
Wind	mild
Elevation	990 ft

GENERAL DATA

Curb weight	**est 3200 lb**
Test weight	est 3370 lb
Weight dist (with driver), f/r, %	52/48
Wheelbase	106.3 in.
Track, f/r	56.5 in./57.1 in.
Length	**174.5 in.**
Width	**67.3 in.**
Height	**52.3 in.**
Ground clearance	3.2 in.
Trunk space	14.5 + 6.0 cu ft

MAINTENANCE

Oil/filter change	3750 mi/3750 mi
Tuneup	30,000 mi
Basic warranty	48 mo/50,000 mi
Dinan powertrain	24 mo/unlimited mi

ACCOMMODATIONS

Seating capacity	**4**
Head room, f/r	38.0 in./34.0 in.
Seat width, f/r	2 x 19.0 in./52.5 in.
Front-seat leg room	43.5 in.
Rear-seat knee room	23.5 in.
Seatback adjustment	75 deg
Seat travel	7.5 in.

INSTRUMENTATION

160-mph speedometer, 8000-rpm tach,
coolant temp, fuel level

FUEL ECOMOMY

Normal driving	17.3 mpg
EPA city/hwy	na
Cruise range	265 miles
Fuel capacity	16.4 gal.

DRIVETRAIN

Transmission			**5-sp manual**
Gear	Ratio	Overall ratio	(Rpm) Mph
1st	4.20:1	13.57:1	(7000) 37
2nd	2.49:1	8.04:1	(7000) 63
3rd	1.66:1	5.36:1	(7000) 95
4th	1.24:1	4.01:1	(7000) 127
5th	1.00:1	3.23:1	est (7000) 157
Final drive ratio			3.23:1
Engine rpm @ 60 mph in 5th			2600

STAGE 1
(Blue Sedan, 3.2-liter engine)

Horsepower............ **257 bhp @ 6000 rpm**
Torque .... **245 lb-ft @ 4000 rpm**

Package price, installed **$9450**

Includes high-flow airbox & filter ($300), big-bore catalyst-back exhaust system ($1300), Stage 3 performance suspension (springs, Koni rebound-adjustable shocks, adjustable anti-roll bars, 0.5-degree negative front camber plates) $1529, 3-piece Dinan wheels and Michelin Pilot SX tires, 245/40ZR-17 ($4080), front strut-tower brace ($350), rear strut-tower brace ($250), Dinan floormats ($150).

STAGE 2
(Purple Coupe, 3.2-liter engine)

Horsepower............ **285 bhp @ 6500 rpm**
Torque .... **267 lb-ft @ 4500 rpm**

Package price, installed **$10,500**

Includes high-flow airbox & filter ($300), high-flow throttle body ($400), low-restriction airflow meter ($469), camshafts ($2000), engine-management chip ($350), big-bore catalyst-back exhaust system ($1300), clutch, pressure plate and lightened single-mass flywheel ($2300), Stage 3 performance suspension (springs, Koni rebound-adjustable shocks, adjustable anti-roll bars, 0.5-degree negative front camber plates) $1529, Toyo Proxes RA1 tires, 235/45ZR-17 ($1072), front strut-tower brace ($350), Dinan floormats ($150).

ACCELERATION				
	Stock BMW M3	Dinan M3 Sedan (Blue)	Dinan M3 Coupe (Purple)	Dinan M3 Coupe (White)
Time to speed, sec				
0–30 mph 2.0		2.0	1.8	2.0
0–40 mph 3.2		3.1	3.0	2.9
0–50 mph 4.3		4.3	4.0	3.8
0–60 mph 5.6		5.6	5.2	4.8
0–70 mph 7.5		7.7	7.2	6.5
0–80 mph 9.2		9.5	8.9	7.8
0–90 mph 11.8		11.9	11.2	9.8
0–100 mph 14.5		14.6	13.8	12.1
Time to distance				
0–1320 ft (¼ mile): 14.2 @ 99.0 mph		14.3 @ 98.8 mph	13.9 @ 100.6 mph	13.5 @ 106.2 mph
BRAKING				
Minimum stopping distance				
From 60 mph .... 114 ft		125 ft	108 ft	118 ft
From 80 mph .... 204 ft		214 ft	202 ft	199 ft
Control.............. excellent		excellent	excellent	excellent
Brake feel........... excellent		excellent	excellent	excellent
Overall brake rating ..... excellent		excellent	excellent	excellent
HANDLING				
Lateral accel (200-ft skidpad): 0.91g		0.92g	0.91g	0.94g
Balance .... mild understeer		mild understeer	mild understeer	mild understeer
Speed thru 700-ft slalom: 63.6 mph		65.8 mph	65.6 mph	65.8 mph
Balance .... mild understeer		mild understeer	moderate understeer	mild understeer
INTERIOR NOISE				
Idle in neutral .... 48 dBA		47 dBA	55 dBA	50 dBA
Maximum, 1st gear...... 79 dBA		83 dBA	80 dBA	72 dBA
Constant 50 mph .... 70 dBA		66 dBA	68 dBA	67 dBA
70 mph .... 73 dBA		71 dBA	70 dBA	69 dBA

Subjective ratings consist of excellent, very good, good, average, poor; na means information is not available.

fractionally slower than the purple coupe, largely a function of all that supercharged torque lighting up the more ride-oriented Toyos off the corners. A sensitive throttle foot is called for. Given a longer track with larger-radius corners, the white car would simply run away and hide.

Our Pomona test impressions reinforced the car's Streets of Willow prowess: 0.94g on the skidpad, 65.8 mph through the slalom and near-record stopping distance from 80. It's interesting to note that all the cars have stock M3 braking systems whose calipers and rotors come straight off the 321-bhp European M3, so you see the difference a gumball tire can make here.

Cool-down lap

AN IMPRESSIVE LOT, these Dinan BMWs. But we do have to take slight exception to his "Performance Without Compromise" mantra. A determined soul could probably burn those Toyos down to the cords in less than 10,000 street miles. While the smooth-road ride is acceptably firm, you wouldn't want to contend with too many frost heaves and chuckholes on a daily basis. And with the suspension adjustments, some of the stock M3's self-centering steering feel is lost.

But all these things are acceptable compromises to an enthusiast with performance on the brain. Any one of these would be an ideal car to commute with during the week, then wring out at a BMW Club time trial or autocross on the weekend. Which is exactly what Steve Dinan had in mind when he built this impressive trio.

BMW M roadster
Another Munich masterpiece

BY PAUL FRERE

GOOD NEWS: BMW's M roadster is a gem. Bad news: The one you're getting in the U.S. in 1998 (for around $45,000) won't be quite as good as our European car. Ours has 321 bhp at 7400 rpm. Yours has the same 240-bhp powerplant found in your U.S.-spec M3. Evidently, BMW thinks the Euro-spec car is too expensive for the U.S. Nevertheless, the U.S. model will be great, with lower gearing to make it accelerate almost as fast as the Euro-model.

This new M roadster has the same widened fenders as the Z3 2.8. These house 17-in. wheels (7.5 in. wide in front, 9 in. wide in back) that wear tires of size 225/45 in front and 245/40 in back. The springs, shock absorbers and anti-roll bars of the new M roadster are all firmer than the 2.8's, and the rear semi-trailing links have been reinforced as well. These carry M3 hubs and pivot on a reinforced crossmember. The M roadster also has the M3's brakes, plus a limited-slip differential (with a 25-percent-stronger locking factor) and a front anti-roll bar that's linked to the MacPherson struts through solid balljoints for quicker response. No significant changes have been made to the Z3's main structure.

The 3.2-liter inline-6, running 11.3:1 compression, comes straight from the M3 and is probably the finest 6-cylinder in the world. It produces more than 100 bhp/liter and ample torque as low as 3200 rpm. This engine pulls without hesitation from 1000 rpm in high gear and is exceptionally smooth.

While the current European M3 has a 6-speed gearbox, the M roadster comes with only five forward ratios. Fitting the 6-speed would have required expensive modification to the floorpan, and the car isn't viewed as a long-distance car, so a cruising gear was deemed nonessential.

In addition to optional roll-hoops behind the driver and passenger, the M roadster comes with a power top, seats and windows, plus three new instruments—a clock and temperature gauges for the oil and outside air. Of note, the steering ratio of 17.8:1 is actually slower than the standard Z3's 15.4:1 because of the quick response of the M roadster's tires.

Externally, the M roadster can be recognized by its four exhaust pipes, its specific front air dam, unique side vents, special wheels and by a badge on its trunk rather than its rear bumper. To compensate for the comparatively heavy engine, the battery has been moved to the trunk, where the spare tire has been replaced by a quick-repair kit and a compressor resulting in a reasonable amount of luggage space.

I recently drove the car in Spain, over a variety of mountain roads, and at the Jerez circuit, a favorite test course of Formula 1 teams. With a test weight of 2975 lb. (220 lb. less than the M3 Coupe), the M roadster has electrifying acceleration, particularly in the lower speed ranges. BMW says it hits 62 mph in 5.4 seconds and reaches the quarter mile in 13.4. Top speed of 155 mph is electronically governed.

What impressed me most about the car was the enormous range of its engine. It has immediate throttle response (thanks to six separate throttle valves!) and is completely vibration-free.

On the road, the well-weighted steering feels accurate and responsive, and rough surfaces don't throw the M roadster off its path. The header of the steeply raked windshield extends to near the driver's head, but it is effective at keeping the wind out of the cabin when running top down.

At the track, the M roadster's excellent balance is fully appreciated. The brakes are fade-resistant, body roll is very limited, and even on tight bends, understeer is almost entirely absent. Nearing the limit, the M roadster feels neutral, with the driver controlling the balance with small corrections to the steering and throttle. With the straightaway in sight, full power can be unleashed to the rear wheels, which fight for grip as the tail drifts out—a wonderful sensation that only lots of power can produce.

This new M roadster is really fun. And if fun has a price, the M roadster is an excellent value. ◉

BMW M3 IMSA RACER

The *real* Ultimate Driving Machine

BY JOE RUSZ
PHOTOS BY HAL CROCKER

"IT JUST DOESN'T get any better," I thought as I tootled along a Southern California highway in a snazzy BMW M3 4-door. Here was a car that looked sensational, went fast, handled great—with the capability of carrying four adults and their luggage. Could anything top this? Probably not on the highway. But in terms of absolutes, BMW did have something better: an M3 4-door that looked outrageous, went even faster, handled fantastically, but forget the passengers and bags. Prototype Technology Group's GTS-3 Bimmer sedan was designed with only one purpose in mind: beating the pants off those pesky Porsche 911s in SportsCar's (formerly IMSA) Exxon Supreme GT championship.

Just when I'd resigned myself to admiring the BMW racer from afar (behind the Armco), serendipity called. Actually, it was Judy Stropus, once Penske Racing's top timer and scorer who years ago put down her watches to embark on a career in racing PR. "Hey," says Judy, "BMW of North America wants to promote their M3 4-door road car so they've built a racing 4-door and they'll all be testing at Road Atlanta. Wanna drive it?" She didn't have to ask twice.

Twenty-three hundred and thirty-two United Airlines frequent flyer miles later, I am standing under the awning beside the PTG transporter, listening to team owner and old racing buddy Tom Milner cite chapter and verse about car number 10. Built by the factory for the European Touring Car Championship, it arrived at PTG's Winchester, Virginia, shops as a bare bodyshell composed of steel floorpan, inner fender panels, firewall, window pillars and roof—and an alu-

■ Pizza platter-size disc brakes ensure that the 4-door racing Bimmer stops as well as its Euro/American suspension makes it handle. Old-style fuel injection with individual throttles, instead of a single throttle body, is used in the sedan. Like a safety briefing on an airplane, crewman's words fall on deaf ears.

minum rollcage designed to stiffen as well as protect. To bring the cage up to SportsCar standards, PTG welded in doorbars and a cross-brace behind the driver's seat. Piece of cake.

Not so, the rest of the transformation. To call the bodyshell a racing car is like saying that the essence of a great cake is flour. Point is, Milner and the PTG crew crammed a lot of goodies (and burned gallons of midnight oil) creating this tasty dessert. You'll have to get the recipe from Milner (then again, he may not give it to you), but here's a list of the essential ingredients: carbon-fiber doors, fenders, decklid, hood and dash; plexiglass side glass; adjustable JRZ coil-over shocks with remote reservoirs; ABS-equipped Brembo vented disc brakes with cross-drilled rotors (14.0-in. front, 12.0-in. rear); BBS wheels (18 x 10½-in. front, 18 x 11.0-in. rear); Yokohama racing slicks (290/640-18 front, 290/680-18 rear); Hewland 6-speed gearbox; and modified BMW 5-Series rear differential with limited slip.

Oops, almost forgot the "yeast," BMW's production dohc 24-valve in-line-6 fitted with European head (with VANOS variable valve timing); custom-made valve springs, cams and pistons; Bosch electronic fuel injection. Serves "more than 400 horsepower," by Milner's admission.

Late in the a.m. number 10 takes to the track for the first time and just as R&T's own Derek Hill is letting the engine stretch its legs, the hinges buckle and the hood flops up against the windshield, which promptly cracks. Watching the PTG crew straighten (and reinforce!) the hinges

and replace the windscreen, I'm thinking that I'll never get to drive the car. But shortly after lunch, Milner looks up from his clipboard: "Better suit up. When the car comes in, it's your turn."

I do. It does and before you can say, "Er, Tom, could you gimme a little more slack in that lap belt," yours truly is jjj-jud-dering out of the pits, slipping the clutch to get the Bimmer (whose trans has 1st gear locked out—to turn the 6-speed into a rules-legal 5-speed) up to speed. Which happens about as quickly as it took you to read this sentence. In a snap, I'm cresting the hill on the exit of Turn 1, heading for Road Atlanta's esses.

A confession: Earlier in the day, driving a stock M3 4-door, I loop it in the last ess—just like I did in the 1982 SCCA Runoffs. The thought of Milner tearing me a new, uh, visor, crosses my mind, but not to worry. The race car sticks to the tarmac like a leech on fly-paper, and two turns later I'm out on the back straight where any idiot can go fast. So I do, rowing the family-size racer through the gears, shifting at 8,000 rpm while marveling at the broadness of the 6-cylinder's powerband. Now I see why Derek, Bill Auberlen, Dieter Quester, Javier Quiros, Tom Hessert and Marc Duez like these cars. And why these BMW M3s have won their class at Daytona and Sebring.

Earlier, during our walk-around tour of the car, Milner casually mentioned that unlike the BMW coupes, the 4-door does not have power-assisted steering. Oh, oh! Shouldn't have cut Nautilus training. But again, my worries are for naught. The unassisted steering feels not the least bit heavy, at

least at Road Atlanta where there are no slow corners.

Although Tom suggested I take about five laps in the car, no one signals as I pass the pits so I press on. As I get comfortable in the car and re-familiarize myself with the track, my lap times come down. Sorry, they're classified. However, you might be interested to know that in qualifying for the Grand Prix of Atlanta, Bill Auberlen turned a 1-minute, 23.6-second lap that was 18.2 sec. quicker than what he got out of the road car.

I marvel at the precision of the Hewland gearbox (did I really make that downshift?). And at how the speed builds on the back straight where I glance down at the digital speedo and see 150 mph, about 15 mph short of what Derek gets later. A Porsche 911 that I waved by in the last turn moves into view, and I begin to reel it in—until I realize that this is not a smart thing to do in the cat-and-mouse game of racing strategy. Just as I'm thinking about how I'll execute my next lap (harder on those brakes, more revs in the corners!), the checker waves, calling an end to the session. Aw, shucks, Dad!

Climbing out of the car, I'm greeted by Milner and Erik Wensberg, BMW of North America's M Brand manager, who says, "You did great." Translated, "Thank you for not turning $200,000 worth of racing car into found art." Pumped on adrenaline I tell Tom, "Wow what a great car drives like a dream just goes like a streak never got a wheel off the handling is fantastic!"

Ultimate Driving Machines will do that to you. ◎

BMW
M ROADSTER

At last, a wolf in Z3 clothing

BY ANDREW BORNHOP
PHOTOS BY JEFF ALLEN

ARE YOU A bit dissatisfied with BMW's 4-cylinder Z3? Me too. It's eye-catchingly muscular, but the tinny-sounding 1.9-liter engine doesn't pack enough punch to back up the car's powerful looks…which is counter to my tastes and not exactly what you'd expect of BMW. Give me a sleeper car over a poser any day. A Miata, for instance, which is significantly less expensive but equally at home on a twisting back road.

BMW's Z.3 2.8 is another story. Its 189-bhp inline-6—complemented by beefier suspension bits and a richer-feeling interior—creates the refined Z3 that BMW needed to build. If there's one thing the Z3 2.8 lacks, however, it's this: a voracious appetite satisfied only by a diet rich in throttle usage and high in lateral g's. In short, the Z3 2.8 is more a polished GT, less a feisty sports car.

Now things have changed. With the April arrival of the M roadster, BMW will finally bring a Z3 to the American market that makes rabid sports-car enthusiasts stand back and say, "Now that's more like it." And if there's any doubt about the M roadster living up to its "mini Cobra" appearance, consider this—it's the quickest BMW ever sold in the U.S.

Glance at our data panel and see why—this South Carolina-built M roadster is basically a potent M3 wearing impressively stiff (and light) Z3 roadster clothing. Underhood is the M3's twincam 3.2-liter inline-6, which sends its 240 bhp to the rear wheels via the M3's 5-speed manual gearbox and a limited-slip differential adorned with enough low-flying cooling fins to turn a potato into a dozen French fries.

Starchy snacks aside, the 3,085-lb. M roadster also benefits from the M3's

monstrous vented disc brakes (more than a foot in diameter) at each wheel, plus a sport-tuned suspension that lowers the ride height by an inch. The rear suspension isn't the M3's multilink arrangement; rather, it's a version of the Z3 2.8's trailing arms, beefed up to handle the significant stresses generated by BMW M GmbH's powerplant.

Compared with the Z3 2.8, the M roadster has firmer springing and damping in front, and a 1-mm-smaller anti-roll bar for improved turn-in response. In back, the springs have actually been softened for better off-the-line traction, and wheel hop is checked by firmer damping. To further reduce understeer, BMW has switched to a 3.5-mm-larger rear bar, which, as in the front, links to the suspension via balljoints for crisp response. What's more, the M roadster wears tire rubber galore—225/45ZR-17s in front and

BMW doles out the nostalgia, courtesy of two-tone coloring and liberal use of chrome. Note the passenger-airbag deactivation switch, just above the shifter that illuminates when headlights are on.

245/40ZR-17s in back. The latter are mounted on 9-in.-wide alloy wheels that really fill out those large rear fenders the M shares with the Z3 2.8.

With Michelin's Laurens Proving Grounds in South Carolina kindly put at our disposal, we probed this Estoril Blue M roadster for what it's worth. Namely, a sprint to 60 mph in a fleet 5.2 seconds and a quarter-mile blast in 14 flat at a heady 98.2 mph. Bye, bye, Boxster. Find a quicker BMW in our Road Test Summary. You can't.

Subjectively, the reassuringly firm brakes of the M roadster get top marks. No surprise, our objective numbers back up that grade. This car stops as quickly as a Corvette, which is to say it can haul itself down from 80 mph in just a speck over 200 ft. Most impressive. And 4-channel ABS removes any hint of drama from our simulated panic stops.

The slalom is trickier. Because the M roadster reacts so sharply to initial steering inputs (the variable-ratio rack comes straight from the M3), it's deceptively easy to crank in too much steering at the first pylon and start the car off on a path that's far curvier (and full of greater lateral forces) than need be. But with minimum steering input and a straight-as-possible path, the M roadster slices through the cones at an outstanding 65.3 mph.

It's the immediate responsiveness, the agility, that makes the M roadster a delight on Michelin's handling

THE COMPETITION

Chevrolet Corvette Convertible

Length: 179.7 in.   **Width:** 73.6 in.   **Height:** 47.7 in.   **Wheelbase:** 104.5 in.
Track, f/r: 62.0 in./62.0 in.   **Curb weight:** 3240 lb

Will many people cross-shop the M roadster and the new Corvette convertible? Probably not. But as a pair of high-performance roadsters listing for less than 45 grand, a comparison makes sense. The much-larger Vette, despite having a luscious aluminum small-block V-8, is less brutal, less rambunctious. At the same time, it manages to get its nose ahead of the Bimmer's in the quarter mile. That's what 345 bhp will do for you, mounted in a sleek open-top chassis that's just as stiff as the new M roadster's. *(Tested: 9/97)*

Current list price	$44,425
Engine	ohv 5.7-liter **V-8**
Horsepower	345 bhp @ 5600 rpm
Torque	350 lb-ft @ 4400 rpm
Transmission	**6-speed manual**
0–60 mph	**5.2 sec**
Braking, 60–0 mph	**118 ft**
Lateral accel (200-ft skidpad)	na
EPA city/highway	18/28 mpg

Porsche Boxster

Length: 169.9 in.   **Width:** 70.0 in.   **Height:** 50.8 in.   **Wheelbase:** 95.1 in.
Track, f/r: 57.3 in./59.4 in.   **Curb weight:** 2755 lb

It's just about impossible to get a Boxster out of shape. With lots of dialed-in understeer and a rear end that's firmly planted to the ground, this Porsche remains impressively composed in a variety of twisty-road environments. The M roadster, on the other hand, demands more of its driver. And in acceleration, Munich's monster easily outdistances Stuttgart's stallion. But before too long, Porsche will come out with the Boxster S, rumored to have 300 bhp. The race goes on... *(Tested: 3/97)*

Current list price	$41,000
Engine	dohc 2.5-liter **flat-6**
Horsepower	201 bhp @ 6000 rpm
Torque	181 lb-ft @ 4500 rpm
Transmission	**5-speed manual**
0–60 mph	**6.1 sec**
Braking, 60–0 mph	**120 ft**
Lateral accel (200-ft skidpad)	0.93g
EPA city/highway	19/26 mpg

1998 BMW M ROADSTER

MANUFACTURER

BMW Manufacturing Corp.
P.O. Box 11000
Spartanburg, South Carolina 29304-4100

PRICE

List price	est $41,900
Price as tested	est $42,853

Price as tested includes std equip. (dual airbags, ABS, air cond, cruise control, heated pwr seats, AM/FM stereo/cassette; pwr windows, mirrors & top; leather upholstery, central locking, rollover protection bars, limited-slip differential, passenger airbag deactivation switch), luxury tax (est $383), dest charge ($570).

0–60 mph	5.2 sec
0–¼ mi	14.0 sec
Top speed	137 mph*
Skidpad	0.89g
Slalom	65.3 mph
Brake rating	excellent

TEST CONDITIONS

Temperature	53° F
Wind	calm
Humidity	na
Elevation	500 ft

SCALE: 10 IN.(254mm) DIVISIONS
DRAWING BY TIM BARKER

ENGINE

Type	cast-iron block, aluminum head, **inline-6**
Valvetrain	dohc 4 valve/cyl
Displacement	192 cu in./3152 cc
Bore x stroke	3.40 x 3.53 in./ 86.4 x 89.6 mm
Compression ratio	10.5:1
Horsepower (SAE)	**240 bhp @ 6000 rpm**
Bhp/liter	76.1
Torque	**236 lb-ft @ 3800 rpm**
Maximum engine speed	6800 rpm
Fuel injection	elect. sequential port
Fuel	prem unleaded, 91 pump oct

CHASSIS & BODY

Layout	**front engine/rear drive**
Body/frame	unit steel
Brakes	
Front	**12.4-in. vented discs**
Rear	**12.3-in. vented discs**
Assist type	vacuum; ABS
Total swept area	491 sq in.
Swept area/ton	294 sq in.
Wheels	cast alloy; **17 x 7½ f, 17 x 9 r**
Tires	Michelin Pilot SX MXX3; **225/45ZR-17 f, 245/40ZR-17 r**
Steering	**rack & pinion**, pwr assist
Overall ratio	17.8:1 (variable, mean ratio)
Turns, lock to lock	3.2
Turning circle	34.1 ft
Suspension	
Front	**MacPherson struts, L-shaped lower arms,** coil springs, tube shocks, anti-roll bar
Rear	**semi-trailing arms,** coil springs, tube shocks, anti-roll bar

DRIVETRAIN

Transmission................ **5-speed manual**

Gear	Ratio	Overall ratio	(Rpm) Mph
1st	4.21:1	13.59:1	(6500) 35
2nd	2.49:1	8.04:1	(6500) 60
3rd	1.66:1	5.36:1	(6500) 90
4th	1.24:1	4.01:1	(6500) 120
5th	1.00:1	3.23:1	(5980) 137*

Final drive ratio	3.23:1
Engine rpm @ 60 mph in 5th	2600

*Electronically limited.

GENERAL DATA

Curb weight	**est 3085 lb**
Test weight	est 3335 lb
Weight dist (with driver), f/r, %	est 51/49
Wheelbase	96.8 in.
Track, f/r	55.0 in./58.7 in.
Length	**158.5 in.**
Width	**68.5 in.**
Height	**49.8 in.**
Ground clearance	na
Trunk space	6.2 cu ft

MAINTENANCE

Oil/filter change	7500 mi/7500 mi
Tuneup	30,000 mi
Basic warranty	48 mo/50,000 mi

ACCOMMODATIONS

Seating capacity	2
Head room	37.0 in.
Seat width	2 x 20.5 in.
Leg room	42.5 in.
Seatback adjustment	22 deg
Seat travel	8.0 in.

INTERIOR NOISE

Idle in neutral	54 dBA
Maximum in 1st gear	85 dBA
Constant 50 mph	73 dBA
70 mph	76 dBA

INSTRUMENTATION

160-mph speedometer, 8000-rpm tach, coolant temp, oil temp, fuel level, analog clock

ACCELERATION

Time to speed	Seconds
0–30 mph	1.8
0–40 mph	2.9
0–50 mph	4.0
0–60 mph	5.2
0–70 mph	7.2
0–80 mph	9.0
0–90 mph	11.6
0–100 mph	14.6

Time to distance	
0–100 ft	2.8
0–500 ft	7.5
0–1320 ft (¼ mi):	14.0 @ 98.2 mph

FUEL ECONOMY

Normal driving	est 22.0 mpg
EPA city/highway	est 20/27 mpg
Cruise range	est 275 miles
Fuel capacity	13.5 gal.

BRAKING

Minimum stopping distance	
From 60 mph	116 ft
From 80 mph	203 ft
Control	excellent
Pedal effort for 0.5g stop	na
Fade, effort after six 0.5g stops from 60 mph	na
Brake feel	excellent
Overall brake rating	excellent

HANDLING

Lateral accel (200-ft skidpad)	0.89g
Balance	mild understeer
Speed thru 700-ft slalom	65.3 mph
Balance	neutral
Lateral seat support	excellent

Subjective ratings consist of excellent, very good, good, average, poor; na means information is not available.

Test Notes...

■ The M roadster launches with authority and beats an M3 sedan in the quarter mile. But the sedan reaches 100 mph first, likely because of its better aerodynamics.

■ Want to know what a firm brake pedal should feel like? Drive this M roadster. BMW and Porsche ought to teach other carmakers about proper brake feel.

■ With its short wheelbase and high power, the M roadster can be teased into gratifying power oversteer on the skidpad. But in steady-state cornering, it mildly understeers.

■ Looking for a sure-fire way to spot an M roadster? It's the Z3 with a quad-tip exhaust, M badges, trunk-mounted license plate and unique wheels and tires that properly fill out the car's muscular flanks. Though M roadsters built for Europe have 321 bhp, the U.S. model pumps out a solid 240.

course. Any time you mix a short wheelbase (10 in. less than the M3's) with gobs of rear-drive power, you're bound to get a car that likes to slide its tail. The M roadster is no exception. Despite a high level of grip from the Michelin Pilots, the rear tires can (and will) break away when you're powering out of a corner or lifting off the throttle and turning in. Nothing spooky here, just enough drama to keep the driver attentive. And sitting so close to the rear wheels—as you do in this traditionally laid-out roadster—only enhances this pendulum feel.

Back to the phenomenal acceleration for a moment. With 240 bhp on tap, a broad band of torque (whose peak of 236 lb.-ft. is reached at 3,800 rpm) and five tightly spaced gear ratios, the M roadster really squirts. Need to pass somebody on the highway? The throaty-sounding inline-6 makes quick duty of it, pulling like a freight train to its 6,500-rpm redline. And around town—where most cars loaf along in 3rd gear—the M roadster cruises comfortably in 4th. This relates directly to the 3.23:1 final drive and gearing so low that 5th isn't even an overdrive. Clutch take-up, by the way, is second-nature, and the short-throw shifter moves firmly from gear to gear with only a bit more resistance than is felt in the Z3 2.8.

As is true of any BMW fit to wear Munich's motorsports badge, the M roadster is endowed with numerous unique pieces, some purely cosmetic, others not. These include new bumper caps, tricolor BMW M badges (in a variety of places), splashes of chrome

trim (inside and out) and exclusive 17-in. alloy wheels. Moreover, the trunklid is different, carrying the BMW roundel on its upper surface and the license plate on its short vertical plane.

The M roadster's air dam has a larger opening because the German-built M engine (which is shipped in assembled form to BMW's plant in Spartanburg, South Carolina) requires more air than the 2.8. And its side ports serve as brake cooling ducts, not places to put foglights. The rear bumper, on the other hand, had to be altered to make room for the M roadster's dual-muffler/quad-tip exhaust, a feature that will appear on all future M cars. Because the passenger-side muffler occupies the space formerly reserved for the spare tire, BMW equips the M roadster with a tiny electric air pump and a fast-acting tire sealer that stow away neatly in the trunk. Also in the trunk is the battery, hung low between the mufflers in a box that is part of the car's unique trunk-floor stamping. This helps with weight distribution, which is pegged by BMW at a smart 51/49.

Other unique bits include a larger, more ovoid rearview mirror (which can get in the way when you're looking toward the apex of a right-hand corner), a pair of stylish but less effective (i.e., smaller) sideview mirrors, two-tone sport seats that offer superb lateral support (particularly for your upper back) and a new center console thats graced with six chrome-trimmed gauges and controls that give the car a warm, decidedly retro feel. That feeling is augmented by chrome trim

around the shift boot and the car's excellent analog gauges, but there's nothing retro about the M roadster's standard level of equipment—it's loaded. A power top, heated power seats, one-touch side windows and air conditioning are all standard, as is beautifully stitched leather that covers much of the interior, even the new thick-rimmed 3-spoke steering wheel.

Taller drivers (those over 6 ft. 2 in. or so) will wish they could move the seat back an additional inch, but the M roadster is nevertheless a comfortable car for most, and its highway ride is on the firm side of comfortable—just what I like. One thing I don't like, however, are the car's limp seatbelt retractors. Twice I shut the door on the belts because they had not retracted properly.

People in the Snowbelt may think again about owning this powerful, wide-tired M roadster, primarily because it doesn't have traction control. It's in the works, says BMW, but it hasn't been tailored to the car yet. BMW says the challenge is in making a system that responds fast enough to catch the explosive wheelspin of this short-wheelbase roadster.

But this sort of concern doesn't detract from a car such as the Shelby Cobra. And it doesn't with the M roadster. This is a well-built weekend car that's refined enough to drive every day. Only 3,000 are planned for the U.S. in 1998, at an estimated price of $41,900 that includes free maintenance for three years or 36,000 miles. Your smiles are guaranteed to last a lot longer.

2000 BMW M5

I confess: 400 bhp redirects my lust

BY DENNIS SIMANAITIS

PHOTOS BY STEPHANE FOULON

■ A most serious 5 Series underneath, the new M5 can be spotted by wider kidney-shaped grille and a gaping lower intake.

FOR A LONG TIME, I LUSTED after the BMW 540i as the perfect 4-door sedan: large enough to be practical, small enough to be nimble and, fitted with its sweet 6-speed manual, sporty enough to be an (fortunate) enthusiast's everyday car.

But I must confess. My lust has been redirected by 400 bhp; this, the power rating of the new BMW M5.

This 5.0-liter V-8 product of BMW's M division first appeared at the 1998 Geneva show, then Frankfurt, then Turin. The M5 is now entering series production, though, alas, it'll be Europe-only at first with the U.S. version coming in the fall of 1999 as a model year 2000 car.

I can hardly wait, my appetite whetted by a couple of days on Bavarian roads ranging from farm paths to *Autobahnen*. In fact, this variety of driving conditions showed off the M5 in brilliant light as an automobile of utterly high performance, yet one that's equally at home just toodling around as well.

Heart of the M5 is its all-new all-aluminum powerplant that pays homage to BMW's smaller V-8, though it's more than simply a punched-out version of the latter. The 5.0-liter has four valves/cylinder actuated by double overhead camshafts, each of which features BMW's variable valve timing via continuous optimization of the camshaft/drive pulley orientation; "Double-VANOS," BMW rightly calls it.

The engine's 400-bhp peak arrives at 6600 rpm. And even more relevant to my manner of driving is its 395 lb.-ft. of torque available as low as 3800. The way I figure it, accelerating hard up to moderate speed is an everyday occurrence; probing a car's top-speed capability comes only once in a while.

I had splendid opportunity for both, however. A Good Neighbor policy with Bavarian farmers kept me from repeatedly verifying BMW's claimed 5.3 seconds to 62.5 mph, but I'll bet this figure is a conservative one. And, once away from muddy roads and Herr Bauer's hay wagon, I found the M5 displaying uncanny stability—and relative tranquility—on the *Autobahn*, even with its speedo touching 260 km/h, a slightly optimistic interpretation of the M5's electronically limited 155-mph maximum.

Aiding this mixed-mode driving is the M5's Sport control, a dash-mounted button that invokes more aggressive operation of its throttle-by-wire and also reduces boost of the car's Servotronic power-assisted steering. With a given twiddle of the accelerator providing enhanced throttle stroke at an increased rate, I believe the Sport button would be just the thing for precise control of power and attitude.

Another M innovation used in the M5 is its quasi-dry-sump lubrication. The engine is fitted with auxiliary oil pumps, one pressure and two vacuum, their operation keyed to lateral-g sensing. In hard cornering, these pumps activate automatically and keep oil from accumulating in outer crannies of the sump and heads.

In traditional Q-ship fashion, all of these technicalities are clothed in 5 Series bodywork that's tweaked in only the most subtle manner. The front air dam has integrated oval foglights and a larger intake scoop. The BMW kidney-shape grilles are widened a tad. Xenon headlights are standard (and I'm sure getting spoiled by xenon's super-white illumination). The side mirrors are different, an underbody diffuser accelerates airflow and helps cool the final drive, and four tailpipes of polished stainless steel provide all the right sounds.

Within the cabin, the handsome instrumentation displays an interesting M innovation as well: The orange region of the tachometer is defined by an illuminated arc that's keyed to engine coolant temperature. On startup, a sensible 4000-rpm limit gradually rises in 500-rpm increments as the engine warms up. There are two choices of ambience: Exclusive, with leather and burled walnut; and Sportive, replacing the wood with aluminum finished to a titanium luster.

As you might guess, I'm the Sportive sort myself. ⬡

BMW
M COUPE

Warning: This coupe can be hazardous to Cougar drivers

BY JOHN MATRAS

PHOTOS BY JEFF ALLEN

Good thing no one was coming the other way. The driver of the Cougar—old style with the "formal roof"—spun his head around like a Linda Blair wannabe as he passed me and drifted into the opposite lane. Had there been oncoming traffic, there would have been a head-on, and the M Coupe I was driving most likely would have been at fault. And all I was doing was waiting at a stop sign.

It was a typical reaction. The BMW M Coupe was new and most likely the first one Mr. Cougar had seen. But with all the good looks of a bulldog, the sawed-off 2-seater caused turned heads, craned necks and dropped jaws no matter where it went. Pumping gas, parked in the high school lot or out on the road, everyone wanted to know what it was, how fast it would go

Pour on the coal exiting a curve and the pocket Bimmer tightens the line.

and how it went around corners. Everyone. From teenage boys to the old ladies at church. So I told them something like this: The M Coupe is a coupe version of the BMW M Roadster which, in turn, is a special high-performance version of BMW's open 2-seater. The M cars are conceived and developed by BMW M, a separate division of the company in Garching, Germany, charged with parenting special high-performance versions of BMW products which are then built else-

where. So in addition to the M Coupe, there's a "lesser" version, the Z3 Coupe 2.8, which is powered by an inline-6 that produces a mere 193 bhp. The M Coupe, like the M Roadster as well as the M3 sedan and convertible, are powered by the big 3.2-liter six that cranks out a healthy 240 bhp at 6000 rpm and 236 lb-ft of torque.

As in the Roadster, the high-output six gives the 3100-lb M Coupe push-you-back-in-the-seat straight-line performance. All the anti-squat in the world can't prevent the nose from rising just a bit when the right pedal is pushed. Unlike the 2.8, the M Coupe is available only with a manual transmission. The stubby lever in the center console works like a good waiter, serving up the next gear with no muss or fuss and just as quick as you need it. The engine dominates the car, filling its compartment from radiator to cowl. With the nose of the big six over the front axle line, the M Coupe almost qualifies as a front mid-engine chassis. The weight distribution is 50/50 front to rear and the driving position is in close proximity to the rear axle.

There's a prodigious amount of rubber under the M Coupe, the offset of the wheels emphasizing the width of the wheels, $7\frac{1}{2}$ in. in front and a full 9.0 in. wide at the rear. The tires are sized appropriately, 225/45ZR-17 in front and a geranium-flattening 245/40ZR-17 at the rear. The Dunlop SP Sports stick well enough for quarter-mile times well under 15 sec with a trap speed knocking at the door of 100 mph. A Corvette and even a Camaro SS will out-accelerate the M Coupe, as

will every new F-car from Italy and those German cars with the same name as the number you call for the police. But not much else, and precious few cars can top both the M Coupe's skidpad and slalom numbers.

Numbers be damned, the M Coupe's handling could be said to make a driver cocky were it not for the car's ability to deliver, with precision, just what was requested. BMW claims the M Coupe is the stiffest car the company has ever made, with none of the Roadster's chassis stiffening being removed when the roof was added. It makes a strong base for the strut-type front and semi-trailing arm rear suspension. BMW accommodated the changes by increasing front caster for more straight-line stability and making the rear springs firmer and the rear anti-roll bar slightly larger.

Pour on the coal exiting a curve and the pocket Bimmer tightens the line, rather than running wider as an ordinary car would. BMW's All Season Traction, plus a limited-slip differential, get credit for the confidence a driver can have with the throttle. It's one of the few traction-control systems that I didn't reflexively turn off every time I started the car, allowing as it does just the modicum of rear wheel slip for ideal cornering, clamping down hard only in really slippery situations, such as loose gravel. It takes the worry out of a short wheelbase and oodles of torque.

But more than just performance, BMW claims to have reinvented, or at least revived, the GT car, as in Grand Touring, when that meant a great getaway vehicle for two people, with no "+2" compromise of a back seat, and just enough luggage room for a weekend trip. The hatchback will also swallow a couple of golf bags. Seating is ideal for two, the M Coupe coming equipped with a leather-covered pair of bum-embracing seats that look like they've been upholstered in Hide of Batman. Neat. As is the chrome trim around the shifter boot and circling the gauges, adding a faint retro touch to the businesslike interior. It's snug, with pockets in the doors and a small bin in the bulkhead behind the seats. And no cupholders. Need more room? Buy a 740iL.

Just about everything on the M Coupe is standard—power doors, mirrors, seats and so on—and factory-installed options are limited to a deeply tinted glass moonroof with power tilt (no slide feature) for $300 and a CD radio for $200. An alarm system, cellular phone, navigation system and trunk-mounted CD changer are available from the dealer.

Wonderful as all this is, however, it's not what made the Cougar driver almost lose control of his car, if not himself. That was the M Coupe's *eigenwillig*, or "determinedly going its own way" shape. Rather than plunking a short coupe bubble top on the roadster or create another clichéd fastback, BMW designers deliberately sought to make something different. It may not be universally admired, but the man-on-the-street response is almost universally thumbs up. There's certainly no doubt about its somewhat aggressive intentions with that L'il Abneresque shape—too muscular for its little barchetta bodywork, bulging with flares and sills and four tailpipes under the rear bumper that wraps around to those meaty rear tires. "It's so ugly ya gotta love it," remarked one observer. That's a compliment, I think. But be forewarned: Even sitting still, the M Coupe is a safety hazard—at least to one Cougar driver.

BMW

M COUPE

PRICE

List price, all POE.................. $41,800
Price as tested.................... $42,816
Price as tested includes std equip. (dual front and side airbags, rear defroster, ABS, rack & pinion power-assist steering, heated seats, cruise control, front spoiler, leather upholstery, remote entry, a/c, AM/FM/cassette/stereo; pwr windows, mirrors, seats & door locks) luxury tax ($446), dest charge ($570).

ENGINE

Type.................. dohc 24-valve inline-6
Displacement..................... 3152 cc
Bore x stroke .... 86.4 x 89.6 mm
Compression ratio................... 10.5:1
Horsepower, SAE net ..... 240 bhp @ 6000 rpm
Torque .... 236 lb-ft @ 3800 rpm
Maximum engine speed .... 6800 rpm
Fuel injection........... elect. sequential port
Fuel requirement .... premium unleaded

GENERAL DATA

Curb weight..................... 3131 lb
Weight distribution, f/r, % 50/50
Wheelbase .... 96.8 in.
Track, f/r.................. 56.0/58.7 in.
Length .... 158.5 in.
Width....................... 68.5 in.
Height .... 50.4 in.
Trunk space.................... 6.7 cu ft

CHASSIS & BODY

Layout.............. front engine/rear drive
Body/frame .... unit steel
Brakes, f/r...... 12.4-in. vented discs/12.3-in. vented discs, vacuum assist, ABS
Wheels.......... cast alloy, 17x7.5 f, 17x9 r
Tires .... Dunlop SP Sport 8080E
225/45ZR-17 f, 245/40ZR-17 r
Steering .... rack & pinion, power assist
Turns, lock to lock 3.2
Suspension, f/r .... MacPherson struts, L-shaped lower arms, coil springs, tube shocks, anti-roll bar/semi-trailing arms, coil springs, tube shocks, anti-roll bar

DRIVETRAIN

Transmission .... 5-speed manual

Gear	Ratio	Overall Ratio	Rpm	Mph
1st	4.21:1	13.59:1	6900	38
2nd	2.49:1	8.04:1	6900	62
3rd	1.66:1	5.36:1	6900	96
4th	1.24:1	4.01:1	6900	129
5th	1.00:1	3.23:1	est 5820	137*

Final drive ratio.................. 3.23:1
Engine rpm @ 60 mph, top gear........ 2550
*Electronically limited

ACCELERATION

Time to speed   Seconds
0–30 mph...................... 2.0
0–40 mph...................... 3.1
0–50 mph...................... 4.2
0–60 mph...................... 5.5
0–70 mph...................... 7.6
0–80 mph...................... 9.4
0–90 mph...................... 12.0
0–100 mph..................... 14.7
Time to distance
0–100 ft...................... 2.9
0–500 ft...................... 7.8
0–1320 ft (1/4 mile)... 14.3 @ 98.7 mph

BRAKING

Minimum stopping distance
From 60 mph................. 125 ft
From 80 mph................. 217 ft
Control .... excellent
Overall brake rating.............. very good

HANDLING

Lateral accel (200-ft skidpad) 0.87g
Speed thru 700-ft slalom.......... 62.3 mph

FUEL ECONOMY

Normal driving .... 19.6 mpg
EPA city/highway .... 19/26 mpg
Fuel capacity................... 13.5 gal.

BMW M5 vs Mercedes-Benz E55

SPORTS-SEDAN
BATTLE

Is there a new champion?

IN FRONT OF PHOTOGRAPHER GUY Spangenberg's large-format camera sit the BMW M5 and the Mercedes-Benz E55 on a vast, desolate Southern California dry lakebed. It's just a couple of hours before the sun finally dips into the horizon. And amazingly, the wind isn't howling this late afternoon like it normally does at this time of the year. It's calm and extremely quiet. Perhaps Mother Nature has decided to take a break so she can witness an extraordinary battle between two of the world's most powerful, technically sophisticated and exciting sports sedans.

In 1999, when we matched the E55 against the Jaguar XJR, the Mercedes took the honors as the best sports sedan. And now a year later, the E55 has to step into the ring once again and defend its crown against the BMW M5. This time, in addition to our usual *Road & Track* road test and subjective evaluations from Feature Editor Sam Mitani and me, we upped the challenge by taking these two cars to the Streets of Willow raceway in Rosamond, California. We recruited our resident racer, Online Services Editor Kim Wolfkill, to properly wring out both

of these cars on the track. You'll find Wolfkill's track impressions in his sidebar later in this story.

The players

THROUGH THE CAMERA LENS, there is nothing obvious on the exteriors of these two German cars to show that they are more than the standard BMW 540i and Mercedes-Benz E430 sedans. The M5's styling is understated, especially with a dark blue-metallic exterior color scheme. In front, the kidney-shape grille is widened and flared outward a bit, with a blackened diagonal mesh hiding the air intake beneath the bumper, flanked by two outboard openings housing the oval foglamps. In profile, only the massive 18-in. shadow-finish chrome wheels and a small lip atop the edge of the trunklid stand out. At the rear, an M5 badge, clear turn-signal/parking-light lenses with a lower valance wrapping around a pair of stainless-steel exhaust tips give hints to this specially tuned version of the 5 Series.

Turn to the E55 and you'll have to look even harder to find exterior design cues to differentiate this AMG

from other silver Mercedes E-Class models. Other than the super-wide 18-in. wheels alongside lower side skirts ending with a pair of chrome-tipped exhaust pipes at the rear, and the "E55" and the "AMG" badge on the decklid, it looks nearly identical to the E430 Sport.

Inside, our M5 sports two-tone blue-and-black leather upholstery, special chrome-ringed instrumentation, an M sport steering wheel and an illuminated shift knob. Also included in the M package are the GPS navigation system and the 14-speaker premium sound system with a CD changer. The E55 comes in a red-and-black combination for the interior leather upholstery, with black bird's-eye maple wood trim. The only options available with the E55 are the portable cellular phone and the trunk-mounted CD changer. All in all, both of these cars offer the same opulence, amenities and safety features you would normally associate with a well-equipped BMW 5 Series or a Mercedes-Benz E-Class luxury sedan.

Weighing almost 400 lb. more than the E55, the 4000-lb. BMW M5 comes well equipped to challenge the reign-

ing champion. Based on the 540i Sport, BMW's Motorsport division bumped the stock M62 4398-cc 282-bhp unit to 4941 cc, enabling the new S62 M5 powerplant to pump out 400 bhp and 369 lb.-ft. of torque. This bumped displacement is accomplished by lengthening the stroke from 82.7 mm to 89.0, and increasing the bore from 92.0 mm to 94.0. Other modifications to the engine include a heavy-duty double-roller timing chain and hollow camshafts for long life and reduced inertia, enlarged intake ports and larger-capacity cooling system to meet the stringent demands of the powerplant. A double VANOS system (variable valve timing) designed specifically for the M5 is also adopted to enhance low- to medium-speed torque delivery, as well as optimizing combustion for reducing harmful emissions.

Making sure all the cylinders in the S62 have access to all the fresh air they need is a top priority. Once the outside air is gobbled up at two points behind the front bumper, it then flows into a carbon-fiber plenum atop the engine. From there, 9.1-in. intake runners funnel the air to the entrance of the cylinders. But gaining access to the actual combustion chambers requires passage through a system of eight individual throttle valves. Usually, separate throttle butterflies are seen only on ultra-performance sports applications, including racing engines. And while previous M 6-cylinder powerplants had the same feature, the M5 V-8 is the first with electronically actuated individual throttles. By having a DC servomotor connected to separate throttle valves housed at each intake port, the engine is able to respond to gas-pedal movements in as little as 120 milliseconds.

In My Opinion...

PATRICK HONG, Road Test Editor

I must admit that before entering into this comparison test my heart had already swayed toward the BMW a bit. I thought the M5 was going to smoke the E55 in every category. Well, I hate to say it, but I was *wrong*. Both of these cars are exceptionally competent sports sedans, if not sports cars with four doors and two extra seats. So my pick basically comes down to which one offers the most fun driving. That would be the M5. It looks cool, sounds great, and the 6-speed manual and the lightning-fast throttle response allow me to be more active in driving, which is the best part about enjoying a sports sedan.

■ The BMW M5 comes to battle with a 400-bhp powerplant, a sporty 6-speed manual transmission, 18-in. tires and shadow chrome wheels. Inside, the driver is treated to special M instrumentation and blue-and-black upholstery.

Tipping the scale at 3620 lb., the E55 comes ready to defend its title armed with the familiar 5.4-liter V-8 that AMG prepares at the Affalterbach factory for Mercedes-Benz. It's a modified version of the 5.0-liter 8-cylinder block that powers the SL500. The AMG engineers stroked the stock powerplant from 4966 to 5439 by installing a different crankshaft with connecting rod journals that are 4 mm farther from the centerline of the crankshaft. The offset increased the stroke by 8 mm to 92.0 mm, bringing it closer to the 97.0-mm bore and thus making the V-8 a nearly "square" engine. The crankshaft is dynamically balanced, with connecting rods and pistons selected specifically for each engine in equal weight-matched sets to ensure the 5.4-liter monster produces smooth power delivery of 349 bhp at 5500 rpm and 391 lb.-ft. of torque at 3000 rpm.

In addition to Mercedes' new generation of V-8s incorporating twin-spark/3-valve, single-overhead-cam technology with low-friction cast-in silicon-aluminum cylinder sleeves, AMG added higher-tension valve springs and lighter camshafts. And to satisfy the E55's thirst for fresh air now with more cubic inches to fill, AMG engineers installed a new dual-tube air cleaner assembly and modified the stock dual-resonance intake manifold with a wider cross-section to increase the airflow.

The road test

ON THE DRAG STRIP, THE TREMENDOUS power available to both of these sedans clearly showed in the performance numbers. Off the line, the BMW quickly grabs hold of the asphalt with

In My Opinion...

SAM MITANI, Feature Editor

After spending more than a week in Germany driving that country's fastest road-going machines, I realized that the name of the game there is top speed. And both the BMW and Mercedes-Benz are *Autobahn* demons of the first order. The difference between the two becomes apparent around a twisty road course. Surprisingly, the BMW exhibited significant understeer through tight corners, while the Mercedes-Benz felt more neutral and precise. Also, the E55 felt noticeably more stable under hard braking. So, despite not having a manual gearbox, my nod in this test goes to the Mercedes-Benz.

■ The reigning champion Mercedes-Benz E55 defends its title with a new Touch Shift 5-speed automatic transmission mated to the familiar AMG-prepared 5.4-liter 349-bhp V-8 engine. The red-and-black leather upholstery adds a little flair to the otherwise serious-looking cockpit.

Hot lapping brings out the true "sport" in this speedy pair

To get a better feel for how the M5 and E55 behave outside the confines of day-to-day street driving, we took them out to the Streets of Willow raceway for some back-to-back hot laps. With a varied assortment of short- and medium-radius corners, the Streets quickly put our two super sedans to the test. If either car had any distinguishing (or disquieting) behavioral traits, they'd reveal themselves here.

First car on the track was the M5. With a fast time of 1:06.96, the BMW lapped the short course nearly one second faster than the big Merc. As might be expected, some of this can be attributed to the M5's 6-speed manual gearbox versus the E55's 5-speed automatic. The 6-speed optimizes the BMW's power by always offering the right gear at the right time. As good as the E55 is at automatically adapting to different driving styles, it's no match for the instantaneous power afforded by the M5's manual. Using the E55's Touch Shift helps matters but still proves less effective than the manual.

In handling, the BMW feels surprisingly light on its feet (especially for a car that weighs 4000 lb.). Relatively flat cornering and good directional control allow the M5 to be pitched into turns at impressively high entry speeds. It reacts quickly to steering input and maintains chassis composure under both heavy braking and acceleration loads.

However, as competent as the M5's handling may be, it's not without fault. Considerable understeer from mid-turn to corner exit

stopped it from turning really quick laps. This consistent push makes it difficult to apply early throttle in medium- to high-speed turns. So while a little understeer is the best way to keep the M5 out of trouble on the street, at the track it prevents the front end from hooking up and fully exploiting the car's otherwise excellent handling.

On the other side of the coin, the E55 carved through the Streets' course with little of the M5's front-end drama. Slightly softer suspension tuning gives the E55 better front bite, allowing power to be applied earlier in the turn. The Mercedes' nose goes where pointed and holds tenaciously in all but high-speed corner exits. Combined with the 5-speed automatic, this setup produces a car that doesn't accelerate as quickly *out* of turns, but carries more speed *through* them.

The E55's lap time of 1:07.77 bears this out—the M5 gets from turn to turn more quickly, but the E55 actually achieves higher speeds in the turns themselves. In the process, the Mercedes also manages to be just a touch more comfortable, and thanks to its automatic transmission, takes less work to hustle around the track.

From a power standpoint, the E55 feels *faster*, while the M5 feels *quicker*. The BMW

literally leaps from corner to corner, whereas the Mercedes needs a fraction more time to gather up a head of steam. Once on a roll, however, the E55 seems to accumulate speed more rapidly. We didn't record top speed at the track, but I believe the Mercedes may have reached a slightly higher velocity at the end of the pit straight.

Never before have two production sports sedans performed so impressively yet remained so civilized. Short of strapping a La-Z-Boy to the roof of your 911, these two hot rods may be the only way of sharing true sports-car performance with four of your bravest friends.—*Kim Wolfkill*

---

modest wheelspin. Once on its way, the engine revs up so fast that it will hit the rev limiter in 1st gear before the tachometer reaches the 7000-rpm indicated redline. You have to shift to 2nd at the 6000 mark in anticipation of the fuel cutoff. The M's Getrag Type D 6-

speed manual transmission is precise; it takes a few trial runs, however, to get used to the clutch takeup for proper launches. The M5 clocked a time of 5.0 seconds from zero to 60 mph, and 13.4 sec. at the quarter-mile marker with the speedometer showing 108 mph.

Catapulting the AMG Mercedes from a standstill is a breeze compared with the M5. New for 2000 is a Touch Shift 5-speed automatic transmission for the E55 adapted from the just introduced S-Class. This system allows the driver to manually select the desired

■ On the track, the M5 is hunkered down and grips the asphalt with confidence and composure. The instant-on electronic throttle response and the precise manual gearbox will bring a smile to any driver.

gear by pushing the gear lever slightly left to downshift, or slightly right to up-shift. Best acceleration times of 5.1 sec. from zero to 60 mph, and quarter-mile times of 13.6 sec. at 106 mph, are recorded not by brake-hold launches or manually shifting, but by simply stomping on the gas pedal and watch-ing the E55 come alive with little wheelspin. The shifting algorithm and the mechanical actuation of the auto-matic transmission are so smooth that you'll notice only a change in engine tone and a slight pause in forward mo-tion as the car shifts to higher gears.

When it's time to hit the brakes be-fore the end of the drag strip, both the M5 and the E55 are more than happy to accommodate with their impressive ABS braking power. Riding on 245/40ZR-18s coupled to 13.6-in. vented discs up front and 275/35ZR-18s mounted with 12.9-in. vented discs bringing up the rear, the Bimmer need-ed only 129 ft. to stop from 60 mph, and 220 ft. to come to a halt from 80. Not bad for a car that weighs two tons.

The Mercedes comes with the exact same tire package as the BMW. Armed with 13.2-in. vented discs at the front and 11.8-in. vented discs at the rear, the E55's innovative Brake Assist, which recognizes emergency braking and automatically applies full-power ABS brake force, turned in stopping distances seen only on high-perform-ance sports cars. From 60 mph, the AMG accomplishes zero momentum in 122 ft. And from 80 mph, a remark-able 208 ft. is all the Mercedes needed to come to a complete stop.

It's obvious that keeping the M5's 400 bhp and the E55's 349 bhp in check requires more skills than you can acquire from a summer's worth of driver education, especially when you are traveling on unfamiliar or slippery roads. Just tell your parents that BMW's Dynamic Stability Control (DSC) and Mercedes' Electronic Sta-bility Program (ESP) can save you from running out of talent. Both sys-tems, with their electronic control unit actuating ABS, traction and yaw con-trol, will help the driver maintain di-rectional stability, preventing extreme understeer or oversteer situations. As for the parents, if and when they de-cide to risk their own money to test their own driving skills, both of the stability-control systems can be turned off with a button in the cockpit. How-ever, it should be noted that the Merce-des' ESP can not be completely turned off; it only allows for a higher thresh-old of yaw movements.

Bear in mind that although the fancy electronics can help you keep the M5 and the E55 on the road, you can't defy the laws of physics. A competent chas-sis design is needed to keep cars on the road. For the BMW, it starts with the standard 5 Series aluminum suspen-sion with anti-roll bars; MacPherson struts and split lower A-arms control the front tires, and a 4-link system is on duty at the rear. Upgrades for the M5 include a limited-slip differential, firmer springs and shocks, with auxil-iary polyurethane springs all around that stiffen under hard cornering. The Mercedes' underpinnings feature up-per and lower A-arms for the front, and a 5-link configuration at the rear. AMG specified 35-percent higher spring rates, thicker anti-roll bars and Bilstein digressive gas-pressurized shocks for the E55. "Digressive" means that the Mercedes will ride softer over smaller bumps at lower speeds, but the shocks firm up as the car is tossed around.

Through our slalom course, the M5's suspension is able to hold the line better and averages a higher speed of 64.7 mph versus the E55's 63.5 mph. The Bimmer exhibits better bal-ance, threading through the cones like a single unit. In contrast, the Mercedes feels a little disjointed, with the rear showing a tendency to dance around a bit before settling down. However, the E55 feels more nimble when it's tossed from side to side. And while the 0.90g skidpad numbers for both sports sedans are identical, the BMW's mod-erate to heavy understeer surprised everyone. The Mercedes, displaying less understeer, is better at keeping its front tires on track around the 200-ft.-diameter circle than the M.

The track test

WITH A STOPWATCH IN ONE HAND and a notepad in the other, I record Kim Wolfkill's lap times as he alter-nates between the M5 and the E55. And after two 5-lap sessions, Wolfkill is able to hustle the BMW across the finish line in a best time of 1:06.96, just beating the 1:07.77 sec. turned in by the AMG.

We all agree that both the BMW and the Mercedes have tremendous amounts of power to scoot you up to speed. The delivery of horsepower and torque is evenly distributed and comes on smoothly throughout the different gears. But the nod goes to the M5 for its deep-throated engine growl as it

■ The E55 is a real surprise on the racetrack. Its automatic transmission is ready to adapt to driver needs, and its chassis is more balanced, exhibiting less under-steer than the M5.

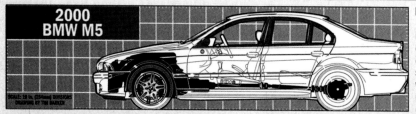

2000 BMW M5

SCALE: 10 in. (254mm) DIVISIONS
DRAWING BY TIM BARKER

List price/Price as tested: $69,400/$73,774
Price as tested includes std equip. (dual airbags, side-impact airbags, head-protection system, ABS, stability control, navigation system, auto. climate control, cruise control, 18-in. wheels, leather upholstery, AM/FM stereo/cassette with 6-CD changer, security, headlamp washer, heated seats, sunroof; pwr seats, windows, mirrors, door locks), gas-guzzler tax ($2100), luxury tax ($1704), dest charge ($570).

2000 Mercedes-Benz E55

SCALE: 10 in. (254mm) DIVISIONS
DRAWING BY TIM BARKER

List price/Price as tested: $69,800/$73,065
Price as tested includes std equip. (dual airbags, side-impact airbags, ABS, stability control, auto. climate control, cruise control, 18-in. wheels, leather upholstery, AM/FM stereo/cassette, security, headlamp washer, heated seats, sunroof; pwr seats, windows, mirrors, door locks), luxury tax ($1670), gas-guzzler tax ($1000), dest charge ($595).

General Data

	BMW M5	Mercedes-Benz E55
Curb weight	**4000 lb**	3620 lb
Test weight	4120 lb	3760 lb
Weight dist (with driver), f/r, %	54/46	55/45
Wheelbase	111.4 in.	111.5 in.
Track, f/r	59.6 in./60.1 in.	60.2 in./59.9 in.
Length	**188.3 in.**	**189.4 in.**
Width	**70.9 in.**	**70.8 in.**
Height	**56.6 in.**	**56.7 in.**

Engine

	BMW M5	Mercedes-Benz E55
Type	dohc 4-valve/cyl **V-8**	sohc 3-valve/cyl **V-8**
Displacement	4941 cc	5439 cc
Bore x stroke	94.0 x 89.0 mm	97.0 x 92.0 mm
Compression ratio	11.0 :1	10.5:1
Horsepower (SAE)	**400 bhp @ 6600 rpm**	**349 bhp @ 5500 rpm**
Torque	**369 lb-ft @ 3800 rpm**	**391 lb-ft @ 3000 rpm**
Maximum engine speed	7000 rpm	6000 rpm
Fuel injection	elect. sequential port	elect. sequential port
Rec. fuel	prem unleaded, 91 pump oct	prem unleaded, 91 pump oct

Chassis & Body

	BMW M5	Mercedes-Benz E55
Layout	**front engine/rear drive**	front engine/rear drive
Body/frame	unit steel	unit steel
Brakes, f/r	**13.6-in. vented discs/ 12.9-in. vented discs;** vacuum assist, ABS	**13.2-in. vented discs/ 11.8-in. vented discs;** vacuum assist, ABS
Wheels	cast alloy; **18 x 8 f, 18 x 9½ r**	cast alloy; **18 x 8J f, 18 x 9J r**
Tires	Michelin Pilot Sport; **245/40ZR-18 f, 275/35ZR-18 r**	Michelin Pilot Sport; **245/40ZR-18 f, 275/35ZR-18 r**
Steering	**recirculating ball,** vari power asst	**rack & pinion,** vari power assist
Overall ratio	14.7:1	15.2:1
Turns lock to lock	3.0	3.3
Suspension, f/r	**MacPherson struts,** coil & polyurethane springs, tube shocks, anti-roll bar/**4-link,** coil & polyurethane springs, tube shocks, anti-roll bar	upper & lower A-arms, coil springs, tube shocks, anti-roll bar/**multilink,** dual lower links, coil springs, tube shocks, anti-roll bar

Accommodations

	BMW M5	Mercedes-Benz E55
Seating capacity	**5**	5
Head room, f/r	37.0 in./35.3 in.	37.8 in./34.5 in.
Front-seat leg room	42.5 in.	44.8 in.
Rear-seat knee room	26.5 in.	26.0 in.
Trunk space	17.3 + 8.1 cu ft	17.9 cu ft

Acceleration

	BMW M5	Mercedes-Benz E55
Time to speed, sec		
0–20 mph	1.2	1.2
0–40 mph	3.1	2.8
0–60 mph	5.0	5.1
0–80 mph	7.9	8.2
0–100 mph	11.7	12.2
Time to distance		
0–1320 ft (¼ mile)	13.4 @ 107.8 mph	13.6 @ 106.0 mph

Braking

	BMW M5	Mercedes-Benz E55
Minimum stopping distance		
From 60 mph	129 ft	122 ft
From 80 mph	220 ft	208 ft
Control	excellent	excellent
Brake feel	excellent	excellent
Overall brake rating	excellent	excellent

Handling

	BMW M5	Mercedes-Benz E55
Lateral accel (200-ft skidpad)	0.90g	0.90g
Balance	moderate understeer	mild understeer
Speed thru 700-ft slalom	64.7 mph	63.5 mph
Balance	mild understeer	mild understeer

Interior Noise

	BMW M5	Mercedes-Benz E55
Idle in neutral	48 dBA	47 dBA
Maximum, 1st gear	72 dBA	70 dBA
70 mph	68 dBA	69 dBA

Fuel Economy

	BMW M5	Mercedes-Benz E55
Normal driving	15.1 mpg	18.7 mpg
EPA city/highway	13/21 mpg	16/23 mpg
Fuel capacity	18.5 gal.	21.1 gal.

Drivetrain

	BMW M5	Mercedes-Benz E55
Transmission	**6-speed manual**	**5-speed automatic**
Gear/Ratio/Overall/(Rpm) Mph		
1st, :1	4.23/11.89/(7000) 40	3.59/10.12/(5800) 40
2nd, :1	2.53/7.11/(7000) 67	2.19/6.18/(5800) 66
3rd, :1	1.67/4.69/(7000) 102	1.41/3.98/(5800) 102
4th, :1	1.23/3.46/(7000) 138	1.00/2.82/(5800) 144
5th, :1	1.00/2.81/est (6460) 155*	0.83/2.11/est (5150) 155*
6th, :1	0.83/2.33/est (5170) 155*	
Final drive ratio	2.81:1	2.82:1
Engine rpm @ 60 mph in top gear	2000	2000

*Electronically limited.

Subjective ratings consist of excellent, very good, good, average, poor; na means information is not available.

■ The M5 and the E55 are nearly equally matched in this battle of sports sedans, with the BMW taking a razor-thin victory here.

builds its pace toward the end of the straight. However, when it's time to dial in steering for the corner, the M5 falls behind the E55 by exhibiting too much understeer. The Mercedes is more balanced, enabling you to step on the throttle sooner out of mid-turn. "The E55 has a quicker and tighter turn-in feel than the M5. I had more fun in the Mercedes than the BMW on this track," Sam Mitani noted. For me, I prefer the more tied-down feel and cohesive movement of the M5 on the track, even if it means living with its understeering nature. Besides, the BMW's 6-speed manual transmission combined with the instant-on throttle response captures more of my enthusiasm than the Mercedes' 5-speed automatic.

And the winner is...

AT THE END OF THE DAY WHEN ALL the points are assigned and totaled, the BMW M5 barely squeezes past the Mercedes-Benz E55 by a mere 0.7 points to take the crown. In the performance category alone, the E55 has a slight lead because its braking and fuel economy numbers beat the M5's by a greater margin. But in the subjective ratings, the M5 comes out ahead because it offers a more enthusiastic feel to the driver. As for the price, even though the BMW is more expensive (about $700) than the Mercedes, the difference is so small in comparison to the total price that both cars receive the same score.

What does all this mean? It means that both the M5 and the E55 are extremely competent and equally matched in the "sports" and the "sedan" categories. You can compare their performance numbers against the likes of Porsches, Corvettes, or even Ferraris, and you'll find the BMW and the Mercedes easily keep pace with these purebred sports cars. And better still, you can enjoy all that and yet be pampered in a spacious and luxurious environment offered by a 4-door sedan. So, trust me, you can't go wrong with either one of them. 🔘

The Results...

Performance		BMW M5	Mercedes-Benz E55
Lap Times	50 pts.	50.0	49.4
0–60 mph	25 pts.	25.0	24.5
Braking, 60–0 mph	25 pts.	23.6	25.0
Slalom	20 pts.	20.0	19.6
Skidpad	20 pts.	20.0	20.0
Fuel economy	10 pts.	8.1	10.0
TOTAL	150 pts.	146.7	148.5

Performance points based on proportional scale.

Subjective Ratings		BMW M5	Mercedes-Benz E55
Engine	10 pts.	9.5	8.5
Gearbox	10 pts.	9.0	8.0
Steering	10 pts.	9.0	8.5
Brakes	10 pts.	8.0	9.0
Ride	10 pts.	9.0	8.0
Handling	10 pts.	8.0	8.5
Controls	10 pts.	8.0	8.5
Build quality	10 pts.	9.0	9.0
Exterior styling	10 pts.	8.5	8.5
Interior styling	10 pts.	9.0	8.0
Front-seat space	10 pts.	9.0	9.0
Rear-seat space	10 pts.	9.0	9.0
Trunk space	10 pts.	8.5	8.5
Noise	10 pts.	8.5	8.5
Driving excitement	10 pts.	9.0	9.0
TOTAL	150 pts.	131.0	128.5

Subjective ratings based on points awarded in each of 15 categories, by two editors.

Price		BMW M5	Mercedes-Benz E55
List price	100 pts.	100.0	100.0

Points-range for price equals average points-range of other categories, with 100 being maximum.

Results		BMW M5	Mercedes-Benz E55
Total points	400 pts.	377.7	377.0
(Total points ÷ 4.0)		94.4	94.3
STANDINGS		**1** BMW M5	**2** Mercedes-Benz E55

BMW M Roadster vs Z8
Can the bulldog catch the greyhound?

BMW M Roadster

THE M ROADSTER IS THE BULLDOG of the BMW family. Stocky in stature, muscular and determined-looking, it packs the power to deliver the performance promised by its looks. Its 240 bhp delivered through fat, 245/40ZR-17 Dunlop SP Sport rear tires, accompanied by the earnest growl of the six in-line cylinders and bark of twin dual exhausts, can punch this car though the 60-mph barrier in 5.4 seconds. Just accelerating up through the gears gives anyone who drives the M Roadster sheer driving pleasure.

With the arrival of its sibling, the Z8, the M Roadster is relegated to being former Top Dog in the open BMW line-up. While admittedly not as graceful, swift and polished as the svelte Z8, its attributes as a sports car keep it proudly in the pack. No lounging on the porch for the M Roadster; it wants to run.

One only need look at the price of the Z8 and at that of the M Roadster, and the value of the Z3-based contender is clear. Its performance numbers are impressive: 0–60 mph in 5.4 sec.; the quarter mile in 14.0 sec.; 0.89g skidpad performance; and an estimated top speed over 135 mph; like we ever *really* drive over 130 in our daily use of a sports car.

This is why we went to Thunderhill Park in Willows, California. On the track, the car does expose some of its bulldog tendencies. Understeer is present through most corners. During high-speed cornering maneuvers, the M Roadster demonstrates slightly nervous behavior, subtly moving around on the suspension, requiring the driver's inputs to be very smooth. Drivers with skill levels less than that of a professional racer will find the understeering characteristic comforting and are unlikely to experience any nervousness at road speeds.

The interior is a great environment for controlling the M Roadster as it vaults through its paces. Its hot-rod style is echoed in the two-tone wrap-around shapes of the dash and chrome-bezeled instruments. The high, bolstered sport seats give excellent support, and the sturdy roll hoops behind the occupants add the sense of security and confidence.

The view out the front of the M Roadster, with the small bulge in the center of the hood and the broad shoulders of the front fenders, gives the illusion of a tight T-shirt stretched across brawny shoulders. Wrapped tightly into the cockpit, it's easy to find yourself tugging at the leash, restless and anxious, to run with the big dogs.—*Bert Swift*

BMW Z8

IF YOU HAVE EVER DISPLAYED ADdictive tendencies, you'd best stay away from the driver's footwell of BMW's Z8, as the skinny pedal down there reigns over the firebreathing 400-bhp, 5.0-liter V-8 that also lurks in the M5's engine bay. Once experienced, you'll have repeated cravings for its shoulder-pinning thrust, near-telepathic throttle response and chunky rumble that burbles from stout-looking chrome pipes.

Yet for all its explosive might, the Z8's M62 engine, driven with its eight throttle butterflies nudged open, is as

BMW M ROADSTER	
Price as tested	$43,743
Engine type	3.2-liter dohc 24V I-6
Horsepower	240 bhp @ 6000 rpm
Torque	236 lb-ft @ 3800 rpm
Transmission	5-speed manual
Tires	Dunlop SP Sport 8080; 225/45ZR-17 f, 245/40ZR-17 r
0–60 mph	5.4 sec
Braking 60-0	121 ft
Lap time	2 minutes, 17.28 sec
Slalom	63.0 mph
Skidpad	0.89g

Swift (below) enjoys the stocky looks and aggressive personality of the M Roadster, with lots of horsepower and torque on tap from a silky-smooth 3.2-liter inline-6. However, argues Kott (opposite), the big-displacement V-8 and the sleeker design of the more sophisticated and addictive Z8 are hard to beat.

docile as Bambi on Valium. Helped by electronic control of both intake and exhaust camshaft timing, this power-plant twists out 85 percent of peak torque (369 lb.-ft.) at a parking-lot crawl—just 1500 rpm.

Equally habit-forming are the Z8's classic roadster proportions, essentially a modernization of the Albrecht Goertz-designed BMW 507 of 1955. Goertz himself has said, "If I were to design the 507 today, it would look like the Z8." And what a handsome, long-snouted profile it vaunts, with a short rear deck that tapers gracefully to a soft edge after bulging powerfully around 18-in. wheels and tires, as svelte as the M Roadster is stocky. But technology is not to be denied, as the high-set taillights, front turn signals and vent-mounted turn-signal repeaters all use neon lights, which flash

to full intensity 10 times quicker than incandescent bulbs. And the structure is an all-aluminum hybrid, with a stressed skin and underlying extruded-aluminum space frame.

M Roadster pilots used to its cramped driving position can stretch out in the Z8's cockpit. Though still snug enough to be intimate, there's a feeling of openness provided by the elegant, hooded instrument cluster that's situated dead center. And the dashboard, whose painted top-third evokes the dark, lacquered wood of a Steinway grand piano, cants noticeably forward to the base of the windshield. The steering wheel itself is a work of art, with three "spokes," each consisting of four silver rods, emanating from a small glossy black hub. There is stitched leather, thick carpet and silver-fobbed controls all done with a spare elegance that evoke a 1920s' Great Gatsby feel.

There is nothing dated, however, about the Z8's handling. Wide, sticky Bridgestone Potenza tires apply that impressive torque effectively; and modern suspension geometries, shock valving and springing limit the roll, dive and squat motions that make the M Roadster seem like a hobbyhorse by comparison. "Composure" sums up this chassis quite nicely, a sentiment echoed by Steve Millen after a few laps around Thunderhill Park: "The

thing with this car is you're going deceivingly quickly arriving at some of these corners at maybe 125, 130…and it's quite smooth the way it does it. All of a sudden you say, 'Gee whiz!'"

Ultimately, we had to give the Z8 (at $135,303 as tested, an expensive habit) back to BMW. Oh, the withdrawal. Transdermal patch, anyone?

—*Douglas Kott*

BMW Z8	
Price as tested	$135,303
Engine type	5.0-liter dohc 32V V-8
Horsepower	400 bhp @ 6600 rpm
Torque	369 lb-ft @ 3800 rpm
Transmission	6-speed manual
Tires	Bridgestone Potenza RE40; 245/45R-18 96W f, 275/40R-18 99W r
0-60 mph	4.5 sec
Braking 60-0	122 ft
Lap time	2 minutes, 13.30 sec
Slalom	62.3 mph
Skidpad	0.92g

BMW M3

Munich redefines the sports car

BY PATRICK HONG • PHOTOS BY GUY SPANGENBERG

MUNICH, Germany—THE LAST TIME WE had the pleasure of wringing out an M3 was in 1997, in our May issue. The 240-bhp 4-door not only raised the performance standards in the sports-sedan category, it also furthered our addiction to BMW's M cars. So when the new E46 3 Series made its debut in 1999, we wasted no time, immediately asking BMW about the next-generation M3. Late last year, BMW finally took the wraps off its newest M3 sports coupe. But rather than wait for the car to arrive in the States to put it through our road test regimen, we traveled across the

Atlantic and met it on its home turf in Munich. Call us impatient.

Originally begun in 1972 as BMW's motorsport division responsible for developing racing touring sedans, the 500-employee M division is now known more for building high-performance-tuned versions of Munich's production cars. Their latest project is transforming the E46 3 Series coupe into a potent M3 sports car. A *sports car?* You're probably protesting the use of this term because it is usually reserved for cars like Ferraris, Lamborghinis, Porsches and Chevrolet Corvettes. But look at the M3's

numbers: 3415-lb. curb weight, 6-speed manual transmission, 3.2-liter inline-6 with 343 bhp (DIN) and 269 lb.-ft. of torque. These figures alone deserve admission into the sports-car category. And unlike previous U.S.-market detuned M3s, the new American version will have a similar output of 333 bhp (SAE) and 262 lb.-ft. of torque.

However, having impressive specifications on paper is no guarantee of "sports-car" status in the real world. That's why we are spending two days and logging over 600 miles on German *Autobahnen* and country roads to evaluate the merits of this new

BMW. European Editor Paul Frère joins us in our fact-finding mission, and we also bring along a Chevrolet Corvette Z06 and a Porsche 911 Carrera for comparison. Our European-spec M3 test car would be duly challenged by the Z06, the nearest competitor in terms of price, and by the 911, the closest contender in power and handling dynamics. Of note, the 911 is on loan to us from our good friends at Ruf Automobile GmbH in Pfaffenhausen.

Traveling in caravan in the M3, the Z06 and the 911, our first day begins with a 3-hour run to Bosch's proving grounds in

Boxberg. After a brief stint in the BMW, I can already report that the car is dangerously addictive. The 3.2-liter inline-6 engine delivers smooth and seemingly endless amounts of torque in any gear, especially with the pistons cranking in the 3000- to 4000-rpm range. The tremendous power on tap is certain to persuade any driver's foot to firmly plant itself on the throttle. The accompanying deep-throated growl through a pair of twin tailpipes sounds like a big-displacement American V-8. There is no

■ Above, BMW's double VANOS variable cam consists of a crankshaft-driven dual chain sprocket system connected to the camshaft via two helical-toothed gearings to vary timing angles. The 3.2-liter M3 powerplant also features low-friction cam followers, six individual throttle butterflies, cross-flow cylinder head cooling, and a quasi-dry sump.

doubt that the M3 can easily keep up with the Z06 and the 911. At speeds in excess of 120 mph, the BMW feels rock solid, with no hint of instability even facing strong crosswinds and damp weather.

The M workshop engineers gave more power to the M3 mostly by retaining the oversquare design and increasing the rpm. Similar to how a Formula 1 race car's V-10 can produce gobs of horsepower at 18,000 rpm with pistons covering about 82 ft. per second, the inline-6 in the BMW, at its 8000-rpm redline, has a piston speed of more than 79 ft. per second. The result is a 6.9-percent increase in horsepower and 4.3-percent improvement in torque over the previous power unit, delivering 343 bhp (DIN) at 7900 rpm and 269 lb.-ft. of torque at 4900 rpm. The M3's specific output of 106 bhp per liter is one of the highest naturally aspirated production 6-cylinders in the world.

Using the previous-generation M3 engine block as the starting point, the stroke was lengthened from 89.6 to 91.0 mm, and the bore increased from 84.6 to 87.0 mm. To cope with higher engine speeds and the 11.5:1 compression ratio, lighter graphite-coated cast-aluminum pistons with forged cracked-steel connecting rods are employed. Cooling for the powerplant comes from oil-injection jets for the pistons and a single-piece 4-valve-per-cylinder head with integrated cross-flow coolant passages for more even distribution of heat. The M3 also uses a quasi-dry-sump system to ensure that the engine is well lubricated even when the car is subjected to high lateral loads

or straight-line acceleration.

BMW's MSS 54 management system, capable of performing 25 million calculations per second, controls the VANOS variable intake and exhaust camshafts to meet the high-revving M3 engine's demand for oxygen and its need to deplete spent air. It is also in charge of relaying throttle input signals to six electronically controlled butterflies directing air into the combustion chambers. One welcome feature is a switch on the instrument panel for sport mode that tells the MSS 54 to change to a more aggressive mapping of gas-pedal travel and throttle butterfly opening, allowing for quicker response as already seen on the Z8.

By the time we reach Bosch's proving ground, it is already late in the evening and a rainstorm has just passed through, leaving the facility slightly damp. Nevertheless, Frère is still able to assess the M3, the Z06 and the 911 individually on the road course and examine the handling characteristics of each car (his analysis can be found in the sidebar). And even though a proper slalom and skidpad result are not possible, I still take a turn in each car and run through our usual handling tests for brief

> "After a brief stint in the M3, I can already report that the car is **dangerously addictive.**"

wet-weather driving impressions.

Through the slalom, both the BMW and the Porsche retain most of their handling characteristics on the slippery asphalt, albeit with less adhesion. The M3 exhibits slightly more understeer than the 911, but feels more nimble and readily sets itself up to attack the next cone. The weighting of the rack-and-pinion power-assisted steering is a touch lighter than I would prefer, but nevertheless is very capable of communicating road conditions to the driver. In the Corvette, while its power and handling prowess in the dry wowed us back in our November cover story, its performance does not translate to wet-weather traction. The Z06's massive torque on tap makes the car tail-happy, so it's nearly impossible to carve any line through the cones in the wet. This, it must be noted, is with the Corvette's excellent stability control switched off.

Around our impromptu skidpad, the BMW can be easily controlled using throttle and steering, sliding on all four tires without much effort. Keeping the M3 from swapping ends and maintaining yaw stability is a torque-sensing rear variable differential lock that sends torque (up to 100 percent) to the wheel with traction. And that's with the Dynamic Stability Control (DSC) turned off! Our friends at *Auto Motor und Sport* magazine tell us that in the dry, their M3 achieved 0.91g compared to their 911's 0.96g on a 200-meter-diameter (764-ft.) skidpad.

On the second day of our trek, Mother Nature cooperates and gives us plenty of sunshine for our M3 acceleration and braking tests, plus handling evaluations on winding German country roads. On the drag strip, the BMW is very easy to launch. Hold the engine at 2500 rpm, drop the clutch, and the powertrain provides the perfect combination of wheelspin and tire grip to propel the car. The precise and short-throw 6-speed manual transmission helps get the M3 to 60 mph in 4.7 seconds, tripping the quarter-mile lights at 13.3 sec. at 106.8 mph. Compared with the 385-bhp Z06, the BMW is only a tenth of a second off in 0–60-mph sprints, and just a few tenths more to the quarter-mile mark. Head-to-head against the 300-bhp Porsche, the M3 comes out on top, beating the 911's 5.0-sec. clocking to 60 mph, and 13.5 sec. to the quarter mile.

What's even more impressive than the M3's forward thrust is its braking power.

Stopping from 60 mph needs a paltry 112 ft., and from 80 mph requires only 200 ft. A quick survey of high-performance sports cars around the world reveals that these results beat or closely match those turned in by Ferrari, Lamborghini and Porsche. BMW tells us even though the cars coming to America will not be fitted with the European-specific cross-drilled compound brake system (above), the 12.8-in. front and 12.9-in. rear vented disc brakes in the States will offer virtually identical performance.

Out on less-traveled German country roads, the M3 feels lighter on its feet than the Z06 and 911. Adhering to the BMW M car principle of "the suspension must always be faster than the engine," the M specialists made a few minor changes for the new M3 to improve the previous model's basic MacPherson strut front and multilink rear suspension. In addition to tweaks in springs, shock absorbers and bushings, the front axle is augmented by a 3-mm-thick aluminum thrust plate bolted onto the bearing points of the two front track con-

trol arms. This ensures rigidity under high lateral loads and sharper handling response. A V-shaped tie-bar added to the rear subframe is also in place for reinforcing the connection to axle components.

The result is an M3 that feels edgier, ready to change direction the instant the driver demands it. Compared with the BMW, the 911 is more relaxed in transitions, needing more aggressive steering input. The bigger size of the Z06 makes the car seem out of place on the narrower European roads. In fact, the American sports car feels a little nervous, a trait exacerbated by a chassis that almost responds too quickly to steering input.

The first-generation M3 set itself apart with exaggerated fenders and a large rear wing. The second M3 iteration lost its unique identity and came dressed in subtler styling cues. The latest BMW sports-car design strikes a perfect blend of E46 3 Series elegance with tight muscular looks. Front and center, an air dam set low to the ground flanked by two cooling air intake scoops clearly conveys an attitude of "get out of my way or I'll swallow you for lunch." The slight bulge atop the aluminum engine cover is not for show; it is necessary to accommodate the M3's new powerplant. Around the side, the BMW gills and flared fender arches stuffed

with massive 18-in. polished-aluminum wheels give the M3 an aggressive and road-hugging stance. Two sets of twin pipes at the rear—a BMW M trademark—tell us that this is a serious sports car.

Inside the cockpit, the first thing you'll notice are super supportive seats with adjustable side bolsters. Everything is wrapped in soft plastic or leather, accented with polished aluminum. And unlike most sports cars, there are two real seats in the back. In fact, the M3 is able to accommodate two adults, swallow all our test gear and photo equipment with no problem. Good luck trying that with the Corvette or the Porsche. At night, the instrument panel and the M-emblem on the gearshift light up in red, giving the cockpit a bit of a fighter-jet ambience. The M3 sacrifices very little interior luxury for sports-car performance.

In just 48 hours of living with the BMW M3, there is no doubt in my mind that this car deserves to be classified as a sports car, not a sports coupe. At a list price of about $45,000, it is a bargain for those who need everyday practicality but who are not willing to sacrifice real sports-car performance. Plus, when you see the Corvette or the Porsche on the road ahead, you'll be able to zoom past and have three of your friends help you wave good-bye.

>>>

The M3's double-spoke light-alloy wheels wearing low-profile 18-in. tires add to the car's muscular look and aggressive stance. Inside, classic BMW circular gauges on the instrument panel, extra-thick padding on the dash and on the steering wheel, super-supportive M sports seats, and polished aluminum-trim accents all around give the driver and passengers a real sports-car feel without sacrificing any luxury appointments.

AT SPEED WITH THE M3'S ADVERSARIES

▷ The BMW M3, Chevrolet Corvette Z06 and Porsche 911 under review are so fundamentally different in their philosophy that a direct comparison is difficult. Yet driving all three back-to-back is certainly illuminating.

Like its forerunners, the current M3 is a development of the present 3 Series BMW, largely re-engineered to make it handle and perform like a real sports car. Its inline-6 shares with Porsche's flat-6 the distinction of having perfect first- and second-order balance. Our test car has Michelin Pilot Sport tires, and according to the factory, its weight distribution is 53/47, near the 50/50 usually considered ideal for handling.

The current 911 has benefited from more than 50 years of development of the rear-engine/rear-drive layout, both in road and racing cars. It is recognized as one of the safest and best-handling road-going sports cars today. The available 300 bhp (DIN) from the 3.4-liter flat-6 engine makes it the least powerful car of the trio. Our test car is on Continental SportContact N1 tires on 18-in. wheels and comes equipped with the optional Stage 1 Sport Suspension from the factory.

The Corvette Z06 is an American legend, powered by the latest version of the 5.7-liter small-block V-8. The Z06's 385 bhp makes it the most powerful car of the trio; but what makes it stand out is its brutish 385 lb.-ft. of torque. Although the Corvette is only 4 in. wider than the Porsche and 3 in. wider than the BMW, it feels like a much bigger car. Tires are Goodyear Eagle F1s, especially designed for the Z06, fitted on 17-in. front and 18-in. rear wheels.

All three cars are equipped with yaw-control systems that can be switched off if required. All cars were driven with it both off and in action. However, in the Corvette there is an extra setting for active handling to turn off traction control, leaving the stability programming on but allowing for higher limits before the system intervenes. In the Porsche, even if the PSM (which also includes traction control) is switched off, the yaw control automatically comes back on whenever the ABS is put into action. This Porsche system also doubles as a differential slip limiter by automatically braking the spinning wheel.

All the test cars' vehicle dynamics are assessed on Bosch's proving ground in Boxberg, a small town located between Heilbronn and Würzburg. The selected road course is the fastest among the various available circuits, but unfortunately it does not include a high-speed turn, and the track is still damp from rain.

BMW M3 HANDLING ANALYSIS

▷ After a few laps with the stability system on, it is switched off because it intervenes too soon. It is certainly effective in keeping the car on the road if the driver makes a mistake; however, it does not allow any insights into how the car handles. When I first drove the M3 in Spain, both on the road and on the Jerez Grand Prix circuit, the car was brilliant, displaying crisp turn-in, excellent grip and first-class traction. The new wheel-speed-sensitive differential made it possible to balance the car in beautifully controlled, smooth 4-wheel drifts by applying appropriate accelerator and steering inputs.

On the narrow, wet road surface

Chevrolet Corvette Z06
Tested: August 2000

Porsche 911 Carrera
Tested: July 1998

■ On the track and under absolutely perfect conditions, the Z06 would probably be the fastest of the trio because of its power advantage. However, in the wet, the M3 and the 911 shine with superior traction, making them better all-around performers. The BMW offers sports-car handling capabilities with all the luxury appointments and room important for everyday use, and at a price that is difficult to beat.

	BMW M3	Chevrolet Corvette Z06	Porsche 911 Carrera
Current list price	est $45,000	$47,500	est $67,000
Engine	dohc 3.2-liter inline-6	ohv 5.7-liter V-8	dohc 3.4-liter flat-6
Horsepower	343 (DIN) bhp @ 7900 rpm	385 bhp @ 6000 rpm	300 (DIN) bhp @ 6800 rpm
Torque	269 lb-ft @ 4900 rpm	385 lb-ft @ 4800 rpm	258 lb-ft @ 4600 rpm
Transmission	6-speed manual	6-speed manual	6-speed manual
0-60 mph	4.7 sec	4.6 sec	5.0 sec
Braking, 60-0 mph	112 ft	123 ft	134 ft
Lateral accel (200-ft skidpad)	0.91g[1]	1.00g	0.91g
EPA city/highway	na	19/28 mpg	19/32 mpg
Length	176.9 in.	179.7 in.	174.4 in.
Width	70.0 in.	73.6 in.	69.5 in.
Height	54.0 in.	47.7 in.	51.4 in.
Wheelbase	107.5 in.	104.5 in.	92.5 in.
Track, f/r	59.4 in./60.0 in.	62.4 in./62.6 in.	57.7 in./58.3 in.
Curb weight	est 3415 lb	est 3115 lb	3080 lb

[1]Courtesy Auto Motor und Sport magazine.

2001 BMW **M3**

BMW of North America, Inc, P.O. Box 1227, Westwood, N.J. 07675, www.bmwusa.com

<table>
<tr><td colspan="2">At a Glance</td></tr>
<tr><td>0–60 mph</td><td>4.7 sec</td></tr>
<tr><td>0–¼ mile</td><td>13.3 sec</td></tr>
<tr><td>Top speed</td><td>155 mph*</td></tr>
<tr><td>Skidpad</td><td>0.91g[1]</td></tr>
<tr><td>Slalom</td><td>na</td></tr>
<tr><td>Brake rating</td><td>excellent</td></tr>
</table>

List Price: est **$45,000**
Price as Tested: est **$47,173**

Price as tested incl std equip. (stability control, traction control, dynamic brake control, limited-slip differential, ABS, heated mirrors, windshield-washer jets & door locks; air conditioning, moonroof; power windows, mirrors & door locks; cruise control, remote locking, AM/FM stereo/cassette, dual front airbags, front-door-mounted side airbags, head-protection airbags, onboard computer, anti-theft alarm), xenon headlamps (est $500), width-adjustable power front seats (est $750), luxury tax (est $343), dest charge (est $570).

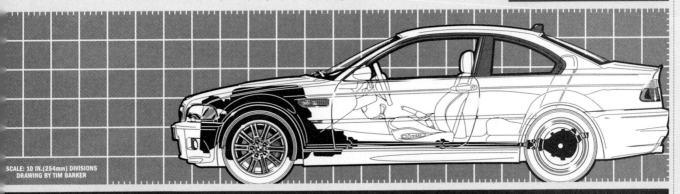

SCALE: 10 IN.(254mm) DIVISIONS
DRAWING BY TIM BARKER

SPECIFICATIONS

Engine

Type	**cast-iron block & alloy head, inline-6**
Valvetrain	**dohc 4-valve/cyl**
Displacement	**198 cu in./3245 cc**
Bore x stroke	**3.43 x 3.58 in./ 87.0 x 91.0 mm**
Compression ratio	**11.5:1**
Horsepower (DIN)	**343 bhp @ 7900 rpm**
Bhp/liter	**105.7**
Torque	**269 lb-ft @ 4900 rpm**
Redline	**8000 rpm**
Fuel injection	**elect. sequential port**
Fuel	**premium unleaded, 91 pump octane**

Warranty

Basic warranty	**4 years/50,000 miles**
Powertrain	**4 years/50,000 miles**
Rust-through	**6 years/unlimited miles**

Chassis & Body

Layout	**front engine/rear drive**
Body/frame	**unit steel**
Brakes: Front	**12.8-in. vented discs**
Rear	**12.9-in. vented discs**
Assist type	**vacuum assist, ABS**
Total swept area	**na**
Swept area/ton	**na**
Wheels	**aluminum alloy; 18 x 8J f, 18 x 9J r**
Tires	**Michelin Pilot Sport; 225/45ZR-18 f, 255/40ZR-18 r**
Steering	**rack & pinion, pwr asst**
Overall ratio	**15.4:1**
Turns, lock to lock	**3.2**
Turning circle	**36.1 ft**

Suspension
Front: **MacPherson struts, double-pivot lower L-arms, coil springs, tube shocks, anti-roll bar**
Rear: **multilink, coil springs, tube shocks, anti-roll bar**

General Data

Curb weight	**est 3415 lb**
Test weight	**est 3595 lb**
Weight dist (with driver), f/r, %	**est 53/47**
Wheelbase	**107.5 in.**
Track, f/r	**59.4 in./60.0 in.**
Length	**176.9 in.**
Width	**70.0 in.**
Height	**54.0 in.**
Ground clearance	**na**
Trunk space	**14.5 cu ft**

Accommodations

Seating capacity	**5**
Head room: Front	**38.5 in.**
Rear	**35.0 in.**
Seat width: Front	**2 x 19.0 in.**
Rear	**48.5 in.**
Front-seat leg room	**46.5 in.**
Seatback adjustment	**65 deg**
Seat travel	**9.0 in.**
Rear-seat knee room	**21.5 in.**

Drivetrain

Transmission:			6-speed manual	
Gear	Ratio	Overall ratio	(Rpm)	Mph
1st	4.23:1	15.30:1	(8000)	40
2nd	2.53:1	9.15:1	(8000)	66
3rd	1.67:1	6.04:1	(8000)	100
4th	1.23:1	4.44:1	(8000)	138
5th	1.00:1	3.62:1	est (7250)	155*
6th	0.83:1	3.00:1	est (6000)	155*

Final drive ratio **3.62:1**
Engine rpm @ 60 mph in top gear **2400**
*Electronically limited.

Instrumentation

300-km/h (186-mph) speedometer, 9000-rpm tachometer, fuel level, coolant temp

Safety

dual front and side airbags, head protection system, rear side airbags*, seatbelt pretensioners, anti-lock braking, traction control yaw control
*Optional

PERFORMANCE

Acceleration

Time to speed	Seconds
0–30 mph	**1.7**
0–40 mph	**2.8**
0–50 mph	**3.7**
0–60 mph	**4.7**
0–70 mph	**6.2**
0–80 mph	**7.8**
0–90 mph	**9.4**
0–100 mph	**11.6**

Time to distance	
0–100 ft	**2.8**
0–500 ft	**7.3**
0–900 ft	**10.4**
0–1320 ft (¼ mile)	**13.3 @ 106.8 mph**

[Graph: MPH vs SEC]

2001 BMW M3
¼ mile: 13.3 sec. @ 106.8 mph

1999 PORSCHE 911 CARRERA
¼ mile: 13.5 sec. @ 105.8 mph

2001 CHEVROLET CORVETTE Z06
¼ mile: 13.0 sec. @ 110.5 mph

Braking

Minimum stopping distance
From 60 mph ......**112 ft**
From 80 mph ......**200 ft**
Control ......**excellent**
Brake feel ......**excellent**
Overall brake rating ......**excellent**

Subjective ratings consist of excellent, very good, good, average, poor; na means information is not available

Fuel Economy

Our driving	**na**
EPA city/highway	**na**
Cruise range	**na**
Fuel capacity	**16.6 gal.**

Handling

Lateral acceleration
(200-m skidpad) ......**0.91g[1]**
Balance ......**mild understeer[1]**
Speed through
700-ft slalom ......**na**
Balance ......**na**
Lateral seat support ......**very good**
[1]Courtesy Auto Motor und Sport magazine

Interior Noise

Idle in neutral	**54 dBA**
Maximum in 1st gear	**86 dBA**
Constant 50 mph	**70 dBA**
70 mph	**74 dBA**

Test Notes:
Off the line, the M3 obtained the best acceleration run using drop-clutch launches with the engine revving at 2500 rpm. The torque delivery from the powerplant is silky-smooth, with no noticeable drop in power with each gearshift. The gear-shift is easy to navigate, albeit a little rubbery in feel. The BMW brakes are exceptional, with fantastic pedal feel. Through our unofficial wet slalom, the M3 understeers around the cones, but nevertheless feels agile.

Test Conditions:

Temperature	Humidity	Elevation	Wind
76° F	na	na	calm

and the slow corners of Boxberg's handling course, the M3 with the stability system turned off displays a surprising amount of understeer. The push is difficult to overcome because when subjected to the comparatively low centrifugal force obtainable on the slippery surface, the car shows little tuck-in if the accelerator is lifted. But when leaving the bend, the new differential ensures excellent grip, even at full throttle and in 2nd gear. With the stability system on, understeer is reduced, but the system intervenes so early that I felt it interfered too much with the driver's action.

◻ The Z06's massive torque-on-demand is impressive, but almost too responsive for slippery roads.

CHALLENGING THE CORVETTE Z06 AND THE 911 CARRERA

▷ The Corvette surprises me by displaying absolutely no understeer, even in tight bends. In the slowest corners the Corvette is probably the fastest of the three cars. With 50 percent more torque than the BMW and the Porsche, it is also the one that by far is most prone to break traction (if the yaw control is switched off). The fastest way around the course is by making the best of the lack of understeer by driving smoothly, trying to keep the car as close to the limit as possible, but never breaking the grip. And if traction

is broken and the tail swings out, it is difficult to catch because of the non-linear feel of the steering, perhaps because of its power assist coming in too quickly after turning a few degrees.

On the slippery track, the Porsche exhibits understeer, though less so than the BMW. It is also easier and requires less time to get it back on course. Even with the relatively low side force applied to the 911, it reacted more to slightly lifting the throttle. The car's stability system in this case makes hardly any difference because it intervenes only if the car gets really out of shape. One is less tempted to switch the Porsche's yaw control off because it leaves more room for the driver to exert his talent.

Based on my on-road and on-track experiences with the M3 here and in Spain, I know that it is a superb-handling car. Of the

three, the BMW also has the best driver's seat. Although it is not necessarily for everyone's taste, personally I like the Porsche's handling better because of its sharper but still moderate liftoff reaction. The 911 also has the most communicative steering, with the BMW a very close second. I like the lack of understeer displayed by the Corvette, but the pleasure is partly marred by the too-brutal operation of the power-assisted steering and of the accelerator pedal. On a proper racetrack in wet weather, the Z06 would probably be the most difficult car of the trio. But under good conditions, the immediate and explosive torque from the Vette is fascinating.

On all three cars, the brakes never showed any sign of fade, though the Porsche's require more force than the other two cars', in exchange for easier modulation.

THE VERDICT...

▷ Because of prevailing weather conditions and because our handling course only included slower corners, it is difficult to draw definite conclusions about the cars' absolute road behavior.

All three cars are very exciting to drive. However, overall, the BMW M3 probably should be declared the winner because, in addition to its stellar handling performance, it also wins points for having four proper seats and by far the largest luggage capacity. It can easily keep up with the other two sports cars, either on the highway or through the twisties. The M3 is also less expensive than the Porsche and about equal in price to the Corvette Z06.—*Paul Frère*

◻ The 911 is an outstanding all-around performer, but the closely matched M3 pulls ahead with better pricing.

2001 BMW M3

Living up to the hype

BY SAM MITANI
PHOTO BY THE AUTHOR

"THE SUSPENSION MUST always be faster than the engine." This is the principle applied to every BMW M car. And with the new, eagerly anticipated third-generation M3, BMW chassis engineers had their work cut out for them because the car's new engine has nearly 40 percent more power than the previous model.

The 2001 M3's 3.2-liter 24-valve inline-6 is 95-percent new—the only shared component carried over from the previous is the quasi-dry-sump oiling system—and offers a number of technological features borrowed from the company's Formula 1 engines. It features the double-VANOS system that continuously varies the timing of both the intake and exhaust valves for maximum power and efficiency, as well as F1-type intake runners that BMW claims account for 7 bhp by themselves.

Turn the ignition key and rev the engine, and you'll hear a deep, rich sound absent in the previous model. Of note here is the engine's piston speed, which at its 8000-rpm redline is nearly the same as that of the Williams-BMW F1 power-plant at its 18,000-rpm peak (79 ft. per second).

The result is a whopping 333 bhp at a high 7900 rpm (that's right, we no longer have to settle for a milder version of the European M3). Torque is rated at 262 lb.-ft. at 4900, most of which is available almost anywhere in the rev range. In fact, about 75 percent of peak torque comes into play at 1000 rpm. Therefore, the moment you press the throttle pedal, whether passing slower traffic or just trying to beat the Porsche 911 sitting beside to you to the next traffic light, you're rewarded with a robust forward lunge. The 6-speed manual gearbox, carried over from the previous model, has a firm feel, with well-defined gates and moderate throws.

So, does the new M3 handle "faster than the engine?" It's a close race, but let's just say the chassis engineers need to be commended. During a half-day of hot-lapping around the Circuito de Jerez racetrack in southern Spain, the M3 performed with the power and grace of a body-building flamenco dancer. Through almost every turn, the new Bimmer cornered flatly, predictably and with flawless balance. The car's rigid body and firmly tuned suspension system—MacPherson struts with aluminum lower control arms up front and a multilink setup at the rear—kept the car stable and body roll minimal.

The M3 did understeer through a couple of the racetrack's hairpins, but by simply modulating the throttle and brake pedal in midcorner, the rear end can easily be positioned in the proper place. (Note: My laps were performed with the Dynamic Stability Control turned off.) The steering, as with most BMW performance cars, displayed razor-sharp precision, maneuvering through tight chicanes with a simple flick of the wheel.

The new M3 looks meaner than the previous car, thanks to an aggressive face highlighted by a restyled front air dam, special "M3" grilles inset just aft of the front wheel openings, a subtle lip on the trunklid and sporty 18-in. forged aluminum wheels. The side mirrors have been redesigned—they're now as functional as they are good-looking. The dimensions of the car are close to a 3 Series Coupe's, with an overall length, width and height of 176.8, 70.1 and 54.4 in., respectively. Wheelbase measures 107.5.

But make no mistake: Despite its appearance as a sedan-based coupe, the new M3 is a pure-blooded sports car. And with a base price of approximately $45,000, it'll match the performance of any sports car in its segment. Look for the new M3 to reach dealer showrooms in January.

BMW M3 Convertible

At first glance, this category may seem an odd matchup of convertible versus sports car. But note: My own personal sports car is a Morgan Plus Four *4-Passenger* Family Tourer, and the M3 is every bit a sports car as well. It's simply a matter of definition.

One driver's definitive view: "The M3 Convertible has everything you could want in an open sports car—rocket-sled acceleration, excellent handling, muscular good looks. It also has decent luggage space and room for more than two people. And throw in the best exhaust note this side of a Ferrari."

"The M3 Convertible is actually *quicker* than the Boxster S," wrote another staff member, "with 333 silky-smooth horsepower on tap. Its styling is aggressive—to my eye, more so than the Boxster's. The Bimmer's tires fill out the wheel wells and give it a great stance."

"This car simply begs to be driven quickly," wrote another, "if only to listen to its wonderfully raspy exhaust bark. Do this with the top down, and it's all the more spectacular."

Most of us spent most of our driving time in this top-stowed mode: "Wick things up to a highway cruising speed, and the exhaust note is replaced by noticeable, though not unbearable, wind noise. With the windows up, even at elevated speed, it's pretty easy to carry on a normal conversation."

"Or enjoy a favorite CD," wrote another.

The M3 top's actuation is electro-hydraulic with automatic latching. The Boxster's is almost as easy, though it does require a manual flip of its center-header-mounted latch. "The best tops—BMW, Ferrari, Jaguar, Porsche—give a signal of some sort to show the action is completed," wrote one staff member. And these tops are so well finished, inside and out, that one of our

LIST PRICE: $54,045   **ENGINE TYPE:** 3.2-liter dohc 24V inline-6   **HORSEPOWER:** 333 bhp @ 7900 rpm   **TORQUE:** 262 lb-ft @ 4900 rpm   **TRANSMISSION:** 6-speed manual   **CURB**

drivers momentarily overlooked he was in a convertible: " 'How odd,' I said to my companion, 'an M3 without a sunroof....' "

M3 Convertible downsides? "Its top cuts into the trunk volume," commented one driver, "though it'll still hold the requisite golf clubs and a couple of small gear bags." It should be noted that the top's well can be collapsed when the top is up, reclaiming a bit of trunk space.

"If I were quibbling," wrote another, "I'd ask for a slightly more mechanical-feeling shifter with a bit shorter throw."

He had it right: quibbling.

On the other hand, the M3/Boxster S decision wasn't taken lightly: "The Boxster S is a *real* sports car," opined one staff member. "It looks like one, it handles like one—and, using its front and rear compartments, I believe it has more trunk space than the M3."

"This was a difficult choice," wrote another pensively, "because I love the Boxster S. Its track manners are exceptional. It makes any driver look like a professional.

"However," he continued, "to select a car for our readers—and for me if I had the money—my vote goes to the M3 Convertible." A critical mass of us agreed.

| lb | 0-60 MPH: 5.1 sec | BRAKING 60-0 MPH: 121 ft | SLALOM: 66.8 mph | SKIDPAD: 0.86g | TESTED: For this article |

> "You get the feeling that BMW finally took the gloves off and put the brass knuckles on for this fight. From the word go, the M3 impresses with a strong shove in the lower back"
>
> —*Bert Swift*
> ASSOCIATE ART DIRECTOR

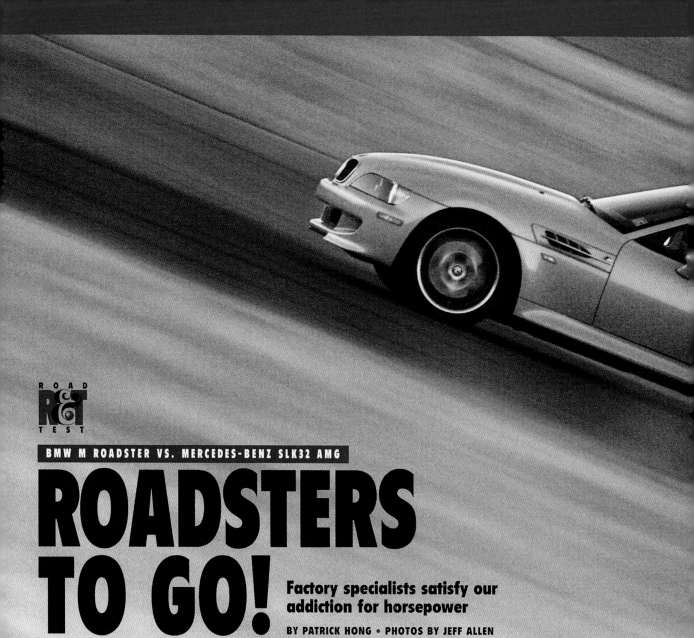

BMW M ROADSTER VS. MERCEDES-BENZ SLK32 AMG

ROADSTERS TO GO!

Factory specialists satisfy our addiction for horsepower

BY PATRICK HONG • PHOTOS BY JEFF ALLEN

WHEN THE 140-BHP BMW Z3 SHOWED UP in 1996, we applauded its contributing to the roadster revolution. Secretly, however, we wished it could have had more horsepower. When Porsche unveiled its 201-bhp Boxster in 1997, we fell in love with its sleek design, but felt it lacked a true sportscar's punch. In 1998, when Mercedes-Benz introduced its supercharged 185-bhp SLK230, we were disappointed once again.

Since then, different variations of the Z3, Boxster and SLK, even the Audi TT and the Honda S2000, have joined the ranks. Although all these cars pump out more than 200 bhp, we still crave more oomph from the roadsters. It's like a drug addiction that we car enthusiasts can't shake—there can never be enough horsepower for a sports car.

Perhaps both BMW and Mercedes-Benz have a few power-hungry fanatics working

in their companies too. That's why they have turned the M Roadster's and the SLK320's keys over to their respective M and AMG in-house motorsports specialists for serious strengthening. The results: a heart-pounding 315-bhp M Roadster and a lightning-quick 349-bhp SLK32 AMG.

So what is the first idea that comes to mind when these two roadsters with the power of Arnold Schwarzenegger show up at the door? Road trip! Senior Editor Andy Bornhop and I, along with photographer Jeff Allen, set out for a two-day Southern California jaunt that included an afternoon stop at Willow Springs Raceway to properly wring out these two muscle-bound beasts.

THE HORSEPOWER RACE

The BMW's 3.2-liter dohc engine is a modified version of the current M3's high-revving S54 power unit. But because of the

M Roadster's smaller dimensions, more restrictive intake and exhaust systems are needed so the S54 can fit beneath the hood. The S54 uses a cast-iron block for compactness and strength. Inertia-reducing, lighter finger-type rocker arms and valve springs connected to BMW's double VANOS (variable valve timing) are part of the aluminum cylinder-head design that helps the engine achieve its 7600-rpm redline capability.

Instead of the usual method of shoe-horning a bigger-displacement engine into a smaller car, AMG decided to supercharge Mercedes-Benz's 3.2-liter sohc V-6. The added force behind the SLK32's power-plant is an IHI (a Japanese company known for building turbochargers) Lysholm-type 14.5-psi-capable super-charger similar to the one used in the Mazda Millenia S. By using an electro-magnetic coupling, the supercharger can

be disengaged under partial load, allowing the V-6 to function as a normally aspirated engine. Only when the driver demands more power is the supercharger engaged, and the activation is not noticeable at all.

On paper, the SLK32 AMG's whopping 349 bhp and 332 lb.-ft. of torque seem to have a clear advantage over the M Roadster's 315 bhp and 251 lb.-ft. of torque. And with the SLK's engine capable of propelling the car with at least 300 lb.-ft. of torque from as low as 2300 rpm all the way up to 6100 rpm, its eagerness to accelerate is obvious.

However, stage the two German pocket rockets together at the drag strip and the SLK's 5.0-second time for 0-to-60-mph acceleration edges out the M Roadster only by a scant 0.1 sec. And quarter-mile sprints showed the AMG pulling slightly ahead with 13.5 sec. at 105.2 mph, again closely followed by the M Roadster's

time of 13.6 sec. at 103.4 mph.

Off the line, the Mercedes' torque delivery is so smooth that you hardly notice you are quickly building up speed. And the AMG SpeedShift 5-speed automatic transmission provides quick and seamless shifting. For the BMW, the significant power disadvantage is made up by the slick 5-speed manual transmission and precise clutch take-up, which give the car just the right amount of wheelspin at the start. And at full power, the engine growl through the M Roadster's exhaust tips is more entertaining than the SLK supercharger's uninspiring whirring sound.

ON THE ROAD

The ability of both cars to serve up more torque as soon as the driver demands it is really the magic of these cars. It doesn't matter if they are driven along mountain roads or passing slower traffic on a two-lane highway, both gobble up the road ahead seemingly without effort. Slide the shifter down a gear and the M Roadster delivers its torque quickly with much impact, as its engine spins toward the 7000-rpm range. For the SLK32, the 332 lb.-ft. can be tapped by simply depressing the throttle to the floor. It comes on progressively and seems endless.

After several stints in both cars, Bornhop comments: "The M Roadster is sort of a neo-Cobra in that it's a high-powered brute not suitable for the timid. That feeling is accentuated by the low-slung seating position and low beltline, which make you feel you are out in the open and almost vulnerable." In contrast, Bornhop describes the SLK32 as a car that is "easy to drive fast and hard to make any big mistakes. It has good overall balance."

For long-distance cruises, both the BMW's and the Mercedes' rides are surprisingly supple given their firmer suspen-

PATRICK HONG, Road Test Editor

In My Opinion... AMG has transformed an ordinary SLK320 into a first-rate sports car. Its outstanding handling dynamics around the racetrack closely match those of the BMW; very impressive. The M Roadster is everything I hoped it would be; it is fast and fun to drive on the racetrack. To choose one car that will satisfy occasional race-driving appetites as well as the rigors of day-to-day livability, my nod goes to the SLK32 AMG.

sion setups compared with their standard roadster siblings. The M Roadster's MacPherson struts, with arc-shaped lower arms up front and semi-trailing arms at the rear, soak up the road bumps without being jarring and still keep the car poised through tight bends. For the SLK32, the front's upper and lower A-arms and the

■ In style and in straight-line performance, the SLK32 AMG beats the BMW, thanks to its AMG body tweaks, attractive alloy wheels and potent engine. The supercharged V-6 is a tight fit, but it's worth the effort because 349 bhp has this delightful way of transforming a pleasant roadster into a ferocious Corvette killer. As good as the automatic is, it's a pity the car isn't available with a manual gearbox.

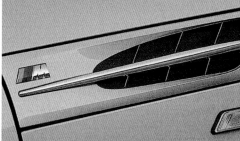

rear's multilinks give up some tautness when pushed hard around a corner, but reward with a more comfortable ride over the concrete slabs on the Interstate.

Top down, wind noise level inside both cockpits is well controlled so that the driver and the passenger do not have to shout at each other to hold a conversation. Top up, nothing can match the quietness provided by the SLK32's convertible hardtop. It really becomes a 2-door sports coupe when the Mercedes' automatic actuators and servos

do their magic and close down the hatch.

As for the M Roadster, its soft-top is well lined on the inside. However, there is still noticeable wind and road noise coming through the passenger cabin. Bornhop writes in his notes: "In the day-to-day real world, the Mercedes is an easier car to live with than the M Roadster. For me, it's more comfortable and its clever folding top keeps out the elements better than the BMW fabric."

Our interior noise measurement tells us that cruising at 70 mph, the BMW registered

77 dBA, while the Mercedes recorded 72 dBA. However, despite the factory claim of 5.1 cu. ft. of cargo capacity, the SLK's two-piece hardtop takes up much of the usable access when it is stowed inside the trunk.

Even though the BMW's classic roadster styling was a hit when it was introduced in 1996, now it appears dated on the road. Only minor detail changes such as updated M logos and gray dials with backlit markings inside the instrument cluster differentiate the new M Roadster from the old. By

Now aided by a double VANOS cylinder head, BMW's brilliant inline-6 produces only a bit more torque than before. But from 6000 rpm to the 7600 redline, the extra 75 horsepower can really be felt as a firm push in the back, regardless of which gear you're in. Retro touches include the chrome hood vents and chrome-trimmed gauges, but they're not carried out with quite the sophistication or quality found in the SLK32. Drivers over 6 feet tall routinely say they'd like a bit more seat travel.

comparison, the Mercedes' wedge shape still manages to look contemporary. A new integrated trunk-mounted spoiler, side skirts and front and rear aprons are AMG styling cues to give the SLK32 an aggressive look.

ON THE TRACK

At first glance, an automatic-transmission-equipped SLK32 appears out of place on a racetrack. But after several hot laps around the Streets of Willow track at Willow Springs Raceway, the SLK32's 5-speed AMG SpeedShift proved to be quite responsive. It is programmed to provide active-braking downshifts, meaning that lon-

gitudinal and lateral acceleration force calculations are performed instantaneously; thus at a pre-set rate of deceleration, the transmission will automatically kick into a lower gear. A lighter torque converter also minimizes slip in 1st gear, and when appropriate, a mechanical lockup clutch is employed in higher gears. Mercedes reports that the AMG SpeedShift provides 35-percent-quicker gearshift response than the standard automatic.

As impressive as the AMG SpeedShift is, it is still no substitute for a manual transmission. The BMW's precisely guided shifter gives the driver absolute control over gear selection, and rewards with pure excitement when a perfectly matched heel-toe-downshift is executed before entering a corner. Even though the Merc's SpeedShift is quick to select the gears, there is still a slight hesitation, whereas the M Roadster gives you power the instant you demand it.

The M engineers have made several improvements to the previous M Roadster's chassis design to enhance the car's handling capabilities. The front suspension sports a wider track for better straight-line stability and employs lightening holes and larger bushings to reduce unsprung weight

and ride harshness. A modified rear subframe housing a heavier-duty differential plus a lowered 1.1-in. ride height are designed into the new M Roadster to improve its overall balance and keep its rear in check through the turns. BMW's Dynamic Stability Control (DSC), its yaw control, is standard on the car.

For the SLK32, AMG engineers exercised

ANDREW BORNHOP, Senior Editor

In My Opinion...
Why the M Roadster over the SLK32? Simple. It has a manual gearbox, it doesn't rely on a supercharger for power and it's much more of a classic roadster, albeit one with brute power. Sure, the Mercedes is competent (and quick!), but you sit so deep inside that you feel isolated from the world, the opposite of what I like in an open-top car. In driver involvement and in overall fun, the BMW wins this battle; it's much more of a sports car at much less of a price.

The Results...

PERFORMANCE

Performance points based on proportional scale (normalization).

		BMW M Roadster	Mercedes-Benz SLK32 AMG
0–60 mph time	30 pts	29.4	30.0
0–¼ mile time	30 pts	29.8	30.0
Slalom	30 pts	29.3	30.0
Skidpad	30 pts	30.0	28.0
Braking, 60–0 mph	30 pts	30.0	27.9
Braking, 80–0 mph	30 pts	30.0	28.3
Fuel Economy	20 pts	20.0	20.0
SUBTOTAL	**200 pts**	**198.5**	**194.2**

SUBJECTIVE RATINGS

Subjective ratings based on points awarded in each of 12 categories by editors and scored based on a proportional scale.

		BMW M Roadster	Mercedes-Benz SLK32 AMG
Driving excitement	20 pts	20.0	17.8
Engine	20 pts	20.0	17.9
Gearbox	20 pts	20.0	16.8
Steering	20 pts	20.0	20.0
Brakes	20 pts	20.0	16.8
Ride	20 pts	20.0	20.0
Handling	20 pts	20.0	17.8
Exterior styling	15 pts	12.5	15.0
Interior styling	15 pts	12.5	15.0
Seats	10 pts	10.0	10.0
Ergonomics/controls	10 pts	9.4	10.0
Luggage space	10 pts	9.4	10.0
SUBTOTAL	**200 pts**	**193.8**	**187.1**

TOTAL POINTS (400 pts) Price independent		**392.3**	**381.3**

PRICE

Points based on a proportional scale; points-range for price equals average points-range of Performance and Subjective categories.

		BMW M Roadster	Mercedes-Benz SLK32 AMG
Price as tested	200 pts	200.0	194.5

TOTAL POINTS (600 pts) Price dependent		**592.3**	**575.8**

Final Standings

1 — BMW M Roadster

2 — Mercedes-Benz SLK32 AMG

---

their chassis-tuning expertise by extending the rear track, adding higher-performance shocks, springs and larger anti-roll bars to firm up the ride and keep unwanted lateral motions in check when negotiating turns. Both cars wear the same tires: Michelin Pilot Sports, size 225/45ZR-17 front, 245/40ZR-17 rear. The SLK32's yaw control system, Electronic Stability Program (ESP), controls the attitude of the car via vented 13.0-in. brake discs in front and 11.8-in. at the rear.

The rack-and-pinion steering on the M Roadster leads the car through chicanes with accuracy and excellent feedback. The SLK32's recirculating-ball unit is nicely weighted and offers quick turn-in response. But despite the SLK32's horsepower advantage, the M Roadster's livelier steering and chassis setup make for a more exhilarating car to drive on the racetrack. And while yaw and traction control can be completely deactivated on the BMW, the Mercedes' system can only be changed to a setting that allows for more wheelslip. This intrudes on the SLK's fun factor, and its ability to let loose and really strut its handling prowess. On the track, we also noticed that the BMW's 12.4-in. front and 12.3-in. rear vented brakes stayed responsive while the Merc's showed signs of fading.

Confirming our seat-of-the-pants feel, an impromptu timed session by Bornhop reveals that the M Roadster is slightly faster than the SLK32 around the Streets of Willow. The Merc's good overall balance and rock-solid grip, however, make it easier to drive fast. Bornhop notes: "The M Roadster is a bit tricky on the track. But there's also a bit more satisfaction involved when you nail a section perfectly. It requires a lot more driver involvement." As for the SLK32, he adds, "I came away impressed with how unflappable the Mercedes is. Too much entry speed will cause it to understeer, but at a slower pace the car feels agile, able to be pitched into corners with confidence that it will stay planted."

THE FINISH LINE

In the race to achieve the most horsepower, the SLK32 AMG dominates the M Roadster. However, taking the entire roadster package into consideration, the decision becomes complicated. Our results box shows that the BMW won this comparison test by coming out ahead in all the categories. It excelled in most of the performance tests, scored big in the subjective ratings and really pulled away in price. However, take a closer look and the points reveal the different focus of each car. The M Roadster edges toward catering to the weekend racer, while the SLK32 AMG takes a more civilized approach. Both roadsters, however, are capable high-powered sports cars and are guaranteed to satisfy power-hungry addicts.

2001 BMW M Roadster

BMW of North America, Inc
P.O. Box 1227, Westwood, N.J. 07675; www.bmwusa.com

List Price: $45,990   **Price as Tested: $47,188**

2002 Mercedes-Benz SLK32 AMG

Mercedes-Benz of North America, Inc
One Mercedes Drive, Montvale, N.J. 07645; www.mbusa.com

List Price: $54,900   **Price as Tested: $58,030**

Price as tested incl std equip. (ABS, front & side airbags, yaw control, traction control, limited-slip differential, retractable soft-top, cruise control, air conditioning, Harman-Kardon 10-speaker AM/FM radio/cassette, anti-theft, power seats, leather upholstery; pwr windows, mirrors & door locks), CD player ($200), luxury tax ($353), dest charge ($645).

Price as tested incl std equip. (ABS, front & side airbags, brake assist, yaw control, retractable hardtop, cruise control, auto. climate control, Bose 6-speaker AM/FM radio/cassette, keyless entry, anti-theft, 6-way power seats, leather upholstery; pwr windows, mirrors & door locks), value pkg (xenon headlamps and washers) $1075, brilliant silver paint ($640), luxury tax ($770), dest charge ($645).

General Data

	BMW M Roadster	Mercedes-Benz SLK32 AMG
Curb weight	**3160 lb**	**3280 lb**
Test weight	3340 lb	3460 lb
Weight dist (with driver), f/r, %	52/48	55/45
Wheelbase	96.8 in.	94.5 in.
Track, f/r	56.0 in./58.7 in.	58.6 in./58.1 in.
Length	158.5 in.	157.9 in.
Width	68.5 in.	67.4 in.
Height	49.8 in.	50.0 in.

Engine

Type	dohc 4-valve/cyl **inline-6**	supercharged sohc 3-valve/cyl **V-6**
Displacement	3246 cc	3199 cc
Bore x stroke	87.0 x 91.0 mm	89.9 x 84.0 mm
Compression ratio	11.5:1	9.0:1
Horsepower (SAE)	**315 bhp @ 7400 rpm**	**349 bhp @ 6100 rpm**
Torque	**251 lb-ft @ 4900 rpm**	**332 lb-ft @ 4400 rpm**
Redline	7600 rpm	6200 rpm
Fuel injection	elect. sequential port	elect. sequential port
Rec. fuel	prem. unleaded, 91 pump oct	prem. unleaded, 91 pump oct

Chassis & Body

Layout	**front engine/rear drive**	**front engine/rear drive**
Body/frame	unit steel	unit steel
Brakes, f/r	**12.4-in. vented discs/ 12.3-in. vented discs;** vac asst, ABS	**13.0-in. vented discs/ 11.8-in. vented discs;** vac asst, ABS
Wheels	cast alloy; **17 x 7½ f, 17 x 9 r**	cast alloy; **17 x 7½ f, 17 x 8½ r**
Tires	Michelin Pilot Sport; **225/45ZR-17 f, 245/40ZR-17 r**	Michelin Pilot Sport; **225/45ZR-17 91Y f, 245/40ZR-17 91Y r**
Steering	**rack & pinion,** power assist	**recirculating ball,** power assist
Overall ratio	16.3:1	15.5:1
Turns lock to lock	3.2	3.1
Suspension, f/r	**MacPherson struts,** arc-shaped lower arms, coil springs, tube shocks, anti-roll bar; **semi-trailing arms,** coil springs, tube shocks, anti-roll bar	**upper & lower A-arms,** coil springs, tube shocks, anti-roll bar; **multilink,** coil springs, tube shocks, anti-roll bar

Accommodations

Seating capacity	**2**	**2**
Head room	37.0 in.	37.0 in.
Leg room	42.0 in.	44.5 in.
Trunk space	5.0 cu ft	7.2 cu ft (top up), 5.1 cu ft (top down)

Acceleration

	BMW M Roadster	Mercedes-Benz SLK32 AMG
Time to speed, sec		
0–20 mph	1.2	1.2
0–40 mph	2.8	2.8
0–60 mph	5.1	5.0
0–80 mph	8.3	8.2
0–100 mph	12.3	12.1
Time to distance		
0–1320 ft (¼ mile)	13.6 @ 103.4 mph	13.5 @ 105.2 mph

Braking

Minimum stopping distance		
From 60 mph	118 ft	127 ft
From 80 mph	211 ft	224 ft
Control	excellent	excellent
Brake feel	very good	good
Overall brake rating	excellent	very good

Handling

Lateral accel (200-ft skidpad)	0.91g	0.85g
Balance	mild understeer	moderate understeer
Speed thru 700-ft slalom	63.5 mph	65.0 mph
Balance	mild understeer	moderate understeer

Fuel Economy

Our driving	19.6 mpg	19.7 mpg
EPA city/highway	17/25 mpg	18/24 mpg
Cruise range	360 miles	345 miles
Fuel capacity	16.6 gal.	18.5 gal.

Interior Noise

Idle in neutral	60 dBA	55 dBA
Maximum, 1st gear	81 dBA	75 dBA
70 mph	77 dBA	72 dBA

Drivetrain

Transmission	**5-speed manual**	**progressive 5-speed automatic**
Gear/Ratio/Overall/(Rpm) Mph		
1st, :1	4.21/13.26/(7600) 41	3.59/11.02/(6200) 37
2nd, :1	2.49/7.84/(7600) 69	2.19/6.72/(6200) 61
3rd, :1	1.66/5.23/(7600) 104	1.41/4.33/(6200) 94
4th, :1	1.24/3.91/(7600) 139	1.00/3.07/(6200) 133
5th, :1	1.00/3.15/(6800) 155*	0.83/2.55/(6000) 155*
Final drive ratio	3.15:1	3.07:1
Engine rpm @ 60 mph in top gear	2100 rpm	2100 rpm

*Electronically limited.

Subjective ratings consist of excellent, very good, good, average, poor; na means information is not available.

Brothers in Arms—
BMW M3
& M3 GTR

Separated at birth, but sharing the same family values

BY KIM WOLFKILL   PHOTOS BY GUY SPANGENBERG

FOR BMW FANS EVERYWHERE, the past year has been an exciting, if not memorable one. Last spring, the introduction of the new E46-based M3 put an end to the Euro-spec-vs.-U.S.-spec engine argument, long a sore point with U.S. owners. Starting with the 2001 model, all M3s come equipped with the same smooth 333-bhp 3.2-liter inline-6. Complemented by an equally entertaining chassis, this more powerful M3 has the sort of performance to go toe-to-toe with perennial

sports-car favorites like the Porsche 911 Carrera and Chevrolet Corvette.

Last racing season, BMW also enjoyed enormous success campaigning its new M3 GTR racer. Based on the E46 platform but powered by a purpose-built 4.0-liter V-8, the controversial M3 GTR completely dominated the 2001 American Le Mans Series (ALMS) season, sweeping both the driver and manufacturer titles in the GT class. However, from its inaugural victory at Sears Point (About the Sport, October 2001) to its

season-ending triumph at Petit Le Mans, the GTR encountered more challenges off the track than on it.

Controversy aside, there's no denying that the GTR is the most highly evolved M3 to ever turn a wheel. From its meticulously crafted chassis to the hand-built V-8, it represents the pinnacle of M3 development.

Which brings us to Sebring International Raceway, the track where, in a cruel twist of fate, the M3 GTR did not compete in this year's 12 Hours of

Sebring (see sidebar). Thanks to BMW of North America and Tom Milner, owner of the Prototype Technology Group racing team, I was given the opportunity to compare the street M3 to PTG's Petit Le Mans-winning M3 GTR. Two distinctly different cars, for sure, but both sharing common DNA, and as such, the same quest for speed.

M3 ROAD CAR

Walk up to the M3 and there's no mistaking it for a standard 3 Series coupe.

Subtle yet suggestive fender flares, 18-in. wheels, sleeker mirrors and a more purposeful nose quietly hint at the serious performance hidden within. Turn the key, stab the throttle and the M3's sporting intentions become self-evident. This car is about more than simply eclipsing its E36 predecessor; it's about totally rewriting the books.

With more horsepower and torque, and one of the industry's sexiest exhaust notes, the engine alone is worth the price of admission. With 3.2 liters of smooth-revving snarl, it belts out a solid 333 bhp and 269 lb.-ft. of torque with power at just about any rpm. Thanks to its larger displacement and such tricky technical items as six individual and electronically controlled throttle butterflies, high-pressure double VANOS valve operation and an 8000-rpm redline, the M3 enjoys a massive 108-bhp advantage over its tamer 330Ci sibling. Or when compared with the previous E36 M3, the new car tromps it by 93 horses on its way to surpassing the vaunted 100-bhp-per-liter mark.

At our test at Sebring, the first order of business is to turn on the Sport mode and flip off the Dynamic Stability Control. Selecting Sport tells the engine-management system to apply a more aggressive map to the gas-pedal travel and throttle butterfly openings, while disengaging the DSC simply makes it easier to slide the car around. In the Sport setting, throttle response feels instantly more reactive and is accompanied by a decidedly more menacing bark from the M3's exhaust. Power on upshifts is almost instantaneous as the car leaps forward with nary a pause in acceleration. Helping matters is a slick 6-speed transmission that makes short work of gear changes to optimize time spent in the meaty part of the powerband. The sweetest range comes between 5000–8000 rpm when the engine just keeps pulling harder and screaming louder.

After a few familiarization laps, it's easy to see why this latest iteration has quickly proven such a favorite among serious enthusiasts. It possesses an instantly reassuring composure that makes it easy to push hard almost right away. Around Sebring's high-speed sweeping Turn 1, for instance, the M3 maintains excellent at-limit balance that allows it to be drifted predictably through the corner's exit lap after lap. At lower speeds, hints of understeer can be easily remedied by simply maintaining light braking to add front bite followed by a welcome dose of the gas pedal.

This track-happy balance comes courtesy of some thoughtful tuning of the MacPherson-strut front and multilink rear suspension along with the M Variable limited-slip differential. At speed, the M3 soaks up Sebring's infamous bumps and surface changes with little protest and puts its power down effortlessly. When a change in attitude is required in most any part of a turn, a little throttle dancing produces the desired result. And despite its rather hefty 3415-lb. curb weight, the M3 still manages to stay relatively light on its feet and handle quick transitions with a surprisingly deft touch. For pure track use the suspension tuning could be firmer, but given the demands of the street, this setup strikes a good compromise between comfort and performance.

The steering, on the other hand, could stand some firming up and a bit less power assist. It lacks some of the trademark feel of previous M3s, instead coming across as overboosted and a little on the light side. This probably doesn't hurt lap times around a racetrack, but it certain affects the overall driving experience on a day-to-day basis. This has been a common complaint of E46 owners in general, so let's hope BMW has been listening.

Steering quibbles aside, it's back to business, as all things that accelerate must also slow down. In the case of the M3, this is dutifully accomplished by a quartet of beefy vented brake rotors (12.8-in. front, 12.9-in. rear) and the accompanying electronic aids (ABS, Dynamic Brake Control). Mysteriously, our test car at Sebring did not exhibit the same level of braking performance we've experienced in other M3s, which have all been excellent. In this case, the Sebring M3 suffered from brake fade to a degree that isn't necessarily reflected in the test numbers but could certainly be felt at higher track speeds.

On the street or at the track, the BMW M3 is a car that you can simply get in and drive. Whether it's the first few turns of an unfamiliar road or the warm-up laps at a new track, there are few cars as easy to feel comfortable with.

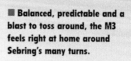

■ Balanced, predictable and a blast to toss around, the M3 feels right at home around Sebring's many turns.

A well-engineered balance of power, performance and civility makes it one of the most enjoyable sports cars around. With that in mind, what better place to start when building a championship-winning race car?

M3 GTR RACER

Purpose-built race cars are designed to do one thing and one thing only—go faster than every other car in the field. With that in mind, the engineers at BMW Motorsport set about building the fastest production-based race car the 2001 ALMS GT-class rules would allow. They utilized data not only from the E46 street-car program, but also valuable technical input from Tom Milner's Team PTG to create a car that would be superior to the 2000 version in every significant way.

As the regulations were written at the

time, this meant they could take a heavily tweaked production E46 unit-body and drop in an all-new specially developed 4.0-liter V-8. Provided BMW also built a street version within a year of the M3 GTR's introduction, it was eligible to compete in the 2001 season. They accomplished that midway through the season, thereby validating the race car, at least in the eyes of the rulebook.

The No. 6 Team PTG M3 GTR represents BMW's interpretation of those rules and the masterfully executed end product. Practically reengineered from the wheels up, the M3 GTR suffers few compromises on its way to being the world's most complete GT-class racer. It goes beyond simply bolting a more powerful V-8 into a revised chassis. The M3 GTR also handles better, brakes better, has better aerodynamics and is a more responsive car overall.

Starting with the chassis, engineers significantly stiffened the unit-body and reworked the suspension design to better accommodate the lower ride height required for racing. The standard MacPherson-strut front and rear multilink configuration remains, but all the major suspension components (shocks, struts, springs, anti-roll bars) are race-tuned and fully adjustable. The front and rear tracks have also been increased significantly to accommodate massive 11 x 18-in. wheels and Yokohama racing slicks. The combination of 15-in. front brake rotors and 6-piston Brembo calipers with 12.3-in. rears and 4-piston calipers delivers stopping power on par with many faster GTS-class cars.

Nestled low and set back in the engine bay sits BMW's now notorious 4.0-liter V-8. Pumping out a claimed 444 bhp and

354 lb.-ft. of torque, this remarkable powerplant makes no secret of its highly developed nature. BMW denies it was originally earmarked for the German DTM series, but it's still tough to hide its very high-tech roots. An oversquare bore and stroke, four valves per cylinder and a 180-degree crankshaft make for a powerful, high-revving mill with an exhaust note more akin to a Formula 1 V-10 than a traditional V-8. And thanks to its featherweight flywheel and vastly reduced reciprocating mass, this V-8 revs quicker than almost any engine in the paddock. A carbon clutch and 6-speed Hewland gearbox round out the powertrain that's easily the most advanced in GT racing.

Strapped in and fired up, the toughest task is getting the M3 GTR out of Sebring's pit lane. The engine's lightweight internals

"Rolling on the throttle **unleashes an intoxicating blast** of smooth, linear power that continues unabated in every gear."

The cockpit, left, includes only the essential controls, switches and instrumentation necessary for racing. Heavily reinforced chassis and rollcage members stiffen the production unit-body while offering extensive driver protection. The trunk, below, houses the carbon-fiber fuel cell and additional bracing. The heart of the M3 GTR is BMW's purpose-built 4.0-liter V-8, right. With more horsepower and torque than the inline-6 it replaced, this controversial engine powered the GTR to driver and manufacturer championships in 2001.

and touchy carbon clutch require a slow constant drag to launch without stalling. Release the clutch any quicker and the engine instantly dies. Out on the track, it's surprisingly easy to drive for such a potent race car. As speeds climb and cornering forces increase, its considerable talents quickly begin to make themselves known.

Immediately apparent is the overwhelming sense of precision. This car goes exactly where it's pointed with no wasted energy or unwanted commotion. It arcs through turns with laser-like accuracy and absolute consistency. Combined with uncanny balance, the GTR inspires confidence in its ample limits. Around corners, over bumps or under braking, it's generally unaffected by what's happening around it. Instead, it allows the driver to concentrate on more important matters like consistency and speed.

Rolling on the throttle unleashes an intoxicating blast of smooth, linear power that continues unabated in every gear. Excellent torque throughout the rev range guarantees strong acceleration out of turns, while individual rev limits for each gear further optimize engine performance. Straight-cut gears make gear-

changes ultra-quick and, like the rest of the car, exceedingly precise.

Rounding out the M3 GTR's bag of tricks is braking performance with few, if any, rivals. Even the almighty Porsches, famous for amazing brakes, can't compete with this M3. Apart from the sheer stopping power, what's more impressive is the uncanny control it possesses under hard braking. Jumping on the binders at 150 mph produces huge deceleration forces without the penalty of unwanted instability. Instead, it tracks true when slowing for corners, takes a solid set turning in, then

rockets out with utter confidence.

While its V-8 engine garnered most of the attention during the 2001 race season, the M3 GTR is about more than just its controversial powerplant. Surrounding this engine is one of the sport's most complete and well-developed race cars. Whether it complies with the spirit of the production-based GT class is still open to debate, but what isn't debatable is that in the world of M3s they don't get any better than this.

HOW SIMILAR ARE THEY, REALLY?

Truthfully, there aren't that many similarities between the street M3 and its M3 GTR sibling. From a technical standpoint, they do share the same unit-body, drivetrain layout, suspension configuration and overall shape, but beyond that, they're two very different cars with entirely different purposes.

However, what they do share are core BMW traits like balance, control and predictability. Even with their wildly disparate goals, both make it easy to get acquainted and up to speed. The street M3 is obviously the milder of the two, but even the GTR, at least by racing standards, is a surprisingly benign car to jump into cold. Both possess a similarly reassuring degree of balance that encourages you to have some fun. So while the M3 and M3 GTR may seem worlds apart, common traits still hold them together, leaving no doubts about their family lineage. ◉

Why no M3 GTR in the ALMS?

Before it had ever turned a lap, the M3 GTR was the center of controversy in the ALMS GT class. A category for production-based cars with road-going counterparts, GT has been the playground of Porsche's GT3R/RS for the previous two seasons. With the arrival of the BMW GTR, however, all that changed as the V-8-powered coupe decimated the competition, winning six straight races en route to both the driver and manufacturer championships.

And while it was built in accordance with the Automobile Club de l'Ouest's (ACO) 2001 homologation requirements (at least one V-8-powered street M3 need be offered for sale within a year of the race car's debut), critics felt the GTR hurt the class and, as Porsche officials put it, violated the "spirit" of the rules.

After all the political chips had fallen, BMW found they'd won the battle but lost the war. For the 2002 season, the ACO drew up stricter eligibility requirements for GT-class cars competing in the 24 Hours of Le Mans and ALMS. Aimed squarely at the M3 GTR, the 2002 rules require GT cars to be based on a vehicle in series production with output of one car per week using an engine derived from a production model built in numbers of 1000 or more.

Any manufacturer unable to meet these criteria is still permitted to compete, but with a 20 percent reduction in their air intake restrictors and the addition of 100 kg. of ballast.

Following careful evaluation and testing over the winter, BMW management concluded that the company could neither meet the required production numbers nor compete effectively with the additional air restrictor and weight penalties. During pre-season testing at Sebring, the restricted M3 GTR was off the pace significantly, turning laps some 3 seconds slower than last year.

Consequently, the BMW Motorsport and Prototype Technology Group teams withdrew from the 2002 ALMS season just two months prior to the 12 Hours of Sebring season-opener. So no more M3 GTR and no Porsche-BMW battles this year. Both BMW and the ALMS say they're hopeful of a return in 2003, but until then, the GT class sadly returns to nearly an all-Porsche affair.—*KW*

2001 BMW **M3**

BMW of North America, Inc
P.O. Box 1227, Westwood, N.J. 07675; www.bmwusa.com

BMW **M3 GTR**

Prototype Technology Group
441 Victory Rd., Winchester, Va. 22602; www.ptgracing.com

st Price: $45,400 **Price as Tested: $53,591**

List Price: $470,000 **Price as Tested: $470,000**

ce as tested incl std equip. (stability control, traction control, dynamic brake control, limited-slip diff, S, air cond, power windows, mirrors & door locks; cruise control, remote locking, dual front airbags & e airbags, head-protection airbags, onboard computer, anti-theft alarm), cold weather pkg (heated front ats & headlight washers, ski bag) $700, Luxury pkg (power moonroof, dual power front seats w/memory, ppa leather, rain-sensing windshield wipers) $3100, adjustable seatback width ($500), titanium silver etallic paint ($475), xenon headlights ($500), AM/FM/CD player ($200), Harman Kardon sound system 675), gas-guzzler tax ($1000), luxury tax ($396), dest charge ($645).

Price as tested incl BMW Motorsport rolling chassis, engine, transmission, electronic data acquisition & telemetry system.

General Data

	BMW M3	BMW M3 GTR
rb weight	**3415 lb**	2425 lb
st weight	3595 lb	2731 lb
eight dist (with driver), f/r, %.	est 53/47	50/50
heelbase	107.5 in.	107.5 in.
ack, f/r	59.4 in./60.0 in.	63.3 in./63.1 in.
ngth	176.8 in.	181.6 in.
dth	70.1 in.	74.8 in.
eight	54.0 in.	52.0–52.4 in. adj.

Engine

pe	dohc 4-valve/cyl **inline-6**	dohc 4-valve/cyl **V-8**
splacement	3245 cc	3997 cc
re x stroke	87.0 x 91.0 mm	94.0 x 72.0 mm
mpression ratio	11.5:1	12.0:1
orsepower (SAE)	**333 bhp @ 7900 rpm**	**444 bhp @ 7500 rpm**
rque	**269 lb-ft @ 4900 rpm**	**354 lb-ft @ 5500 rpm**
edline	8000 rpm	8500 rpm
el injection	elect. sequential port	elect. sequential port
ec. fuel	prem. unleaded, 91 pump oct	Elf race fuel, 100 oct

Chassis & Body

yout	**front engine/rear drive**	**front engine/rear drive**
ody/frame	unit steel	steel, fiberglass/unit steel
akes, f/r	**12.8-in. vented discs/ 12.9-in. vented discs;** vac asst, ABS	**15.0-in. vented discs/ 12.3-in. discs**; driver adjustable balance bar
heels	aluminum alloy; **18 x 8J f, 18 x 9J r**	forged aluminum, **18 x 11**
res	Michelin Pilot Sport; **225/45ZR-18 f, 245/40ZR-18 r**	Yokohama Racing; **290/650-18 f, 290/680-18 r**
eering	**rack & pinion**, power assist	**rack & pinion**, vari power assist
Overall ratio	15.4:1	na
Turns lock to lock	3.0z	1.25
uspension, f/r	**MacPherson struts**, double-pivot lower L-arms, coil springs, tube shocks, anti-roll bar/**multi-link**, coil springs, tube shocks, anti-roll bar	**MacPherson struts**, coil springs, adj tube shocks, adj anti-roll bar/**central link**, coil springs, adj tube shocks, adj anti-roll bar

Accommodations

eating capacity	**5**	**1**
ead room, f/r	38.5 in./35.0 in.	na
eat width	35.0 in.	na
ont-seat leg room	46.5 in.	na
ar-seat knee room	21.5 in.	na
eat travel	9.0 in.	na
unk space	10.7 cu ft	na

Acceleration

	BMW M3	BMW M3 GTR
Time to speed, sec		
0–20 mph	1.7	1.5
0–40 mph	2.8	2.1
0–60 mph	4.7	3.3
0–80 mph	7.8	4.9
0–100 mph	11.6	7.1
Time to distance		
0–1320 ft (¼ mile)	13.3 @ 106.8 mph	11.3 @ 125.3 mph

Braking

Minimum stopping distance		
From 60 mph	112 ft	94 ft
From 80 mph	200 ft	165 ft
Control	excellent	excellent
Brake feel	excellent	excellent
Overall brake rating	excellent	excellent

Handling

Lateral accel (200-ft skidpad)	0.89g	na
Balance	mild understeer	na
Speed thru 700-ft slalom	66.6 mph	na
Balance	mild understeer	na

Fuel Economy

Our driving	na	4.8 mpg
EPA city/highway	16/24 mpg	na
Fuel capacity	16.6 gal.	26.4 gal.

Interior Noise

Idle in neutral	54 dBA	na
Maximum, 1st gear	86 dBA	na
70 mph	74 dBA	na

Drivetrain

Transmission	**6-speed manual**	**6-speed manual**
Gear/Ratio/Overall/(Rpm) Mph		
1st, :1	4.23:1/15.30:1/(8000) 40	2.50:1/8.66:1/(7500) 69
2nd, :1	2.53:1/9.15:1/(8000) 66	2.07:1/7.16:1/(7500) 83
3rd, :1	1.67:1/6.04:1/(8000) 100	1.69:1/5.85:1/(7500) 102
4th, :1	1.23:1/4.44:1/(8000) 138	1.38:1/4.79:1/(7500) 125
5th, :1	1.00:1/3.62:1/est (7250) 155*	1.18:1/4.10:1/(7500) 146
6th, :1	0.83:1/3.00:1/est (6000) 155*	1.04:1/3.62:1/(7500) 165
Final drive ratio	3.62:1	3.75:1
Engine rpm @ 60 mph in top gear	2400 rpm	3604 rpm

*Electronically limited.

Subjective ratings consist of excellent, very good, good, average, poor; na means information is not available.

BMW M3

SMG makes the clutch pedal obsolete

BY SAM MITANI • PHOTOS BY MARC URBANO

"IMAGINE A TRANSMISsion that not only works with you, but can make you feel like a professional race driver." That's how the brochure of BMW's new SMG (Sequential M Gearbox) reads. A pretty hearty claim. From any other manufacturer, we'd dismiss this statement as unsubstantiated marketing fodder, but coming from a company such as BMW—which has long been involved in all types of racing—it warrants closer inspection. Online Services Editor Kim Wolfkill and I drove the M3 with SMG to the Streets of Willow Springs, a tight road course near Los Angeles, to see if we would indeed "feel like a professional race driver."

But before we get into the actual driving, here's a little background on the SMG. (See Technology Update, January 2002, for full details.) The SMG is a manual gearbox that also has the capability to perform like a fully automatic transmission. Manual shifting is performed sequentially through a shift lever or paddles located behind the steering wheel.

Unlike "smart automatics," which also allow the driver to choose gears manually (a la Porsche Tiptronic), the SMG has done away with the torque-converter/planetary-gear setup, allowing the drive to be more direct and shift times more immediate. It's one of a few such systems on the market today, the others being manufactured by Magneti-Marelli (used by Alfa Romeo, Aston Martin, Ferrari and Maserati) and Toyota, whose SMT is in the MR2 Spyder.

The SMG has a total of 11 settings, six in manual mode (S1 through S6), and five in automatic (A1 through A5), adhering to the company's recent pattern of over-complicating its technology features. In both modes, level 1 is the most docile with levels A5 and S6 being the most performance-oriented. In S6, the upshifts are so fast they tend to be abrupt, and you can only activate it with the traction control system turned off.

On the way to the track, the M3 with SMG proved a delight. In dense freeway traffic, the gearbox in A3 behaved like a conventional automatic, with the driver required to do nothing more than operate the throttle and brake pedal. I chose A3 here because in A5 the system waits until engine speed reaches about 5000 rpm before upshifting; in A1 or A2, it does so too early. Wolfkill, who was in a conventional 6-speed manual M3 right behind me, told me his stop-and-go commute was rather more unpleasant.

There's a brief lapse in the application of power as the system readies to grab a higher gear, which tends to jerk you forward, as if someone had lightly shoved you in the back. Despite the slight inconvenience, it beats having to operate a manual in stop-and-go traffic.

Driving near 10/10ths on the track, the SMG performed flawlessly. In S6, upshifts and downshifts were lightning quick, and you could hear the system matching engine revs on each downshift. BMW claims that the SMG can make shifts in 0.08 second, faster than most of us can with conventional gearboxes. After sampling the SMG, we each lapped the course in the M3 equipped with the conventional manual gearbox.

The conventional manual was nice, too, but the SMG was quicker and more comfortable because it allowed us to concentrate more on steering, braking and accelerating, without experiencing any sacrifice in lap times.

Wolfkill liked it too. "Whether it's on the street or at the track, the SMG takes the work out of shifting. For highly experienced drivers, I suspect the biggest advantages at a racetrack will be the greatly reduced upshift times, but there's also no denying the convenience of paddle shifters; just ask any Formula 1 driver."

There are those who dislike the system. Executive Editor Douglas Kott is among them, saying he'd take a conventional 6-speed any day. "SMG's auto mode (lurch/pause/lurch) is certainly inferior to a conventional automatic's operation. And with a standard box, there's a far more satisfying interaction with the machine."

So the SMG is not for everyone. But for its $2400 price, I'd take it in a heartbeat simply because it offers the best of both worlds: On the freeway, SMG provides a luxury that you just can't get with a conventional stick shift, and at the track, well, it makes you feel like a race driver.

■ **BMW's SMG transmission** has a total of 11 auto and manual settings, and can be operated via the shift lever or steering wheel-mounted paddles. Dash display for program mode mimics the pictogram on the shifter.